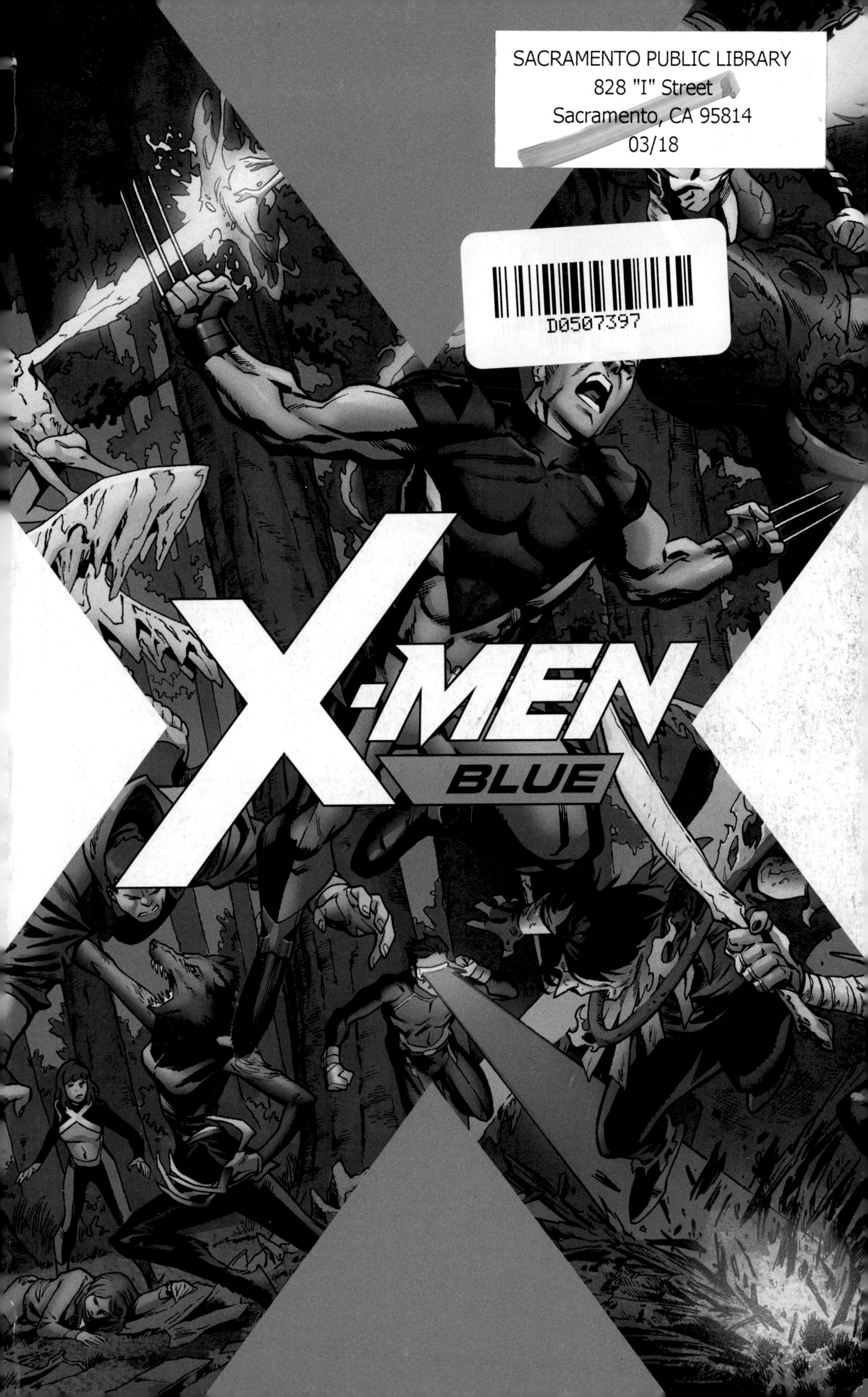
X-MEN
BLUE

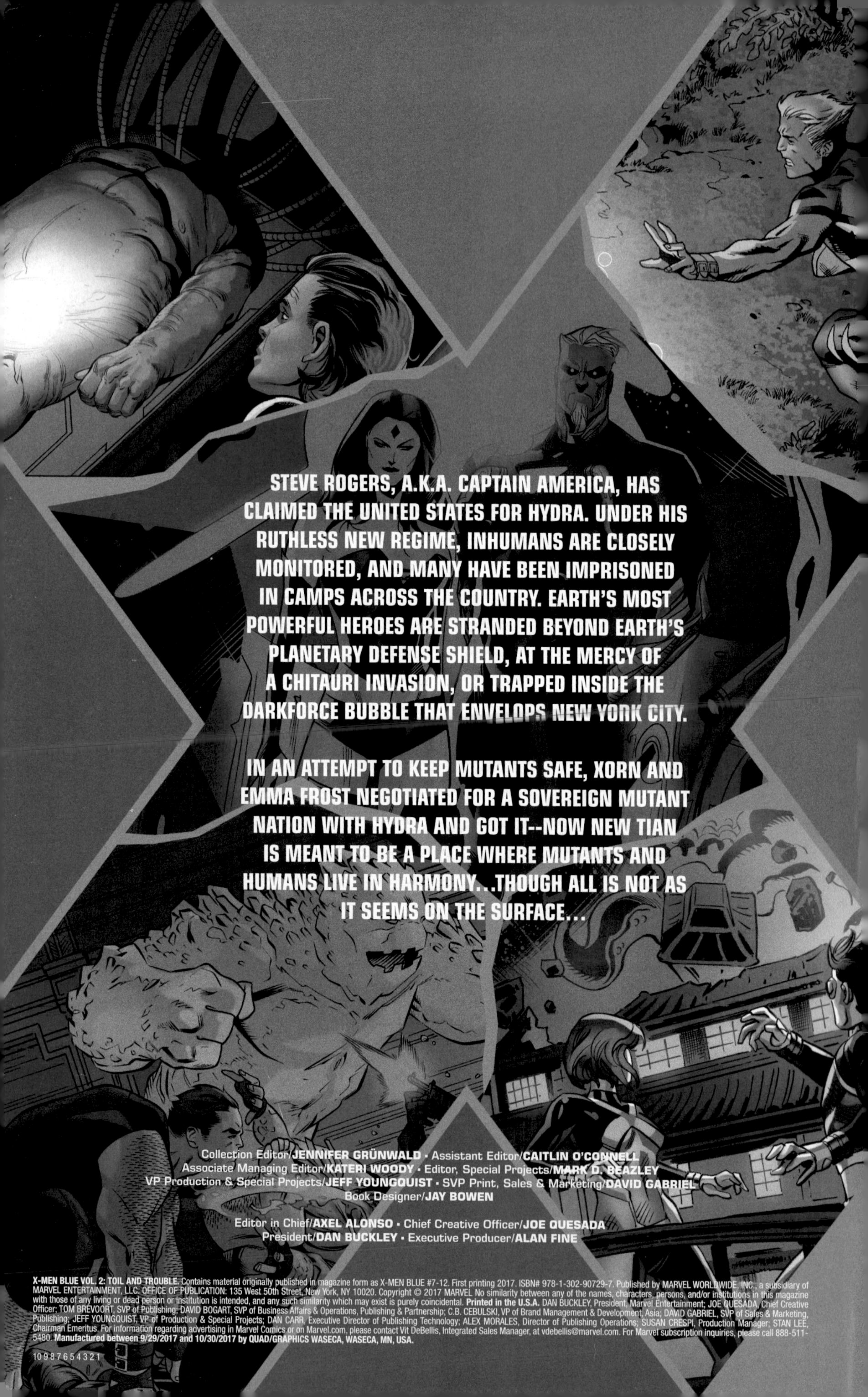

STEVE ROGERS, A.K.A. CAPTAIN AMERICA, HAS CLAIMED THE UNITED STATES FOR HYDRA. UNDER HIS RUTHLESS NEW REGIME, INHUMANS ARE CLOSELY MONITORED, AND MANY HAVE BEEN IMPRISONED IN CAMPS ACROSS THE COUNTRY. EARTH'S MOST POWERFUL HEROES ARE STRANDED BEYOND EARTH'S PLANETARY DEFENSE SHIELD, AT THE MERCY OF A CHITAURI INVASION, OR TRAPPED INSIDE THE DARKFORCE BUBBLE THAT ENVELOPS NEW YORK CITY.

IN AN ATTEMPT TO KEEP MUTANTS SAFE, XORN AND EMMA FROST NEGOTIATED FOR A SOVEREIGN MUTANT NATION WITH HYDRA AND GOT IT--NOW NEW TIAN IS MEANT TO BE A PLACE WHERE MUTANTS AND HUMANS LIVE IN HARMONY...THOUGH ALL IS NOT AS IT SEEMS ON THE SURFACE...

Collection Editor/**JENNIFER GRÜNWALD** • Assistant Editor/**CAITLIN O'CONNELL**
Associate Managing Editor/**KATERI WOODY** • Editor, Special Projects/**MARK D. BEAZLEY**
VP Production & Special Projects/**JEFF YOUNGQUIST** • SVP Print, Sales & Marketing/**DAVID GABRIEL**
Book Designer/**JAY BOWEN**

Editor in Chief/**AXEL ALONSO** • Chief Creative Officer/**JOE QUESADA**
President/**DAN BUCKLEY** • Executive Producer/**ALAN FINE**

X-MEN BLUE VOL. 2: TOIL AND TROUBLE. Contains material originally published in magazine form as X-MEN BLUE #7-12. First printing 2017. ISBN# 978-1-302-90729-7. Published by MARVEL WORLDWIDE, INC., a subsidiary of MARVEL ENTERTAINMENT, LLC. OFFICE OF PUBLICATION: 135 West 50th Street, New York, NY 10020. **Printed in the U.S.A.** DAN BUCKLEY, President, Marvel Entertainment; JOE QUESADA, Chief Creative Officer; TOM BREVOORT, SVP of Publishing; DAVID BOGART, SVP of Business Affairs & Operations, Publishing & Partnership; C.B. CEBULSKI, VP of Brand Management & Development, Asia; DAVID GABRIEL, SVP of Sales & Marketing, Publishing; JEFF YOUNGQUIST, VP of Production & Special Projects; DAN CARR, Executive Director of Publishing Technology; ALEX MORALES, Director of Publishing Operations; SUSAN CRESPI, Production Manager; STAN LEE, Chairman Emeritus. For information regarding advertising in Marvel Comics or on Marvel.com, please contact Vit DeBellis, Integrated Sales Manager, at vdebellis@marvel.com. For Marvel subscription inquiries, please call 888-511-5480. **Manufactured between 9/29/2017 and 10/30/2017 by QUAD/GRAPHICS WASECA, WASECA, MN, USA.**

10 9 8 7 6 5 4 3 2 1

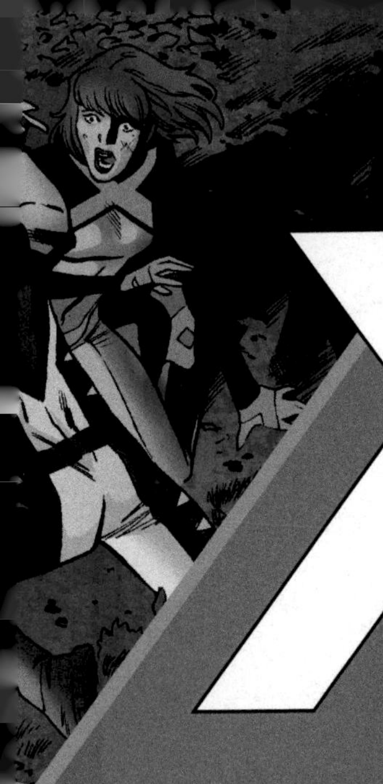

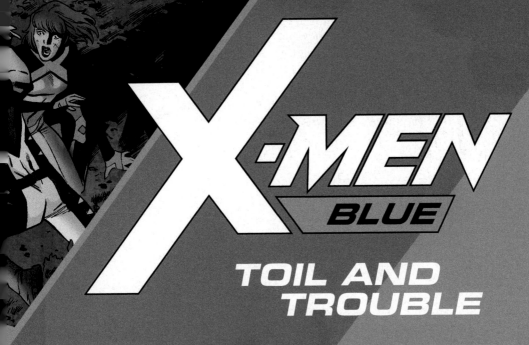

X-MEN BLUE

TOIL AND TROUBLE

Writer/**CULLEN BUNN**

ISSUES #7-9

Pencilers/**CORY SMITH**
with **JOEY VAZQUEZ** (#8) & **THONY SILAS** (#9)
Inkers/**CORY SMITH** (#7, #9) & **TERRY PALLOT** (#8)
with **THONY SILAS** (#9)
Colorist/**MATT MILLA**
with **IRMA KNIIVILA** (#9)
Cover Art/**ARTHUR ADAMS** & **PETER STEIGERWALD**

ISSUE #10

Penciler/**GIOVANNI VALLETTA**
Inker/**SCOTT HANNA**
Colorist/**GURU-eFX**
Cover Art/**ARTHUR ADAMS** & **JASON KEITH**

ISSUES #11-12

Penciler/**DOUGLAS FRANCHIN**
Inker/**SCOTT HANNA**
Colorist/**GURU-eFX** with **MATT YACKEY** (#12)
Cover Art/**ARTHUR ADAMS** & **PETER STEIGERWALD**

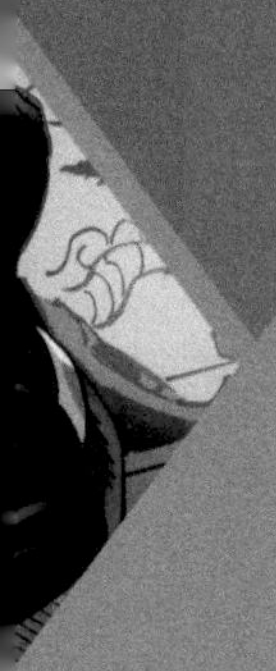

Letterers/**VC's JOE CARAMAGNA** (#7-10, #12)
& **CORY PETIT** (#11)

Assistant Editor/**CHRISTINA HARRINGTON**
Editor/**MARK PANICCIA**

X-MEN CREATED BY **STAN LEE** & **JACK KIRBY**

7

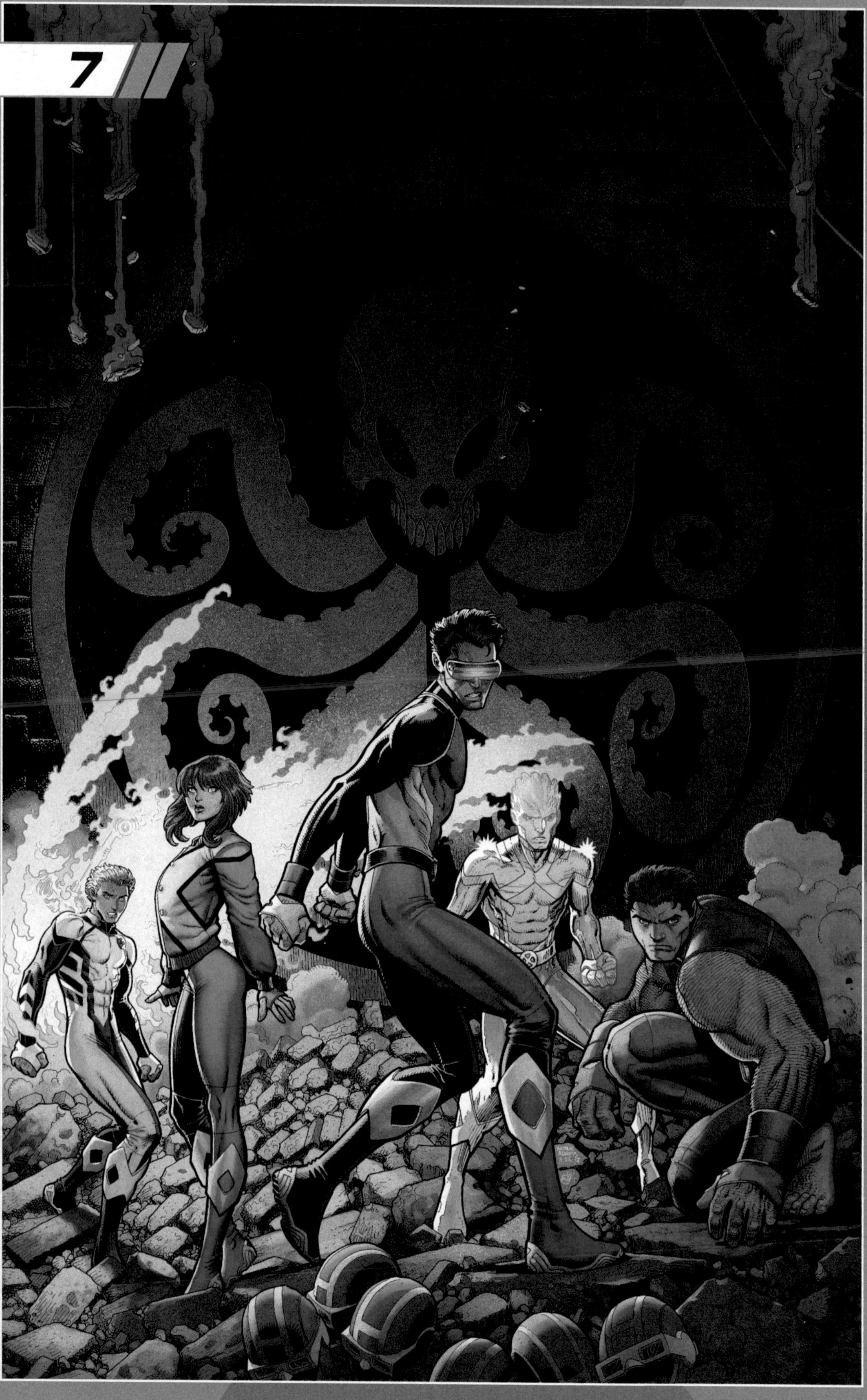

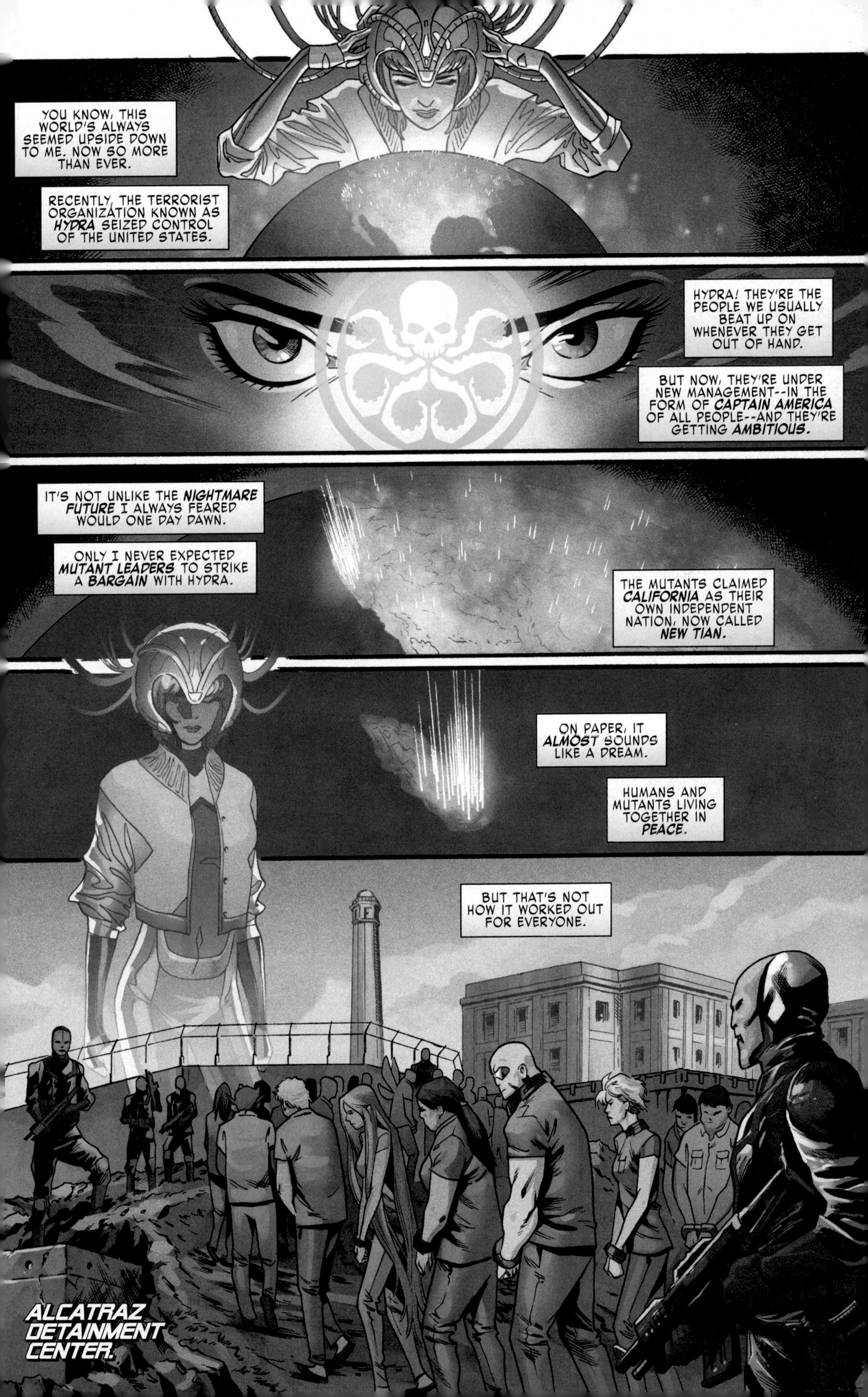

YOU KNOW, THIS WORLD'S ALWAYS SEEMED UPSIDE DOWN TO ME. NOW SO MORE THAN EVER.
RECENTLY, THE TERRORIST ORGANIZATION KNOWN AS HYDRA SEIZED CONTROL OF THE UNITED STATES.
HYDRA! THEY'RE THE PEOPLE WE USUALLY BEAT UP ON WHENEVER THEY GET OUT OF HAND.
BUT NOW, THEY'RE UNDER NEW MANAGEMENT--IN THE FORM OF CAPTAIN AMERICA OF ALL PEOPLE--AND THEY'RE GETTING AMBITIOUS.
IT'S NOT UNLIKE THE NIGHTMARE FUTURE I ALWAYS FEARED WOULD ONE DAY DAWN.
ONLY I NEVER EXPECTED MUTANT LEADERS TO STRIKE A BARGAIN WITH HYDRA.
THE MUTANTS CLAIMED CALIFORNIA AS THEIR OWN INDEPENDENT NATION, NOW CALLED NEW TIAN.
ON PAPER, IT ALMOST SOUNDS LIKE A DREAM.
HUMANS AND MUTANTS LIVING TOGETHER IN PEACE.
BUT THAT'S NOT HOW IT WORKED OUT FOR EVERYONE.
ALCATRAZ DETAINMENT CENTER.

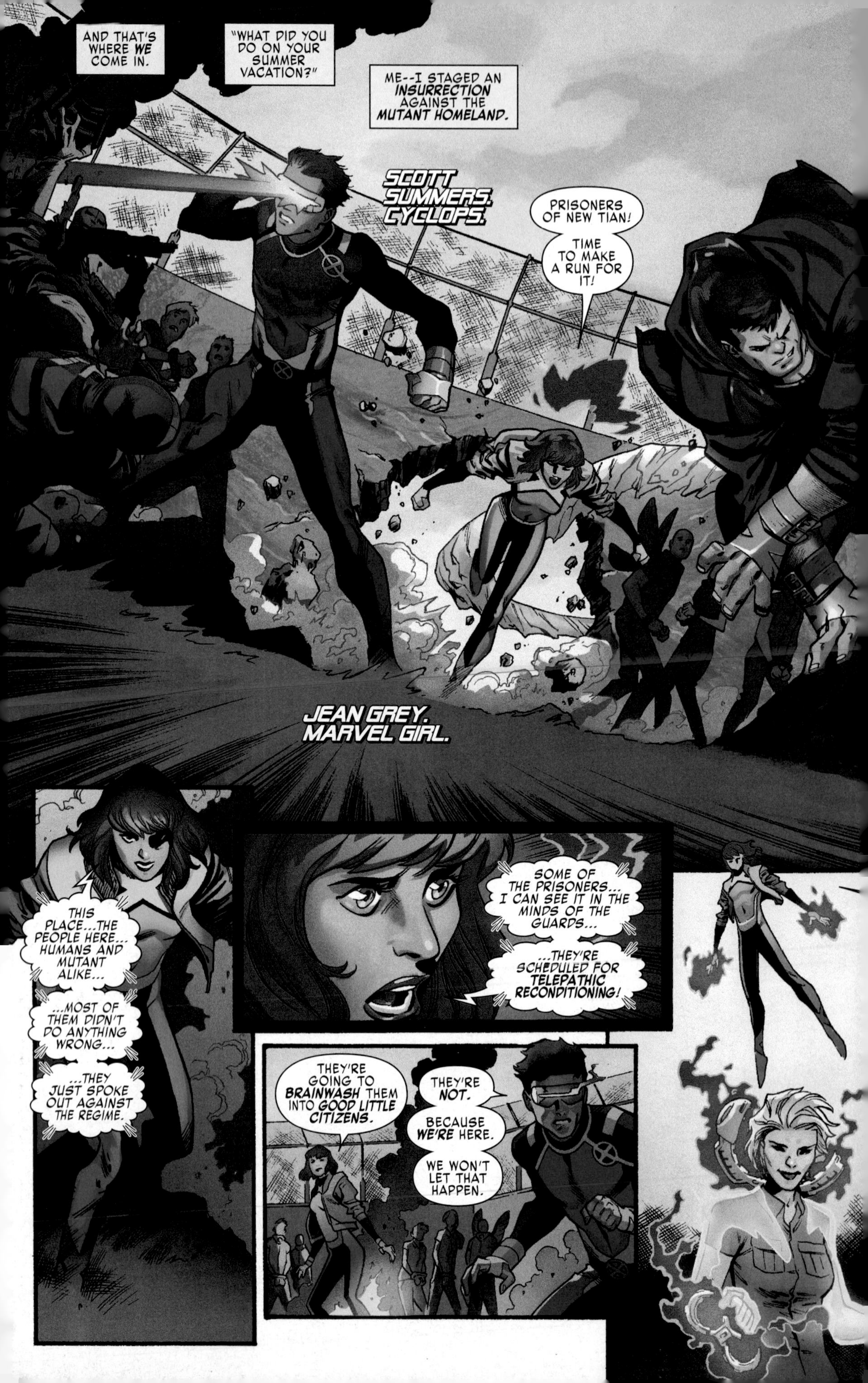
AND THAT'S WHERE WE COME IN.
"WHAT DID YOU DO ON YOUR SUMMER VACATION?"
ME--I STAGED AN INSURRECTION AGAINST THE MUTANT HOMELAND.
SCOTT SUMMERS. CYCLOPS.
PRISONERS OF NEW TIAN!
TIME TO MAKE A RUN FOR IT!
JEAN GREY. MARVEL GIRL.
THIS PLACE...THE PEOPLE HERE... HUMANS AND MUTANT ALIKE...
...MOST OF THEM DIDN'T DO ANYTHING WRONG...
...THEY JUST SPOKE OUT AGAINST THE REGIME.
SOME OF THE PRISONERS... I CAN SEE IT IN THE MINDS OF THE GUARDS...
...THEY'RE SCHEDULED FOR TELEPATHIC RECONDITIONING!
THEY'RE GOING TO BRAINWASH THEM INTO GOOD LITTLE CITIZENS.
THEY'RE NOT.
BECAUSE WE'RE HERE.
WE WON'T LET THAT HAPPEN.

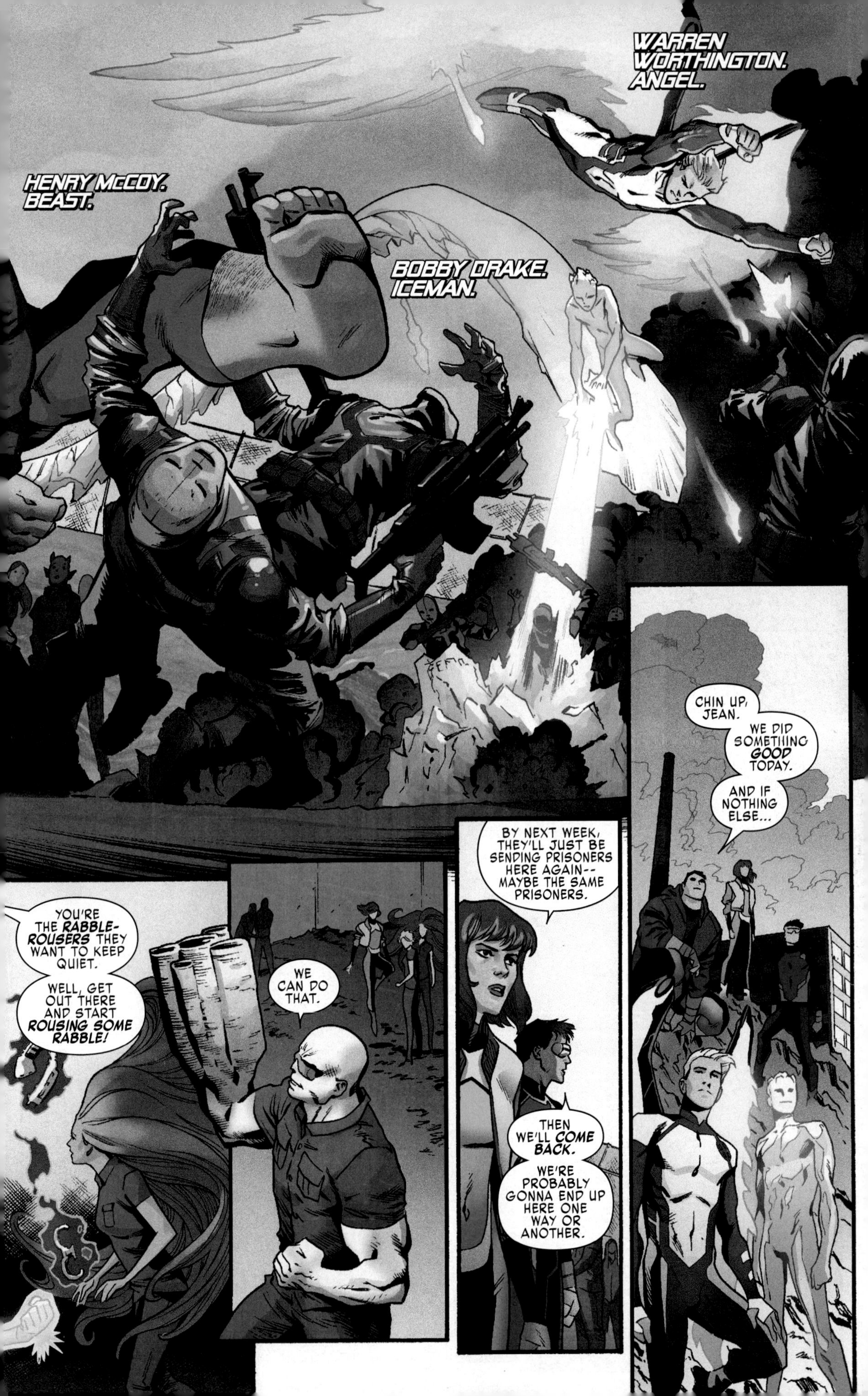
WARREN WORTHINGTON. ANGEL.
HENRY McCOY. BEAST.
BOBBY DRAKE. ICEMAN.
YOU'RE THE RABBLE-ROUSERS THEY WANT TO KEEP QUIET.
WELL, GET OUT THERE AND START ROUSING SOME RABBLE!
WE CAN DO THAT.
BY NEXT WEEK, THEY'LL JUST BE SENDING PRISONERS HERE AGAIN-- MAYBE THE SAME PRISONERS.
THEN WE'LL COME BACK.
WE'RE PROBABLY GONNA END UP HERE ONE WAY OR ANOTHER.
CHIN UP, JEAN.
WE DID SOMETHING GOOD TODAY.
AND IF NOTHING ELSE...

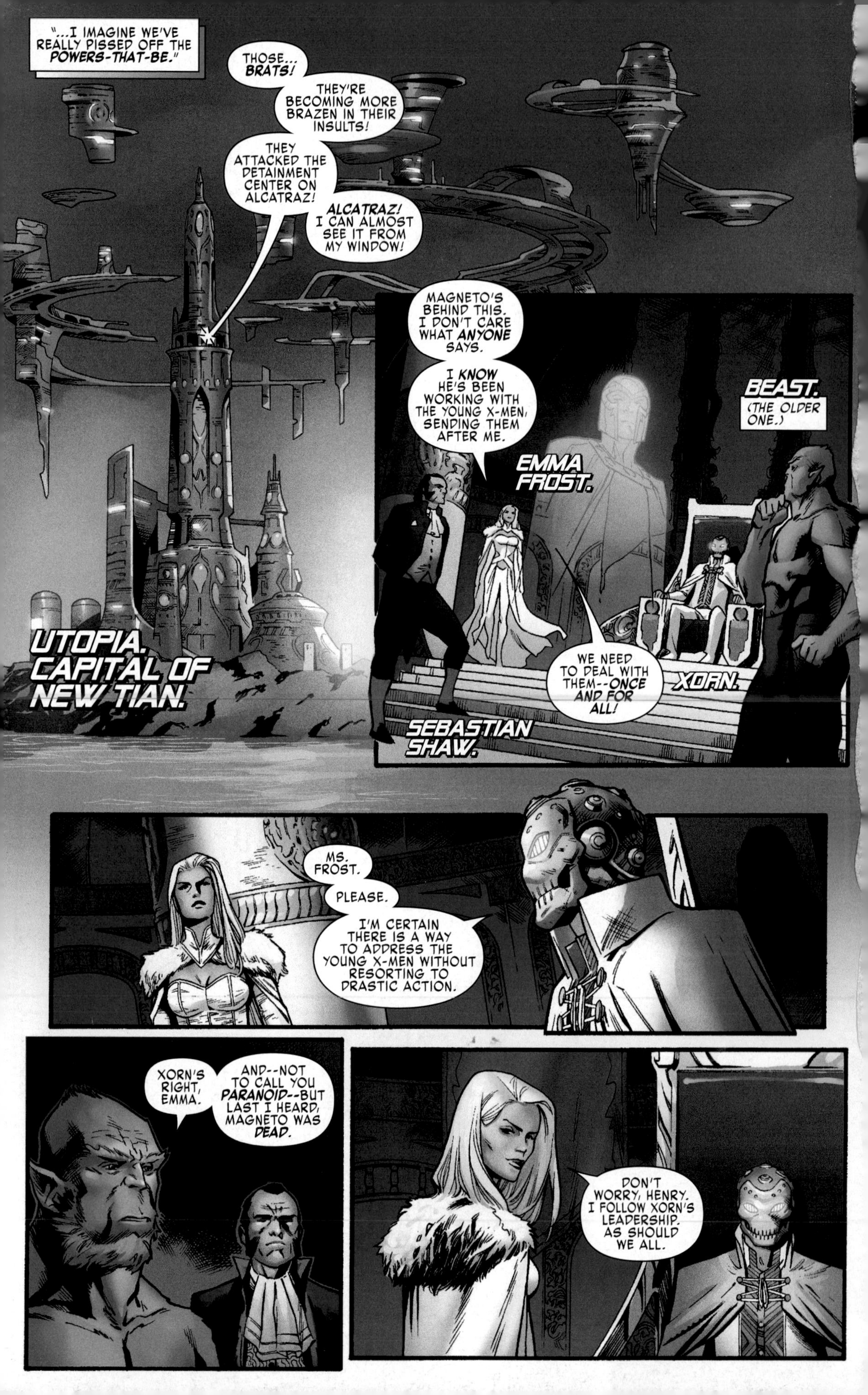
"...I IMAGINE WE'VE REALLY PISSED OFF THE POWERS-THAT-BE."
THOSE... BRATS!
THEY'RE BECOMING MORE BRAZEN IN THEIR INSULTS!
THEY ATTACKED THE DETAINMENT CENTER ON ALCATRAZ!
ALCATRAZ! I CAN ALMOST SEE IT FROM MY WINDOW!
UTOPIA. CAPITAL OF NEW TIAN.
MAGNETO'S BEHIND THIS. I DON'T CARE WHAT ANYONE SAYS.
I KNOW HE'S BEEN WORKING WITH THE YOUNG X-MEN, SENDING THEM AFTER ME.
EMMA FROST.
BEAST.
(THE OLDER ONE.)
WE NEED TO DEAL WITH THEM--ONCE AND FOR ALL!
XORN.
SEBASTIAN SHAW.
MS. FROST.
PLEASE.
I'M CERTAIN THERE IS A WAY TO ADDRESS THE YOUNG X-MEN WITHOUT RESORTING TO DRASTIC ACTION.
XORN'S RIGHT, EMMA.
AND--NOT TO CALL YOU PARANOID--BUT LAST I HEARD, MAGNETO WAS DEAD.
DON'T WORRY, HENRY. I FOLLOW XORN'S LEADERSHIP. AS SHOULD WE ALL.

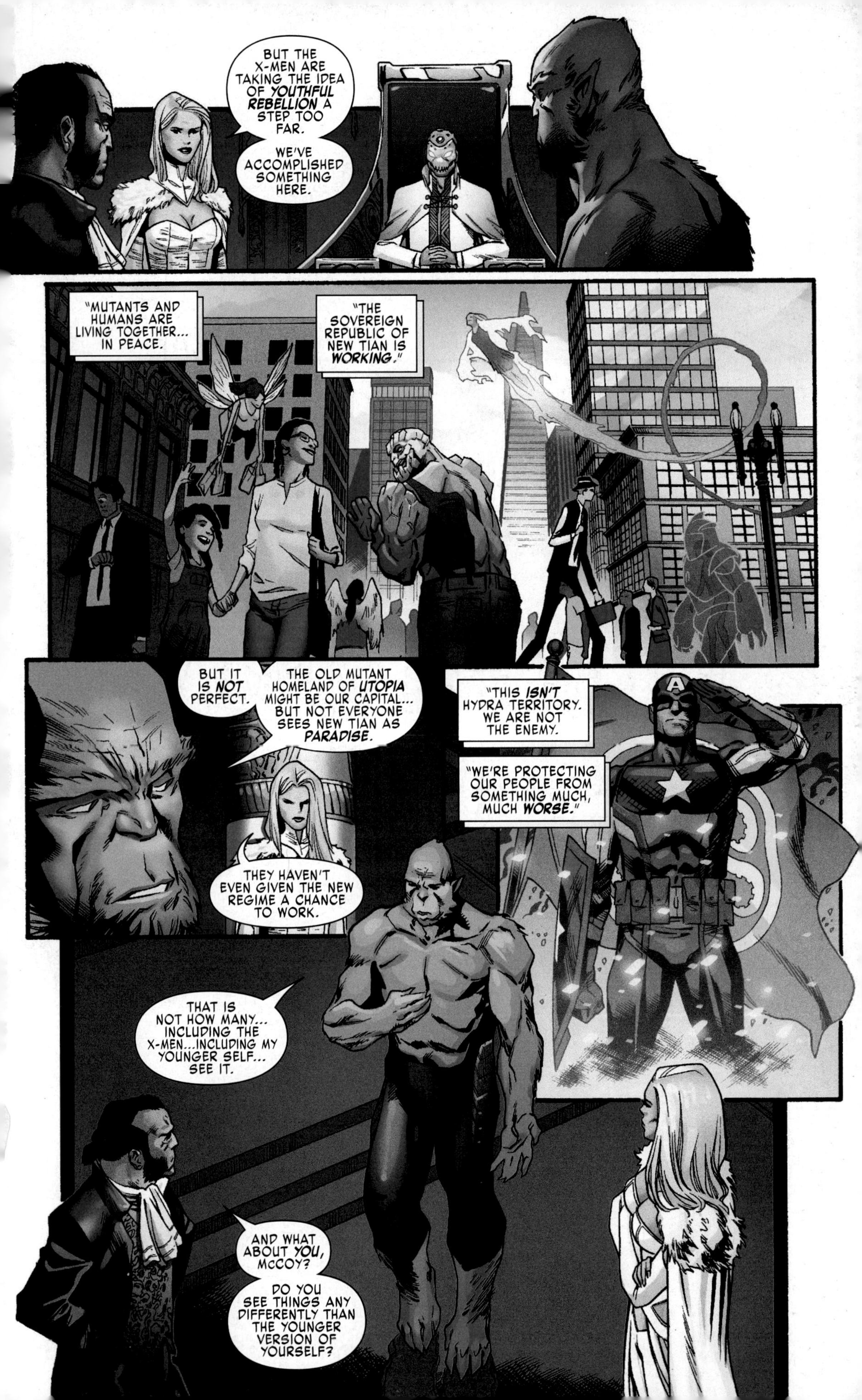
BUT THE X-MEN ARE TAKING THE IDEA OF YOUTHFUL REBELLION A STEP TOO FAR.
WE'VE ACCOMPLISHED SOMETHING HERE.
"MUTANTS AND HUMANS ARE LIVING TOGETHER... IN PEACE.
"THE SOVEREIGN REPUBLIC OF NEW TIAN IS WORKING."
BUT IT IS NOT PERFECT.
THE OLD MUTANT HOMELAND OF UTOPIA MIGHT BE OUR CAPITAL... BUT NOT EVERYONE SEES NEW TIAN AS PARADISE.
"THIS ISN'T HYDRA TERRITORY. WE ARE NOT THE ENEMY.
"WE'RE PROTECTING OUR PEOPLE FROM SOMETHING MUCH, MUCH WORSE."
THEY HAVEN'T EVEN GIVEN THE NEW REGIME A CHANCE TO WORK.
THAT IS NOT HOW MANY... INCLUDING THE X-MEN...INCLUDING MY YOUNGER SELF... SEE IT.
AND WHAT ABOUT YOU, McCOY?
DO YOU SEE THINGS ANY DIFFERENTLY THAN THE YOUNGER VERSION OF YOURSELF?

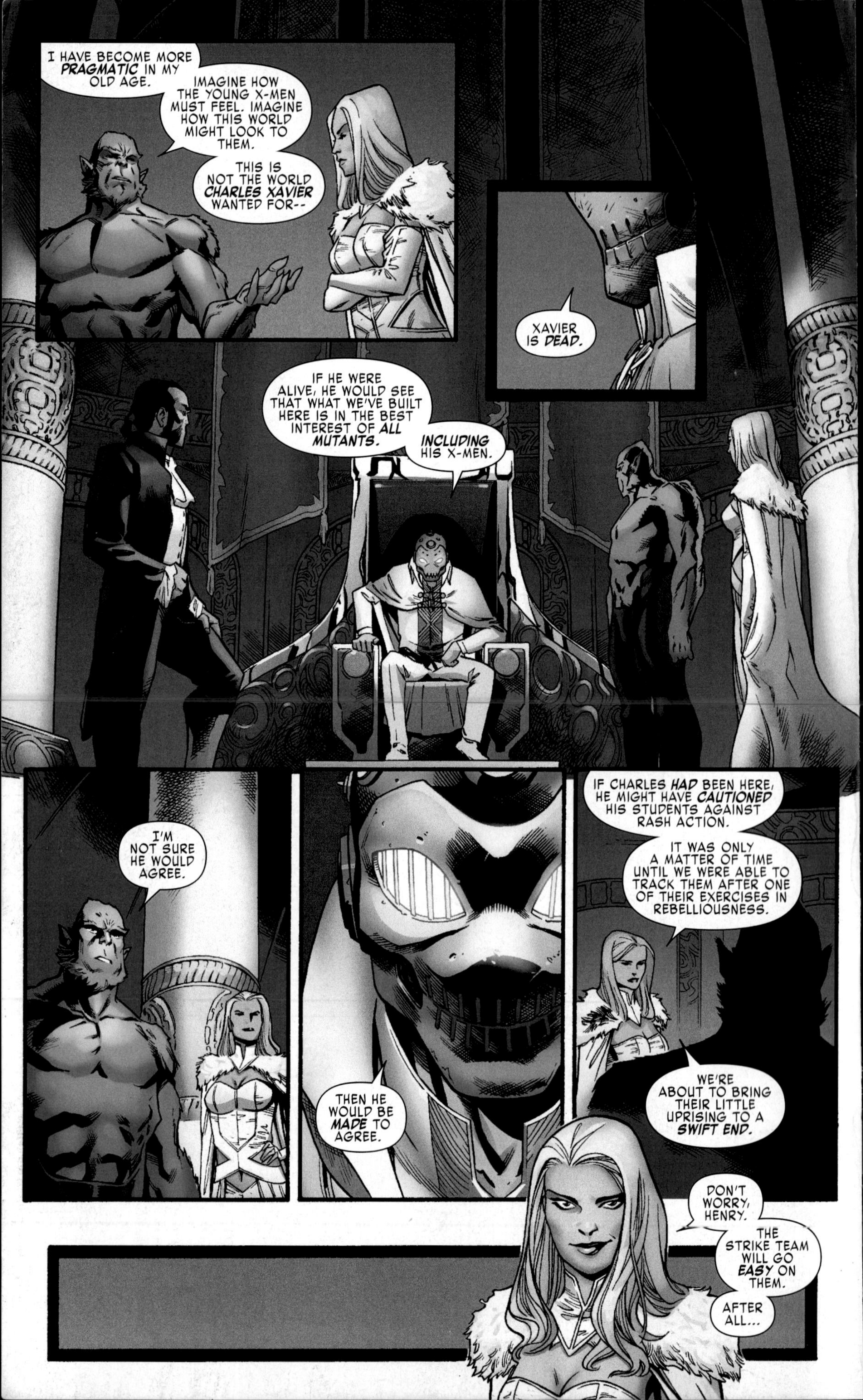
I HAVE BECOME MORE PRAGMATIC IN MY OLD AGE.
IMAGINE HOW THE YOUNG X-MEN MUST FEEL. IMAGINE HOW THIS WORLD MIGHT LOOK TO THEM.
THIS IS NOT THE WORLD CHARLES XAVIER WANTED FOR--
XAVIER IS DEAD.
IF HE WERE ALIVE, HE WOULD SEE THAT WHAT WE'VE BUILT HERE IS IN THE BEST INTEREST OF ALL MUTANTS.
INCLUDING HIS X-MEN.
I'M NOT SURE HE WOULD AGREE.
THEN HE WOULD BE MADE TO AGREE.
IF CHARLES HAD BEEN HERE, HE MIGHT HAVE CAUTIONED HIS STUDENTS AGAINST RASH ACTION.
IT WAS ONLY A MATTER OF TIME UNTIL WE WERE ABLE TO TRACK THEM AFTER ONE OF THEIR EXERCISES IN REBELLIOUSNESS.
WE'RE ABOUT TO BRING THEIR LITTLE UPRISING TO A SWIFT END.
DON'T WORRY, HENRY.
THE STRIKE TEAM WILL GO EASY ON THEM.
AFTER ALL...

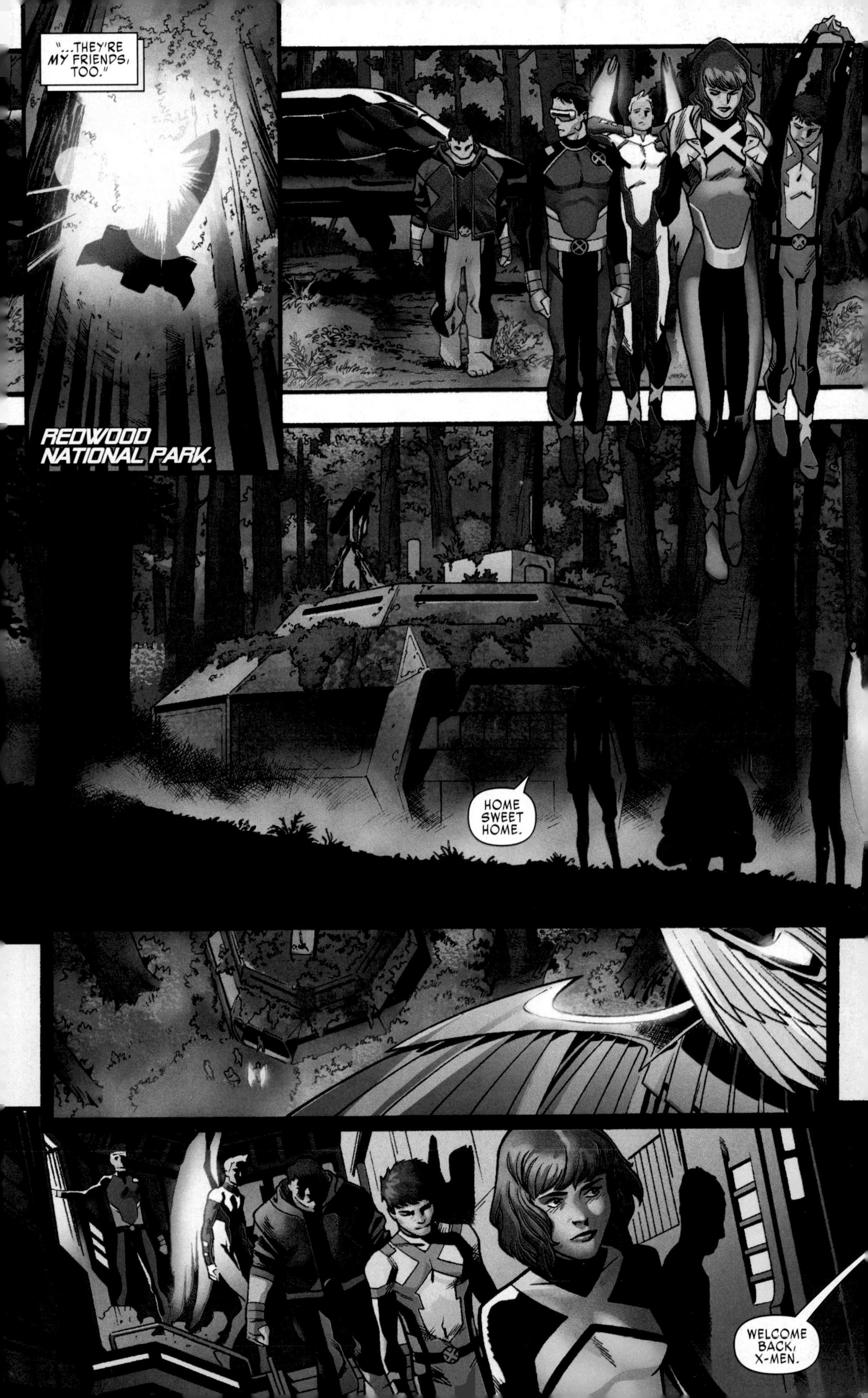
"...THEY'RE MY FRIENDS, TOO."
REDWOOD NATIONAL PARK.
HOME SWEET HOME.
WELCOME BACK, X-MEN.

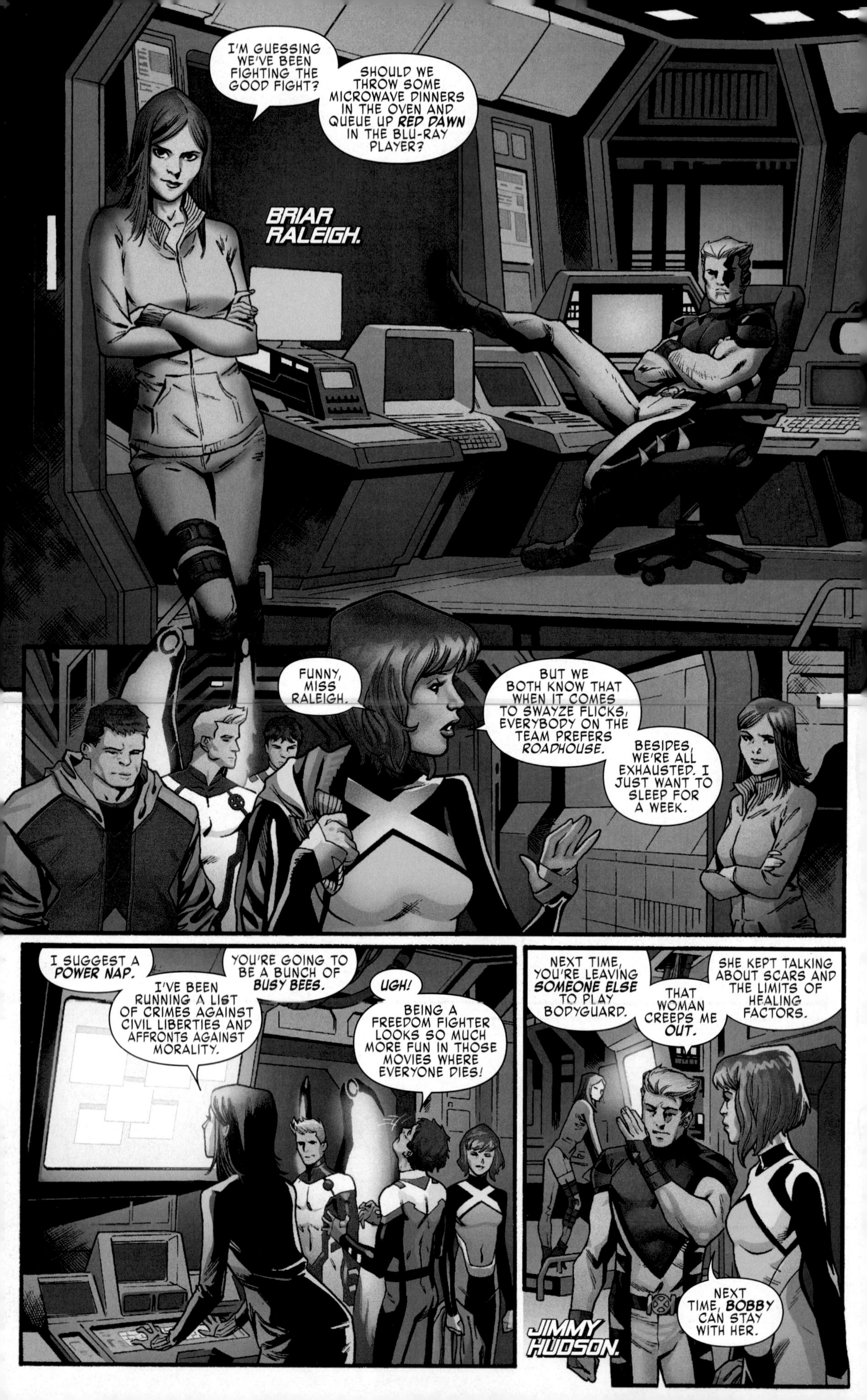
I'M GUESSING WE'VE BEEN FIGHTING THE GOOD FIGHT?
SHOULD WE THROW SOME MICROWAVE DINNERS IN THE OVEN AND QUEUE UP RED DAWN IN THE BLU-RAY PLAYER?
BRIAR RALEIGH.
FUNNY, MISS RALEIGH.
BUT WE BOTH KNOW THAT WHEN IT COMES TO SWAYZE FLICKS, EVERYBODY ON THE TEAM PREFERS ROADHOUSE.
BESIDES, WE'RE ALL EXHAUSTED. I JUST WANT TO SLEEP FOR A WEEK.
I SUGGEST A POWER NAP.
I'VE BEEN RUNNING A LIST OF CRIMES AGAINST CIVIL LIBERTIES AND AFFRONTS AGAINST MORALITY.
YOU'RE GOING TO BE A BUNCH OF BUSY BEES.
UGH!
BEING A FREEDOM FIGHTER LOOKS SO MUCH MORE FUN IN THOSE MOVIES WHERE EVERYONE DIES!
NEXT TIME, YOU'RE LEAVING SOMEONE ELSE TO PLAY BODYGUARD.
THAT WOMAN CREEPS ME OUT.
SHE KEPT TALKING ABOUT SCARS AND THE LIMITS OF HEALING FACTORS.
NEXT TIME, BOBBY CAN STAY WITH HER.
JIMMY HUDSON.

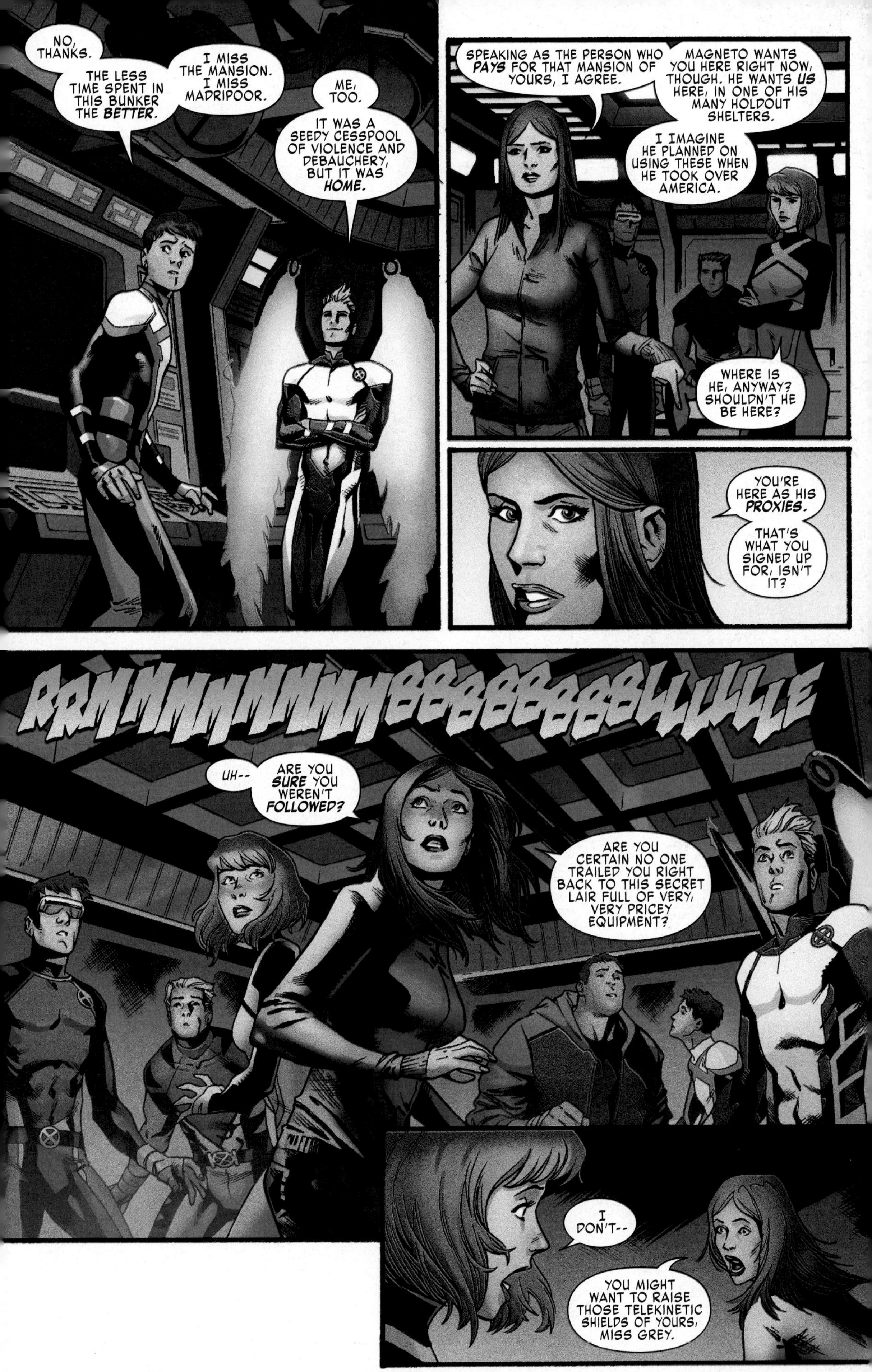
NO, THANKS.
THE LESS TIME SPENT IN THIS BUNKER THE BETTER.
I MISS THE MANSION. I MISS MADRIPOOR.
ME, TOO.
IT WAS A SEEDY CESSPOOL OF VIOLENCE AND DEBAUCHERY, BUT IT WAS HOME.
SPEAKING AS THE PERSON WHO PAYS FOR THAT MANSION OF YOURS, I AGREE.
MAGNETO WANTS YOU HERE RIGHT NOW, THOUGH. HE WANTS US HERE, IN ONE OF HIS MANY HOLDOUT SHELTERS.
I IMAGINE HE PLANNED ON USING THESE WHEN HE TOOK OVER AMERICA.
WHERE IS HE, ANYWAY? SHOULDN'T HE BE HERE?
YOU'RE HERE AS HIS PROXIES.
THAT'S WHAT YOU SIGNED UP FOR, ISN'T IT?
RRMMMMMMMMMBBBBBBBBBLLLLLE
UH--
ARE YOU SURE YOU WEREN'T FOLLOWED?
ARE YOU CERTAIN NO ONE TRAILED YOU RIGHT BACK TO THIS SECRET LAIR FULL OF VERY, VERY PRICEY EQUIPMENT?
I DON'T--
YOU MIGHT WANT TO RAISE THOSE TELEKINETIC SHIELDS OF YOURS, MISS GREY.

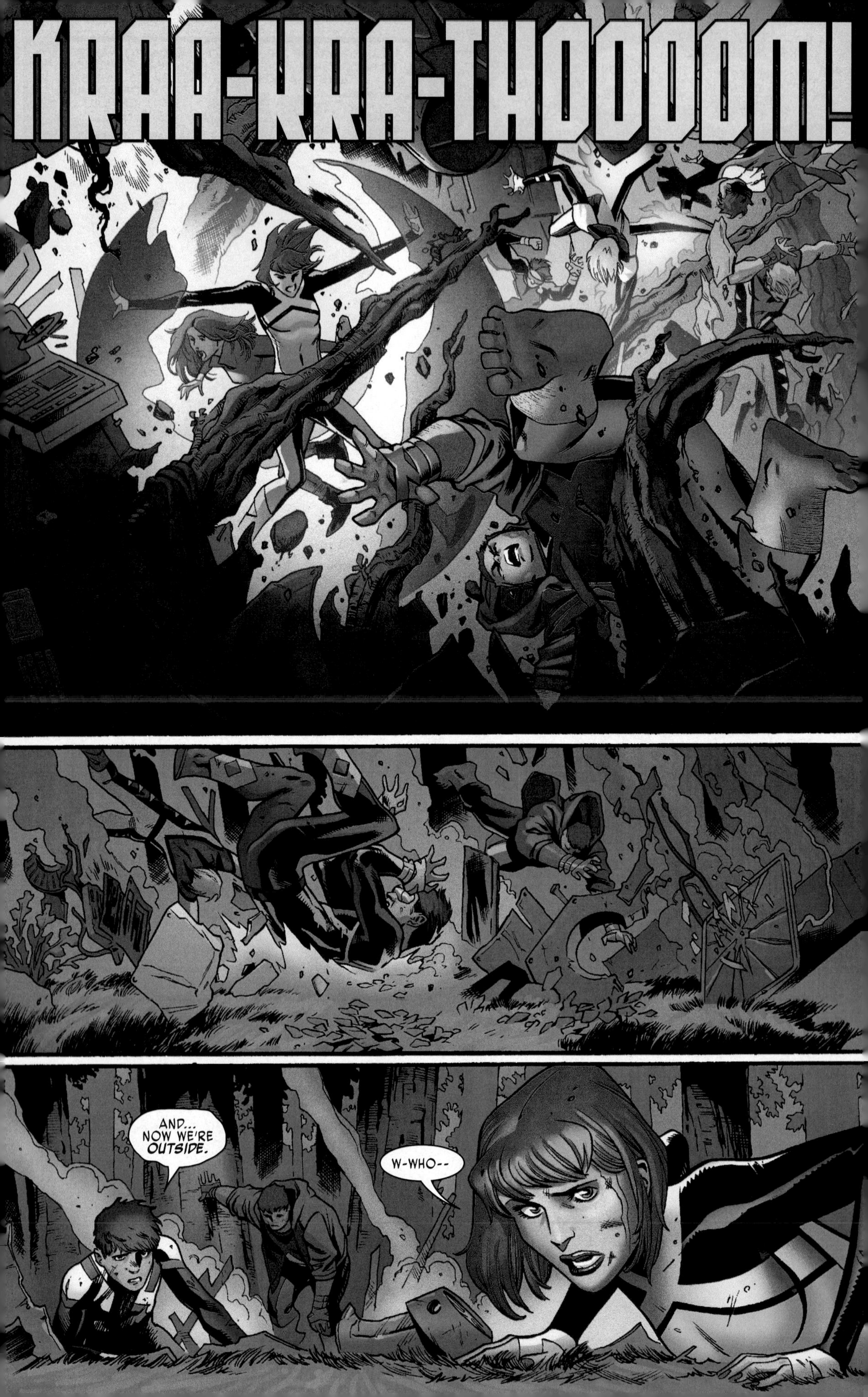
KRAA-KRA-THOOOOM!
AND... NOW WE'RE OUTSIDE.
W-WHO--

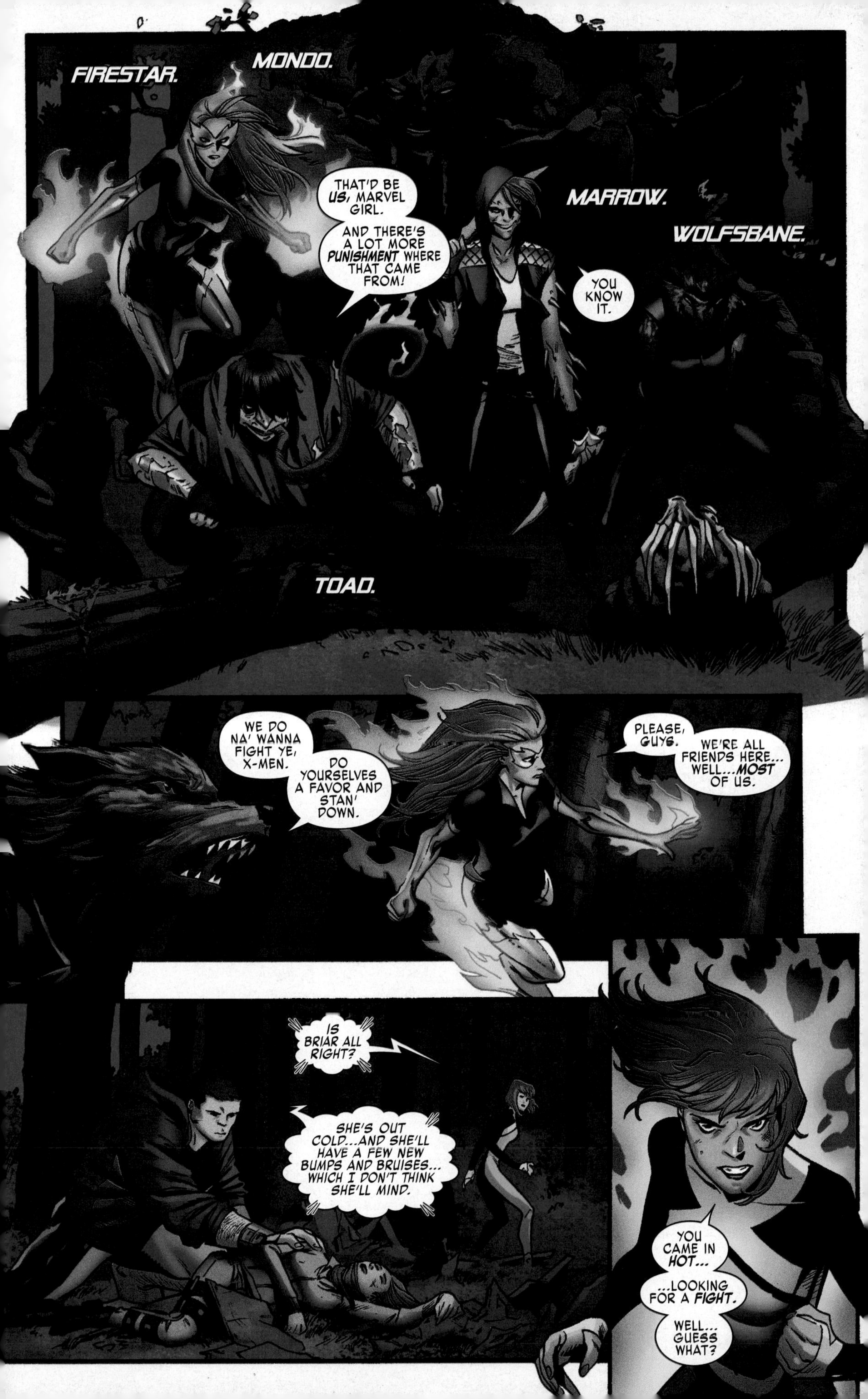
FIRESTAR.
MONDO.
THAT'D BE US, MARVEL GIRL.
AND THERE'S A LOT MORE PUNISHMENT WHERE THAT CAME FROM!
MARROW.
WOLFSBANE.
YOU KNOW IT.
TOAD.
WE DO NA' WANNA FIGHT YE, X-MEN.
DO YOURSELVES A FAVOR AND STAN' DOWN.
PLEASE, GUYS.
WE'RE ALL FRIENDS HERE... WELL...MOST OF US.
IS BRIAR ALL RIGHT?
SHE'S OUT COLD...AND SHE'LL HAVE A FEW NEW BUMPS AND BRUISES... WHICH I DON'T THINK SHE'LL MIND.
YOU CAME IN HOT...
...LOOKING FOR A FIGHT.
WELL... GUESS WHAT?

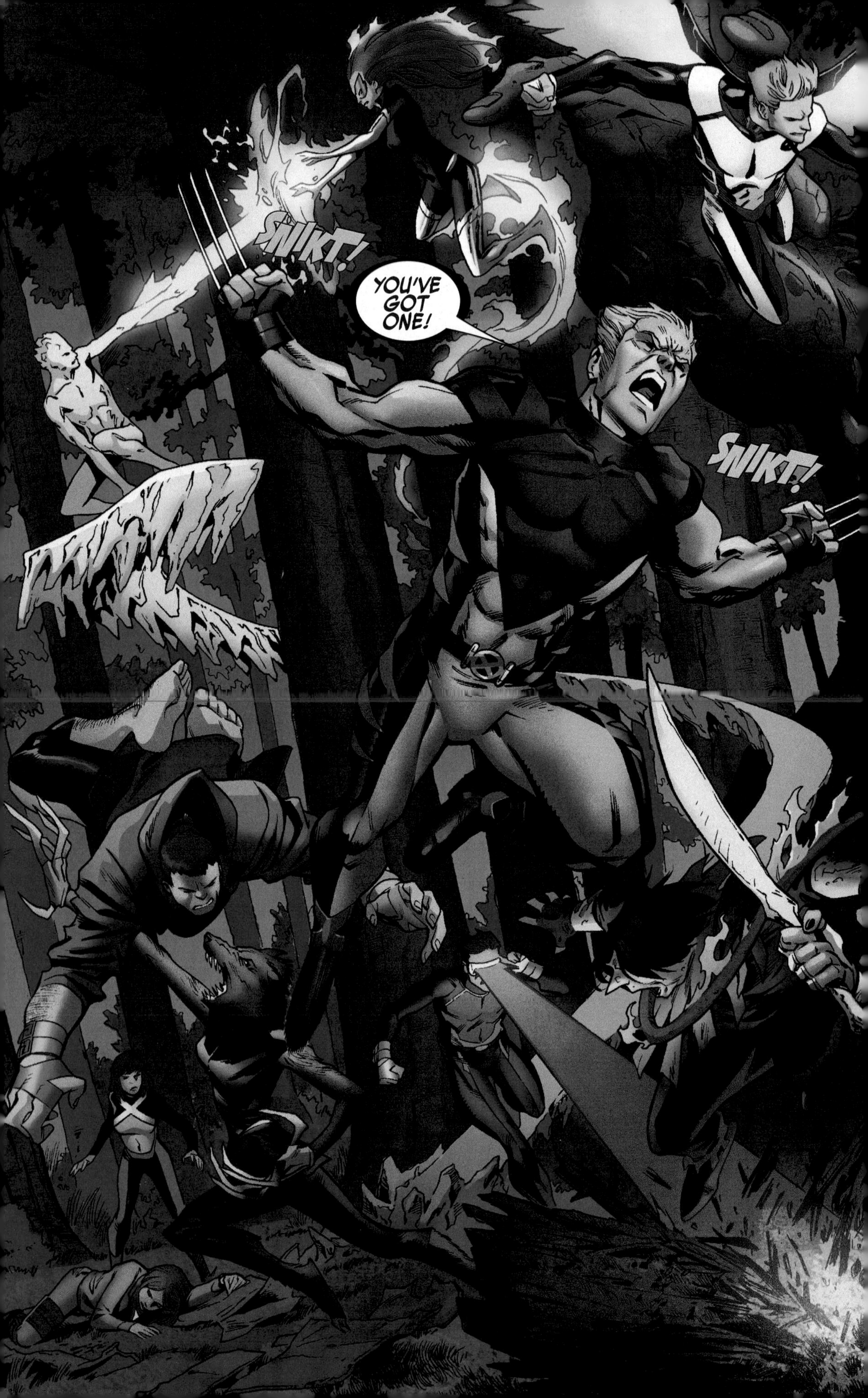
SNIKT!
YOU'VE GOT ONE!
SNIKT!

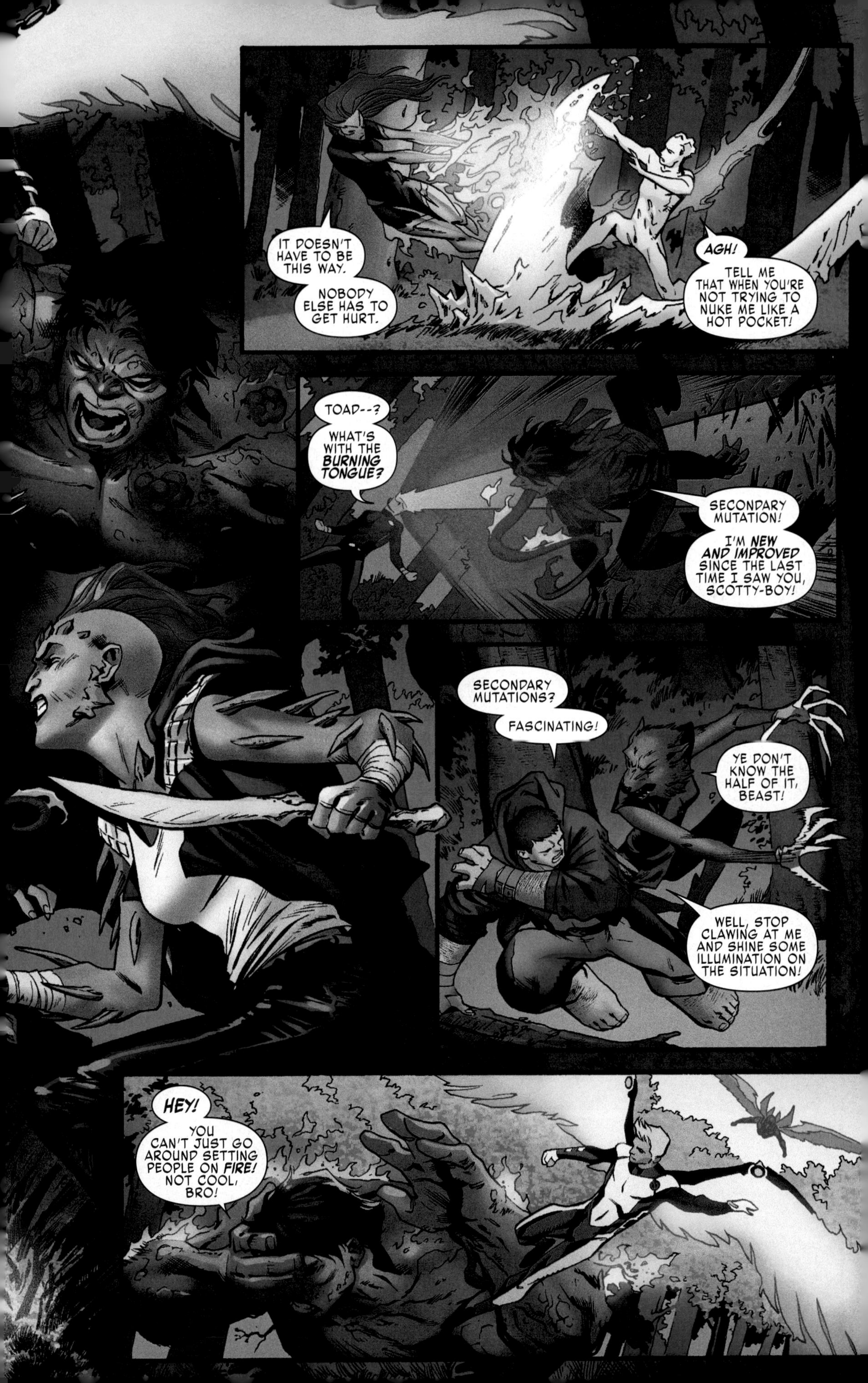

IT DOESN'T HAVE TO BE THIS WAY.
NOBODY ELSE HAS TO GET HURT.
AGH!
TELL ME THAT WHEN YOU'RE NOT TRYING TO NUKE ME LIKE A HOT POCKET!
TOAD--?
WHAT'S WITH THE BURNING TONGUE?
SECONDARY MUTATION!
I'M NEW AND IMPROVED SINCE THE LAST TIME I SAW YOU, SCOTTY-BOY!
SECONDARY MUTATIONS?
FASCINATING!
YE DON'T KNOW THE HALF OF IT, BEAST!
WELL, STOP CLAWING AT ME AND SHINE SOME ILLUMINATION ON THE SITUATION!
HEY!
YOU CAN'T JUST GO AROUND SETTING PEOPLE ON FIRE! NOT COOL, BRO!

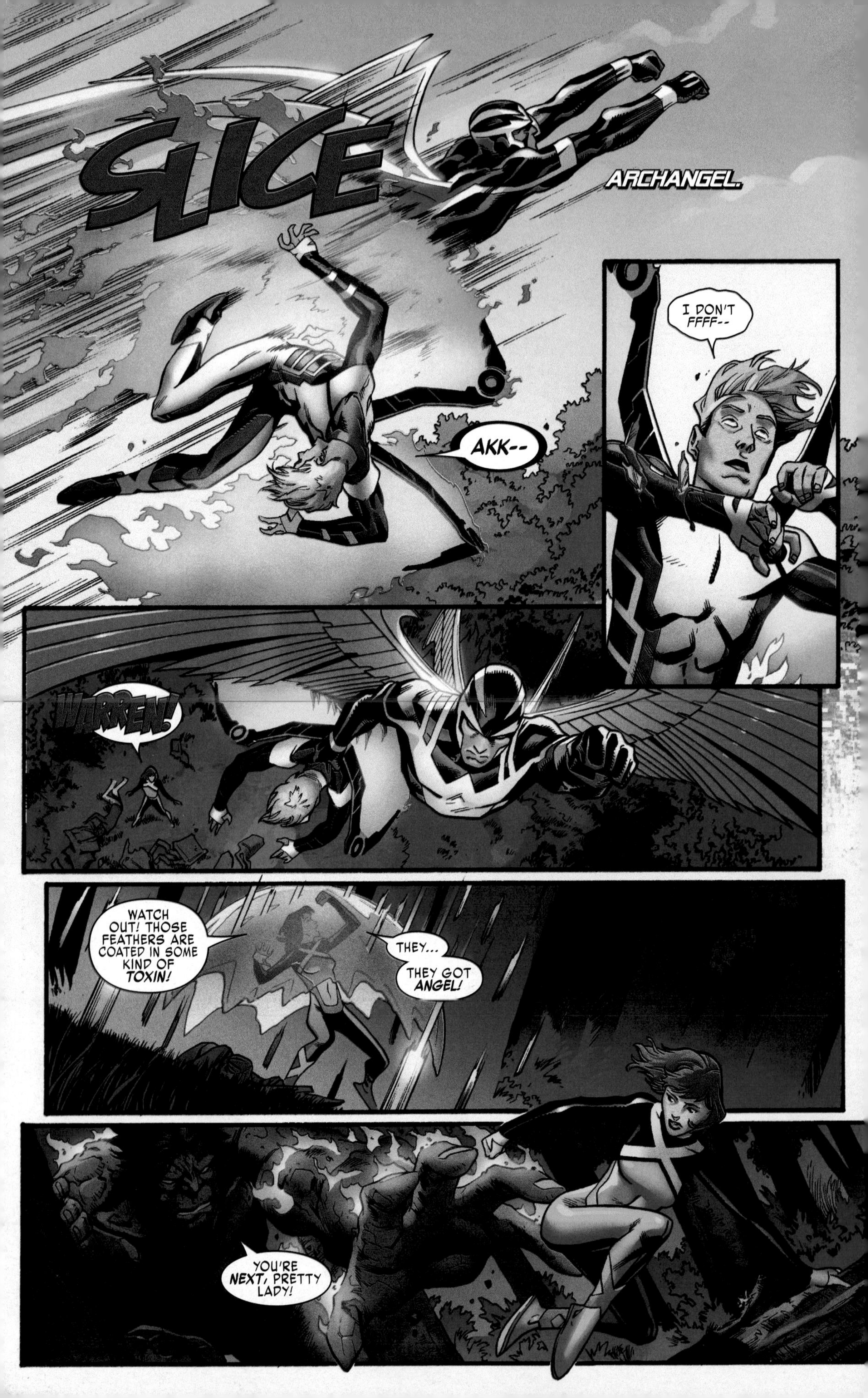
SLICE
ARCHANGEL.
AKK--
I DON'T FFFF--
WARREN!
WATCH OUT! THOSE FEATHERS ARE COATED IN SOME KIND OF TOXIN!
THEY...
THEY GOT ANGEL!
YOU'RE NEXT, PRETTY LADY!

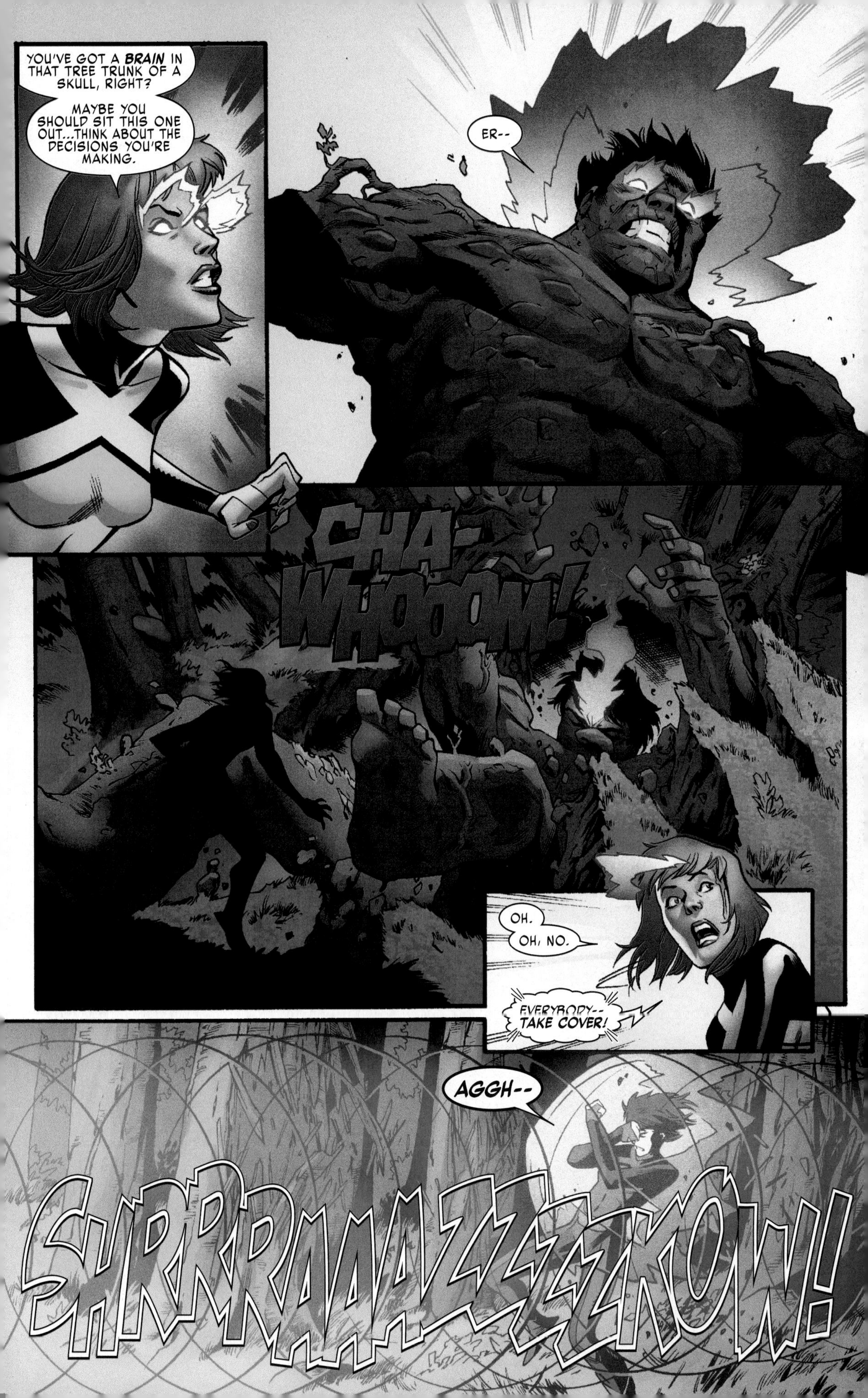
YOU'VE GOT A BRAIN IN THAT TREE TRUNK OF A SKULL, RIGHT?
MAYBE YOU SHOULD SIT THIS ONE OUT...THINK ABOUT THE DECISIONS YOU'RE MAKING.
ER--
CHA-WHOOOM!
OH.
OH, NO.
EVERYBODY-- TAKE COVER!
AGGH--
SHRRRAAAZZZZKOW!

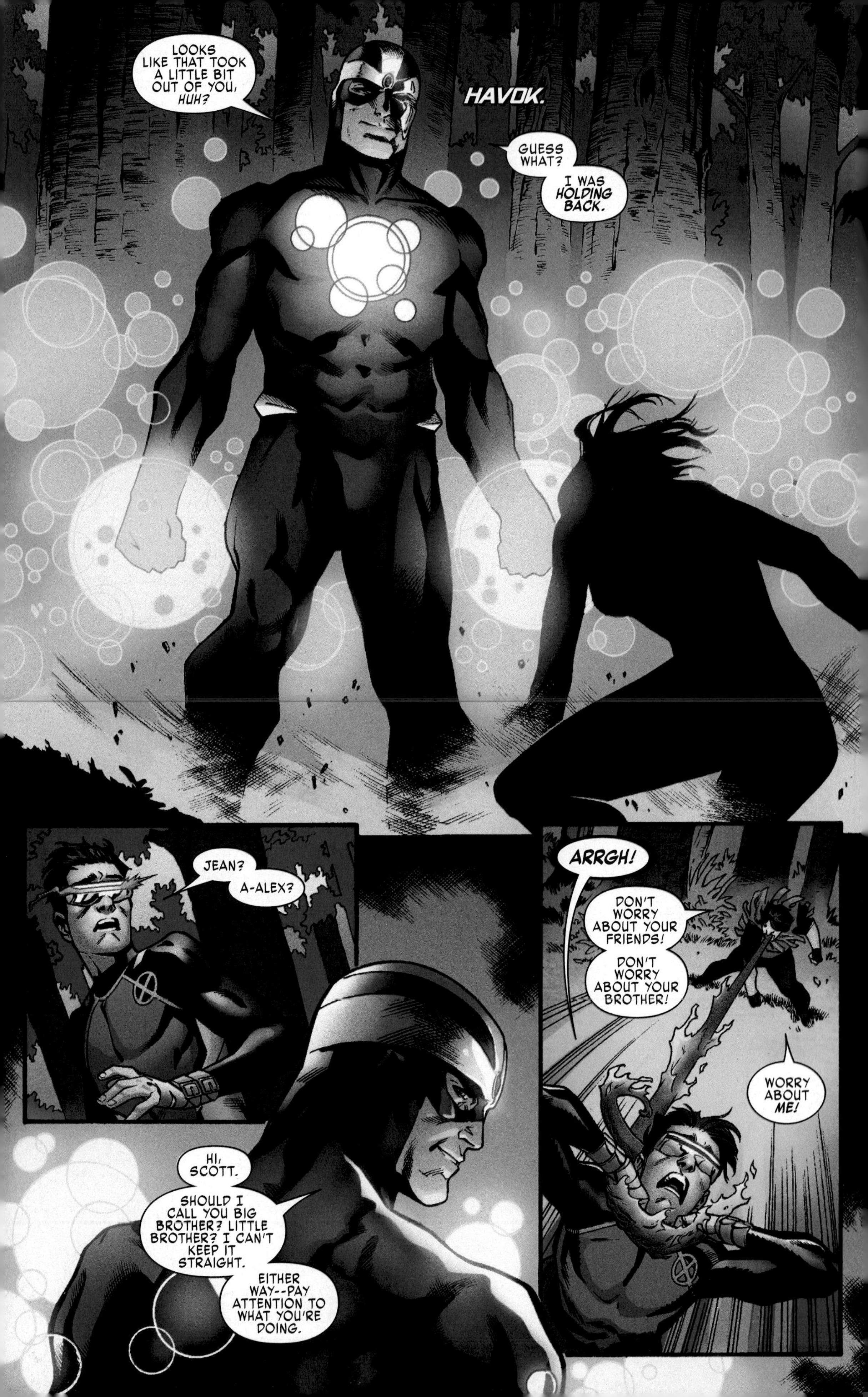
LOOKS LIKE THAT TOOK A LITTLE BIT OUT OF YOU, HUH?
HAVOK.
GUESS WHAT?
I WAS HOLDING BACK.
JEAN?
A-ALEX?
HI, SCOTT.
SHOULD I CALL YOU BIG BROTHER? LITTLE BROTHER? I CAN'T KEEP IT STRAIGHT.
EITHER WAY--PAY ATTENTION TO WHAT YOU'RE DOING.
ARRGH!
DON'T WORRY ABOUT YOUR FRIENDS!
DON'T WORRY ABOUT YOUR BROTHER!
WORRY ABOUT ME!

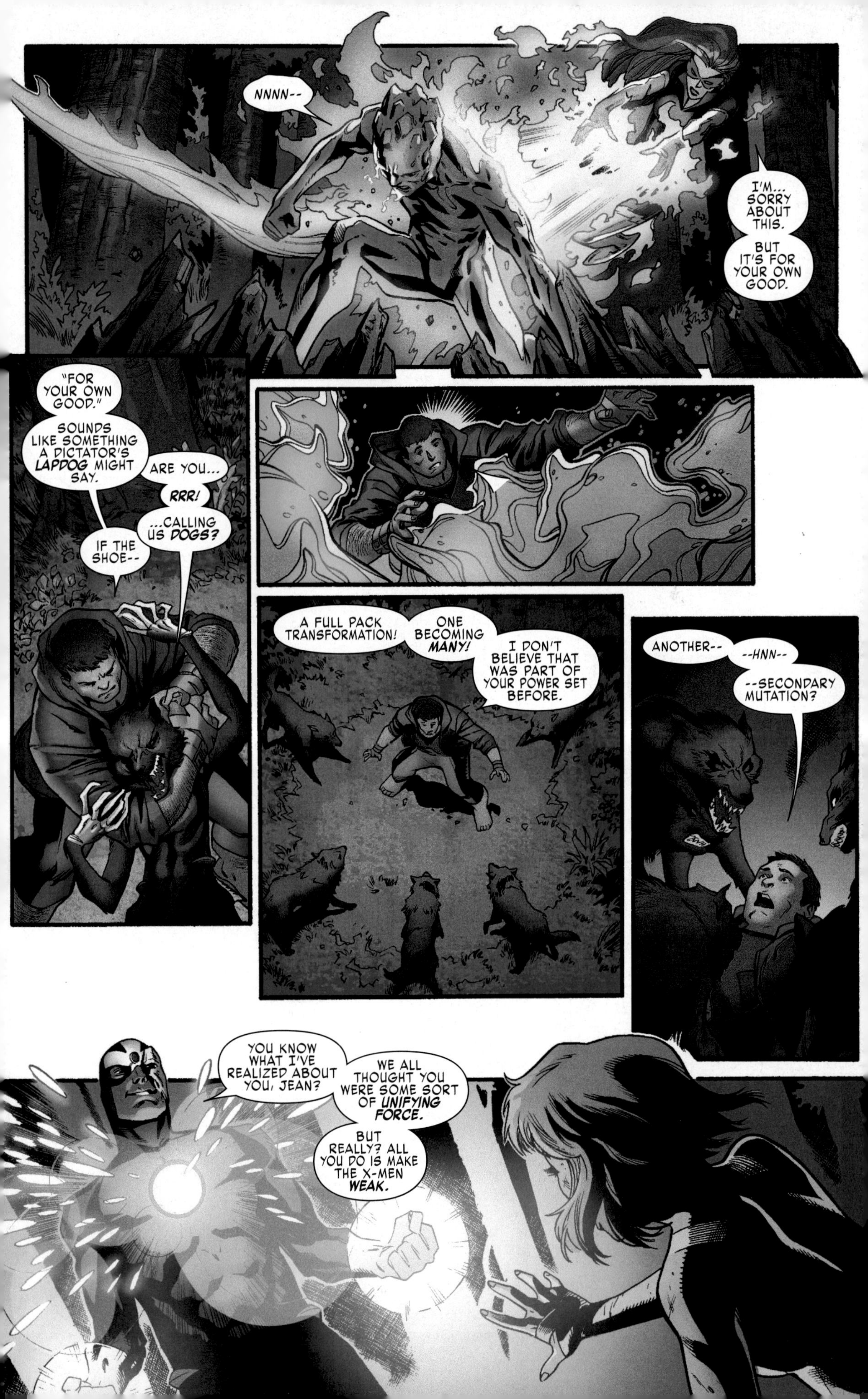
NNNN--
I'M... SORRY ABOUT THIS.
BUT IT'S FOR YOUR OWN GOOD.
"FOR YOUR OWN GOOD."
SOUNDS LIKE SOMETHING A DICTATOR'S LAPDOG MIGHT SAY.
ARE YOU...
RRR!
...CALLING US DOGS?
IF THE SHOE--
A FULL PACK TRANSFORMATION!
ONE BECOMING MANY!
I DON'T BELIEVE THAT WAS PART OF YOUR POWER SET BEFORE.
ANOTHER--
--HNN--
--SECONDARY MUTATION?
YOU KNOW WHAT I'VE REALIZED ABOUT YOU, JEAN?
WE ALL THOUGHT YOU WERE SOME SORT OF UNIFYING FORCE.
BUT REALLY? ALL YOU DO IS MAKE THE X-MEN WEAK.

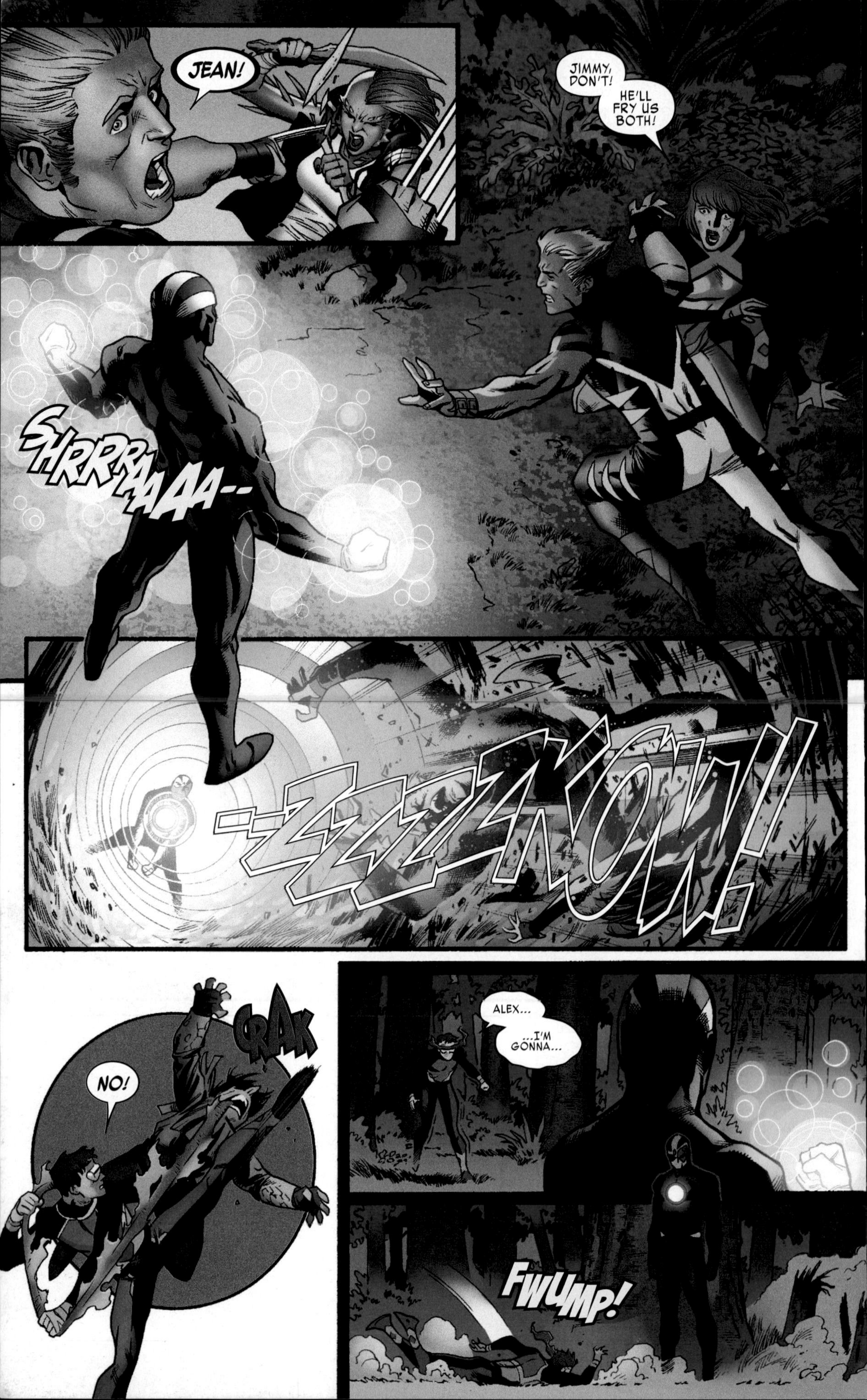
JEAN!
JIMMY, DON'T!
HE'LL FRY US BOTH!
SHRRRAAAA--
-ZZZZKOW!!
CRAK
NO!
ALEX...
...I'M GONNA...
FWUMP!

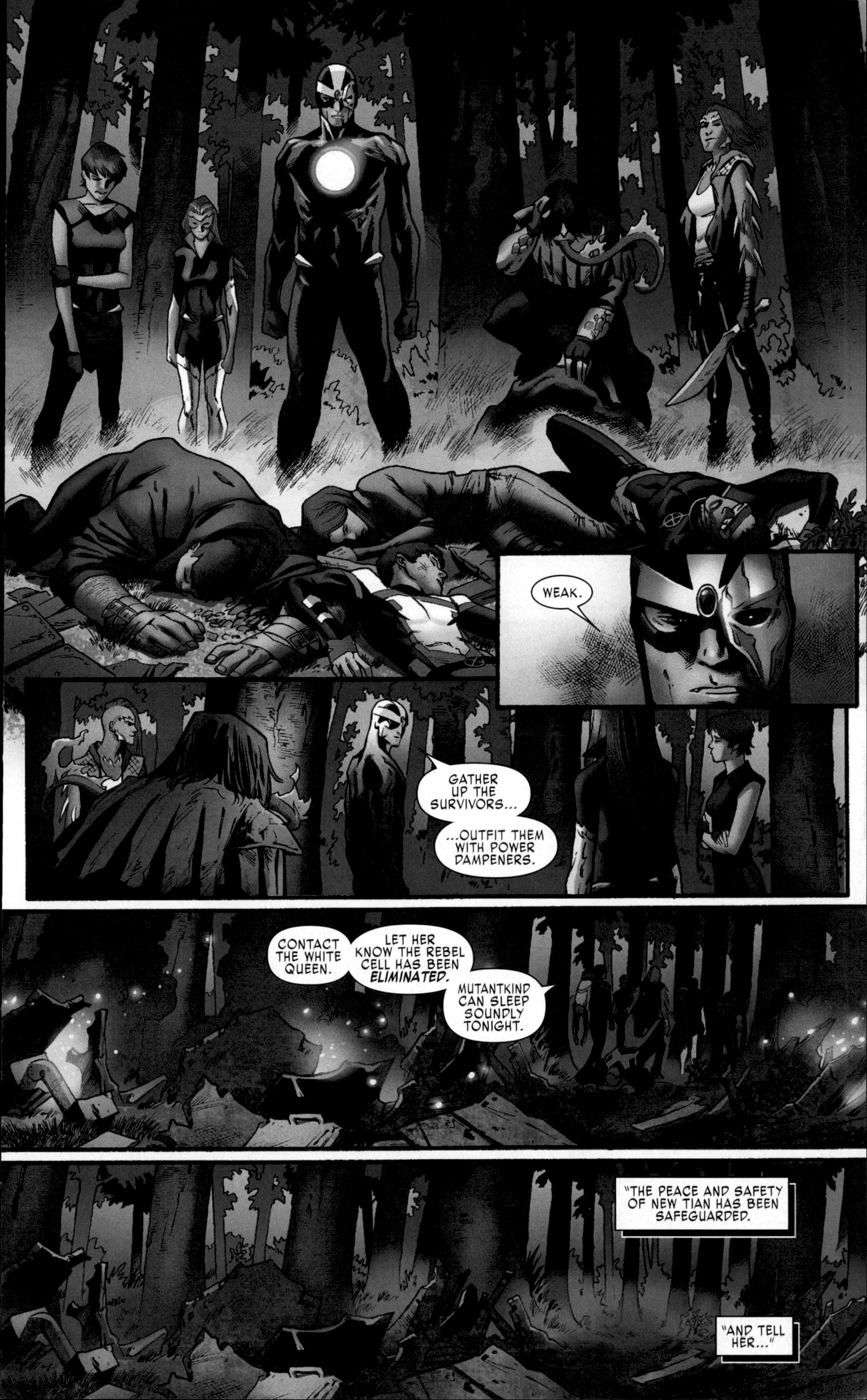
WEAK.
GATHER UP THE SURVIVORS...
...OUTFIT THEM WITH POWER DAMPENERS.
CONTACT THE WHITE QUEEN.
LET HER KNOW THE REBEL CELL HAS BEEN ELIMINATED.
MUTANTKIND CAN SLEEP SOUNDLY TONIGHT.
"THE PEACE AND SAFETY OF NEW TIAN HAS BEEN SAFEGUARDED.
"AND TELL HER..."

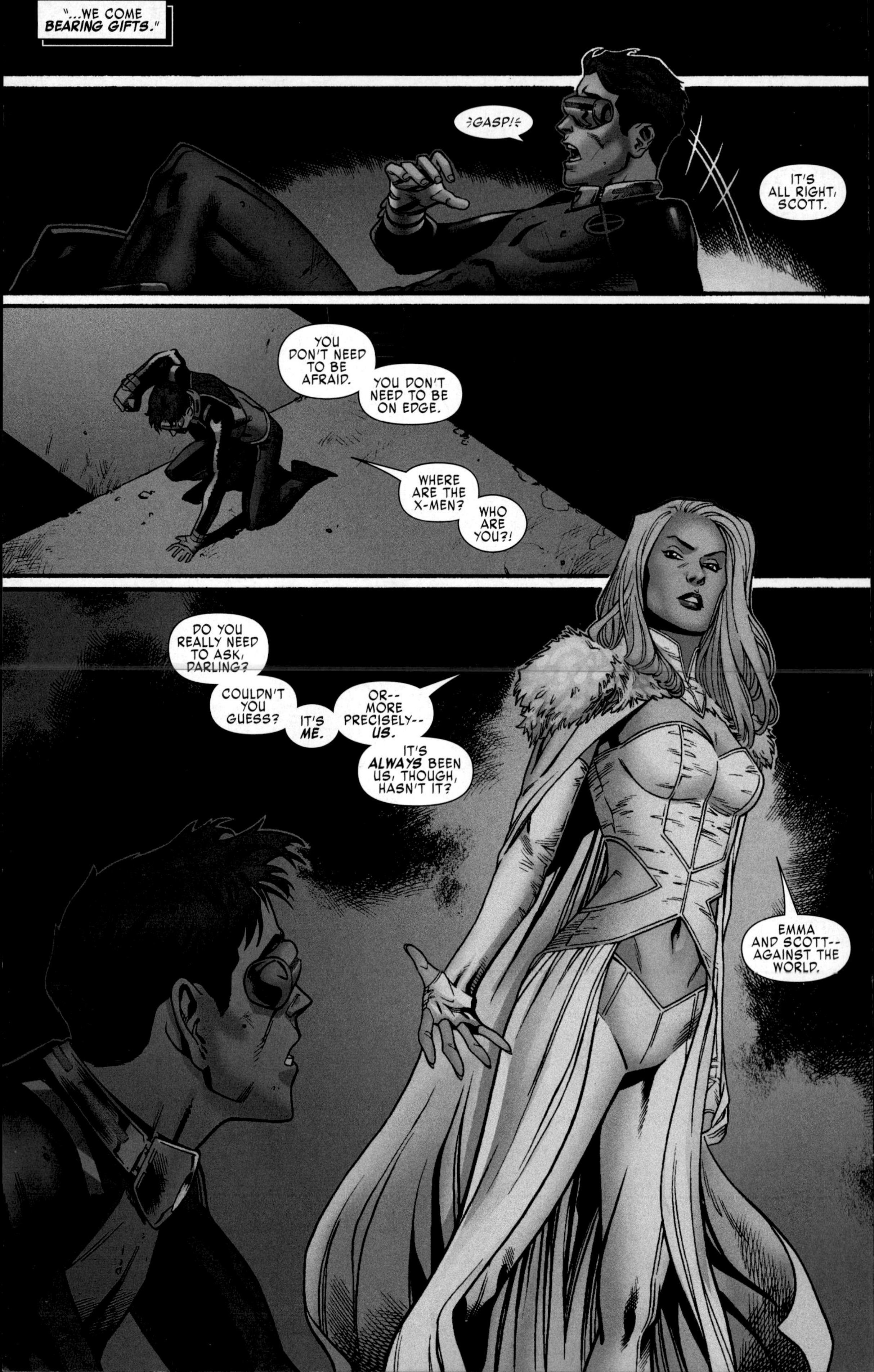
"...WE COME BEARING GIFTS."
≠GASP!≠
IT'S ALL RIGHT, SCOTT.
YOU DON'T NEED TO BE AFRAID.
YOU DON'T NEED TO BE ON EDGE.
WHERE ARE THE X-MEN?
WHO ARE YOU?!
DO YOU REALLY NEED TO ASK, DARLING?
COULDN'T YOU GUESS?
IT'S ME.
OR-- MORE PRECISELY-- US.
IT'S ALWAYS BEEN US, THOUGH, HASN'T IT?
EMMA AND SCOTT-- AGAINST THE WORLD.

8

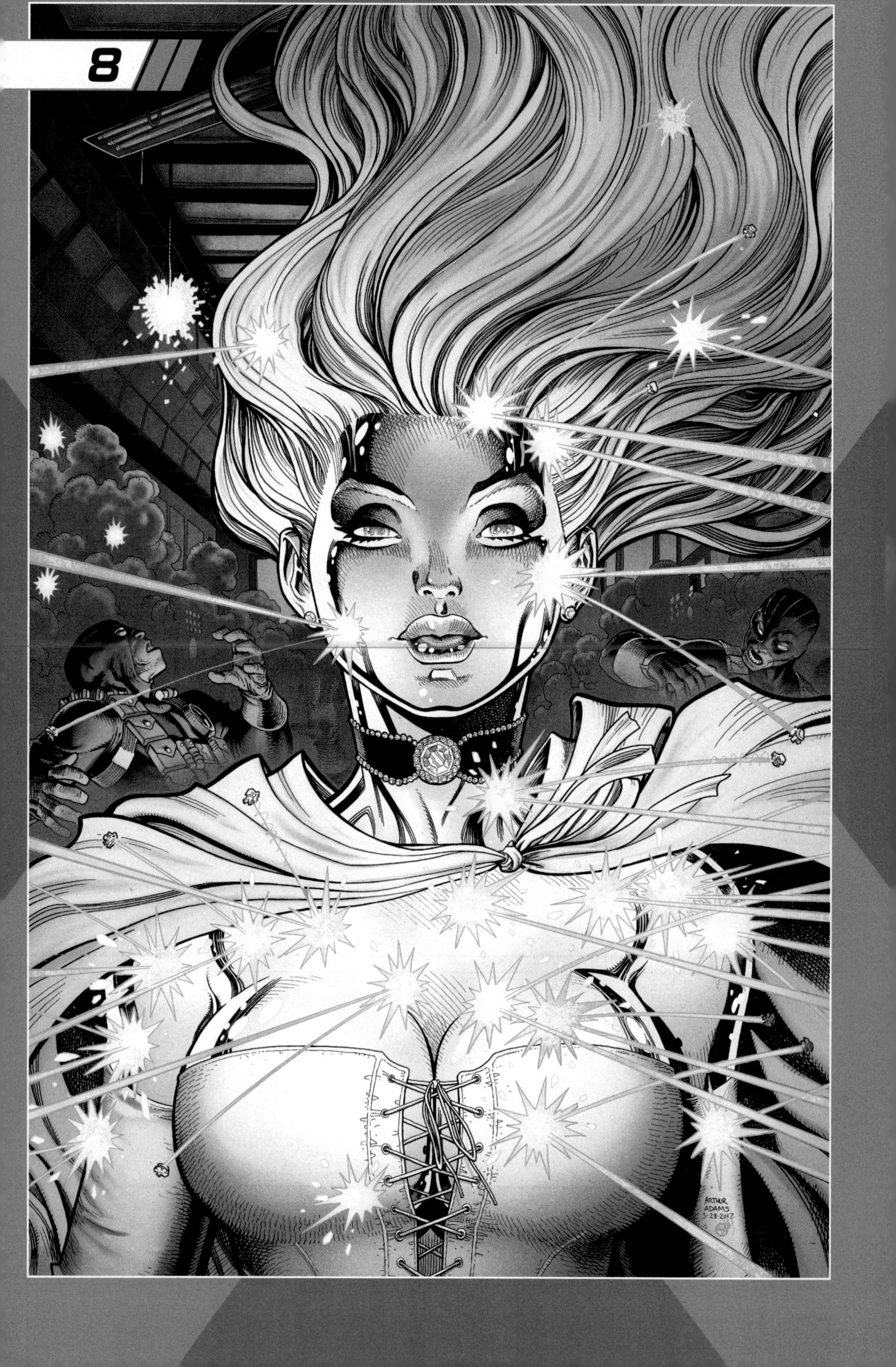
ARTHUR
ADAMS
3-28-2017

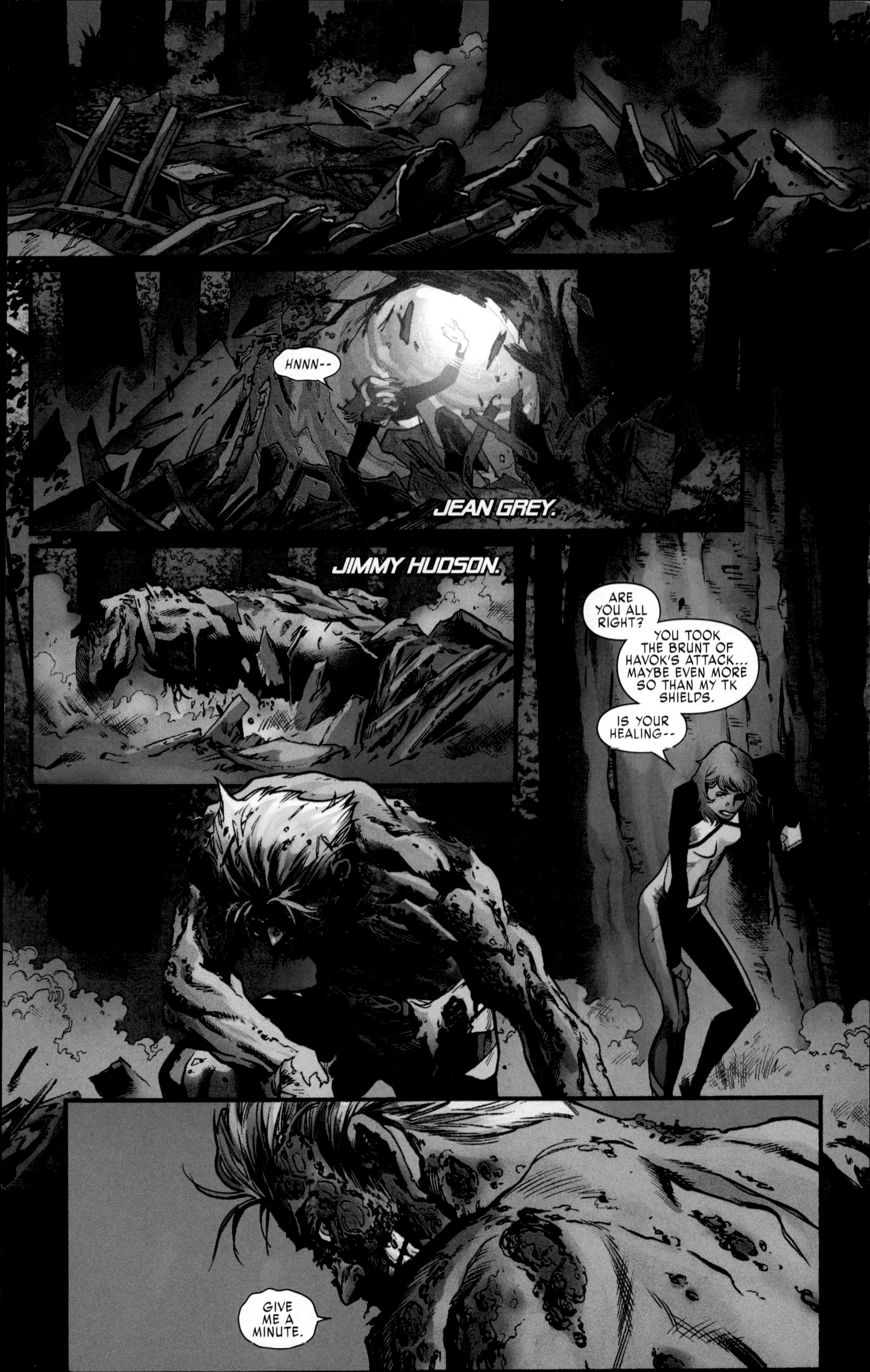
HNNN--
JEAN GREY.
JIMMY HUDSON.
ARE YOU ALL RIGHT?
YOU TOOK THE BRUNT OF HAVOK'S ATTACK... MAYBE EVEN MORE SO THAN MY TK SHIELDS.
IS YOUR HEALING--
GIVE ME A MINUTE.

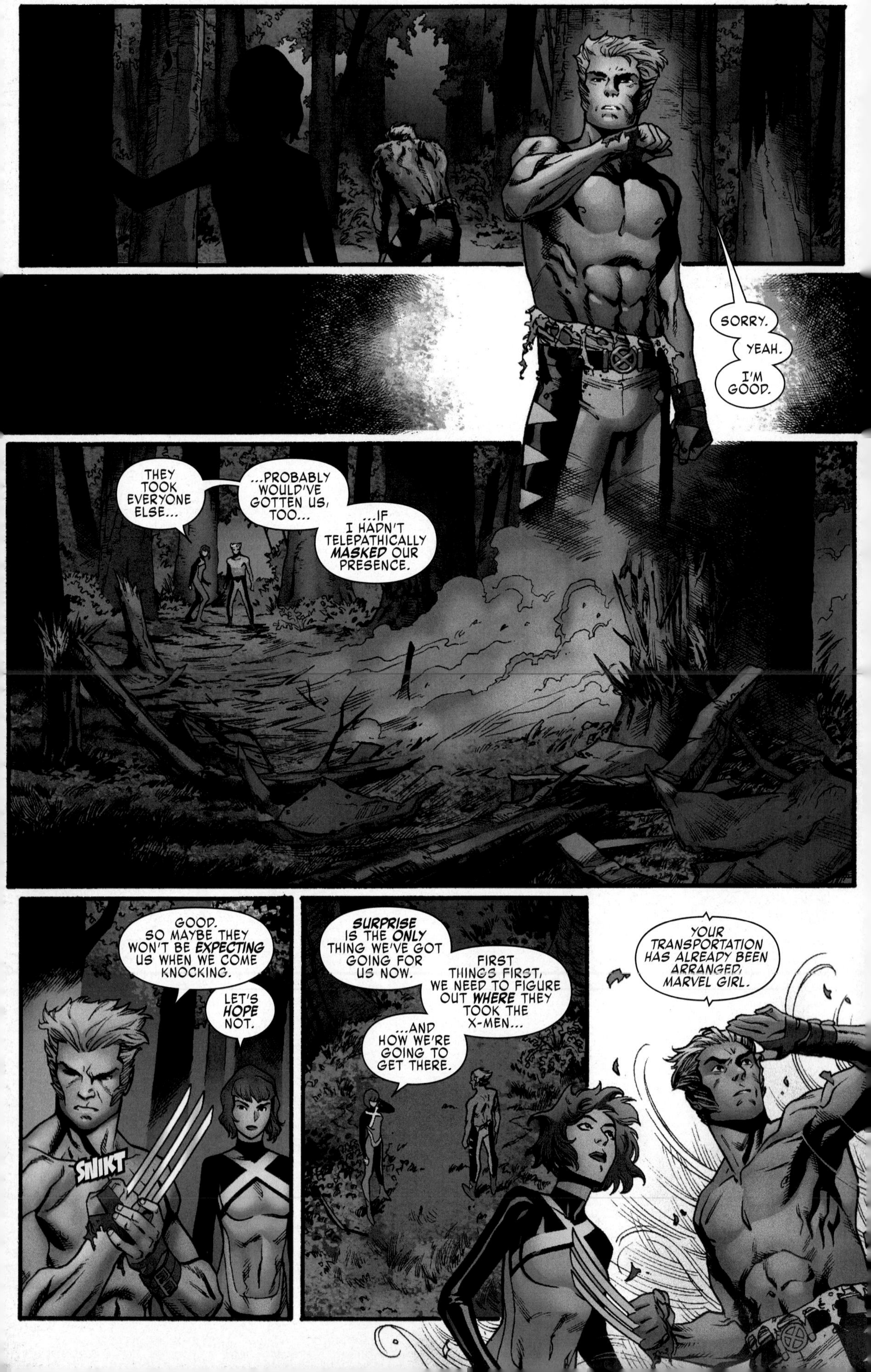
SORRY.
YEAH.
I'M GOOD.
THEY TOOK EVERYONE ELSE...
...PROBABLY WOULD'VE GOTTEN US, TOO...
...IF I HADN'T TELEPATHICALLY MASKED OUR PRESENCE.
GOOD. SO MAYBE THEY WON'T BE EXPECTING US WHEN WE COME KNOCKING.
LET'S HOPE NOT.
SNIKT
SURPRISE IS THE ONLY THING WE'VE GOT GOING FOR US NOW.
FIRST THINGS FIRST, WE NEED TO FIGURE OUT WHERE THEY TOOK THE X-MEN...
...AND HOW WE'RE GOING TO GET THERE.
YOUR TRANSPORTATION HAS ALREADY BEEN ARRANGED, MARVEL GIRL.

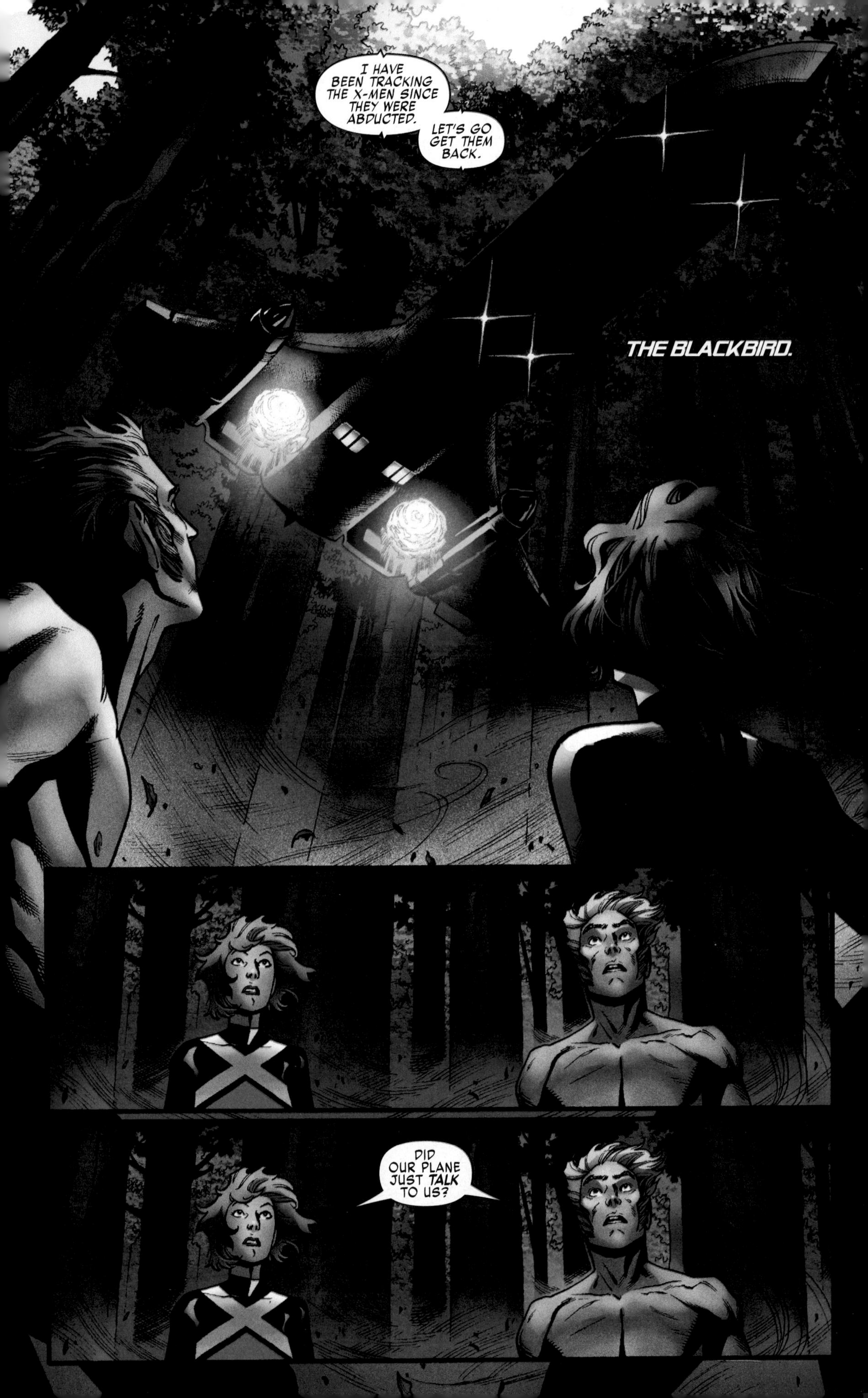

I HAVE BEEN TRACKING THE X-MEN SINCE THEY WERE ABDUCTED.
LET'S GO GET THEM BACK.
THE BLACKBIRD.
DID OUR PLANE JUST TALK TO US?

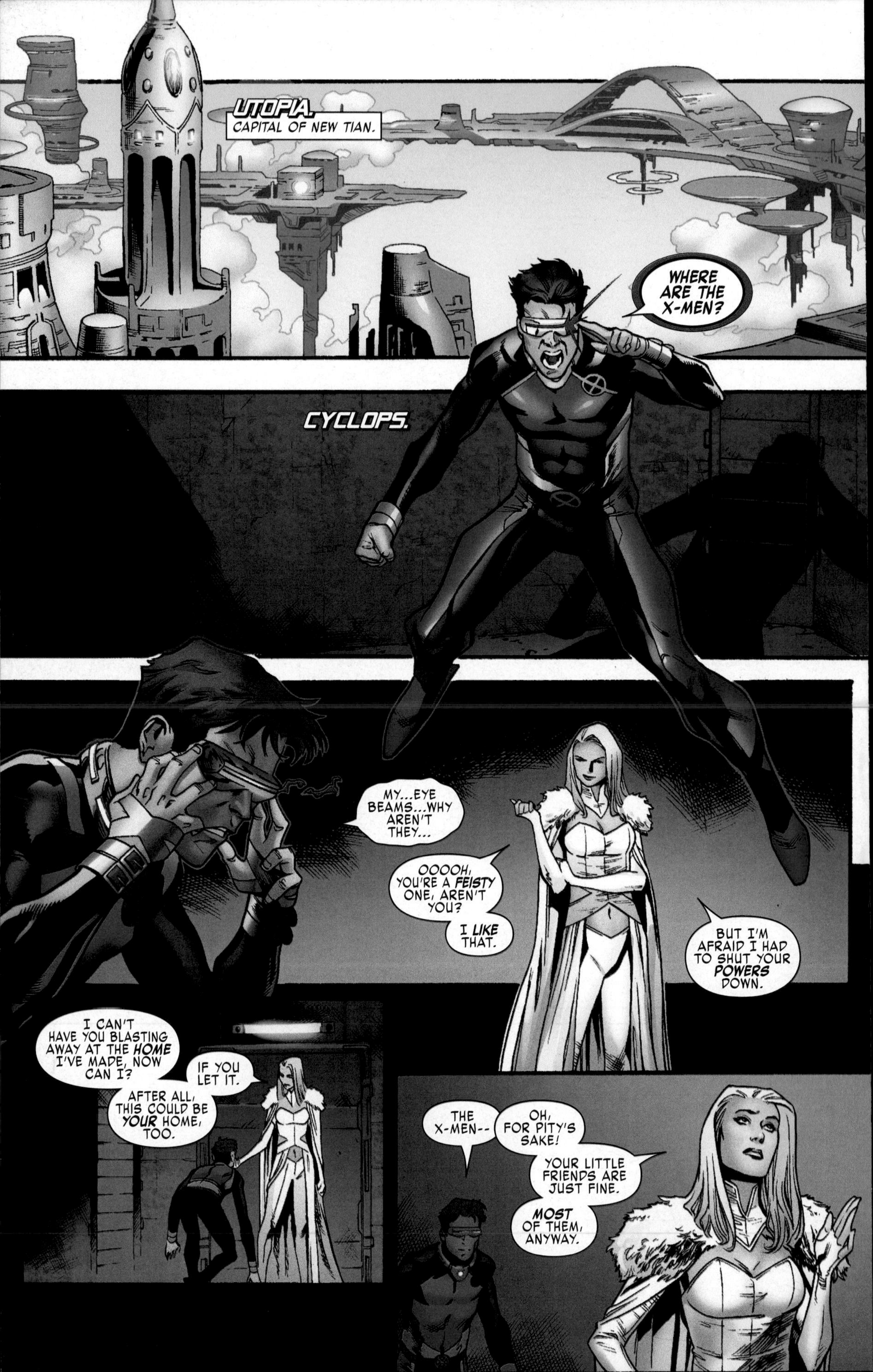
UTOPIA.
CAPITAL OF NEW TIAN.
WHERE ARE THE X-MEN?
CYCLOPS.
MY...EYE BEAMS...WHY AREN'T THEY...
OOOOH, YOU'RE A FEISTY ONE, AREN'T YOU?
I LIKE THAT.
BUT I'M AFRAID I HAD TO SHUT YOUR POWERS DOWN.
I CAN'T HAVE YOU BLASTING AWAY AT THE HOME I'VE MADE, NOW CAN I?
IF YOU LET IT.
AFTER ALL, THIS COULD BE YOUR HOME, TOO.
THE X-MEN--
OH, FOR PITY'S SAKE!
YOUR LITTLE FRIENDS ARE JUST FINE.
MOST OF THEM, ANYWAY.

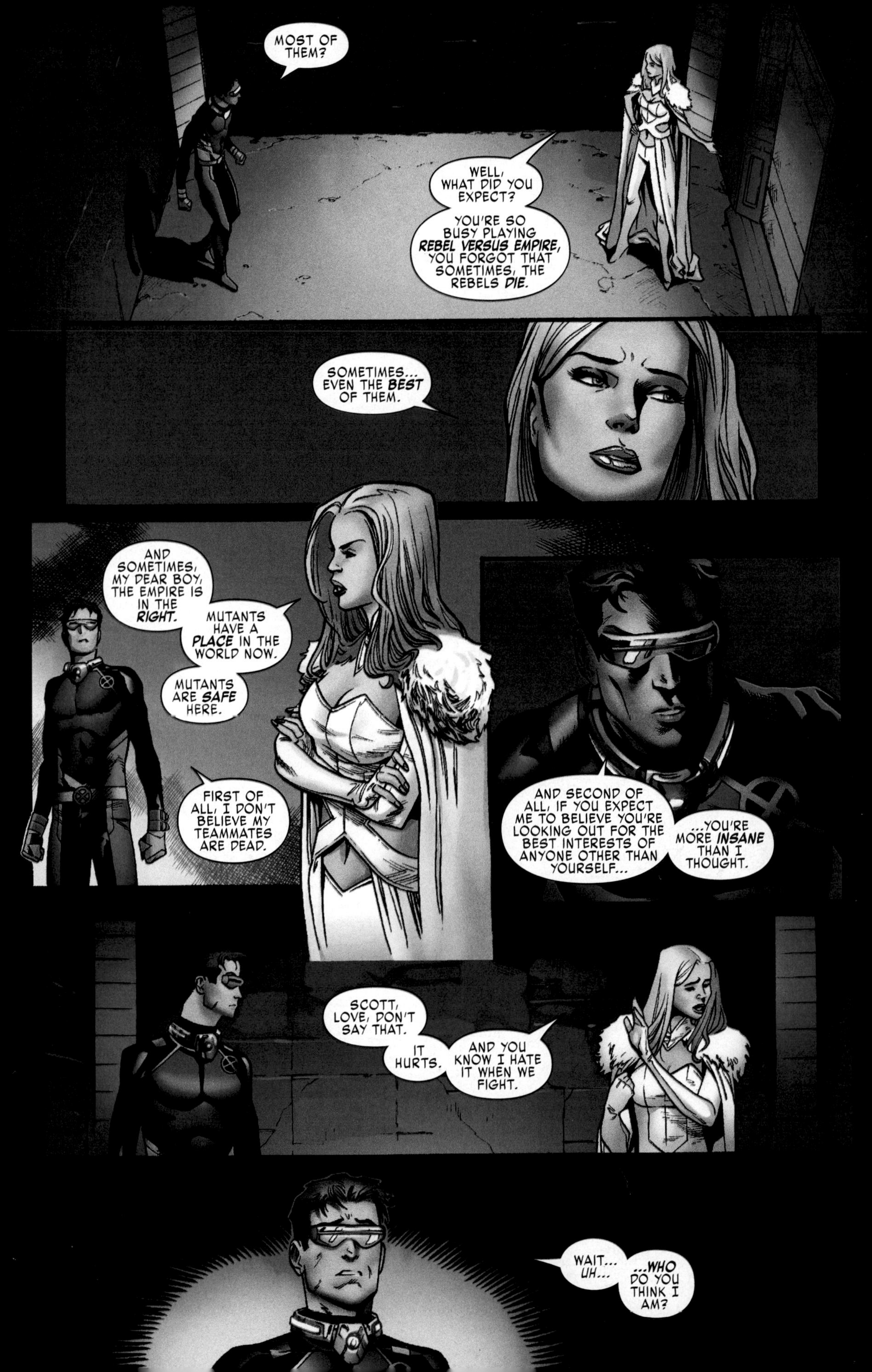
MOST OF THEM?
WELL, WHAT DID YOU EXPECT?
YOU'RE SO BUSY PLAYING REBEL VERSUS EMPIRE, YOU FORGOT THAT SOMETIMES, THE REBELS DIE.
SOMETIMES... EVEN THE BEST OF THEM.
AND SOMETIMES, MY DEAR BOY, THE EMPIRE IS IN THE RIGHT.
MUTANTS HAVE A PLACE IN THE WORLD NOW.
MUTANTS ARE SAFE HERE.
FIRST OF ALL, I DON'T BELIEVE MY TEAMMATES ARE DEAD.
AND SECOND OF ALL, IF YOU EXPECT ME TO BELIEVE YOU'RE LOOKING OUT FOR THE BEST INTERESTS OF ANYONE OTHER THAN YOURSELF...
...YOU'RE MORE INSANE THAN I THOUGHT.
SCOTT, LOVE, DON'T SAY THAT.
IT HURTS.
AND YOU KNOW I HATE IT WHEN WE FIGHT.
WAIT... UH...
...WHO DO YOU THINK I AM?

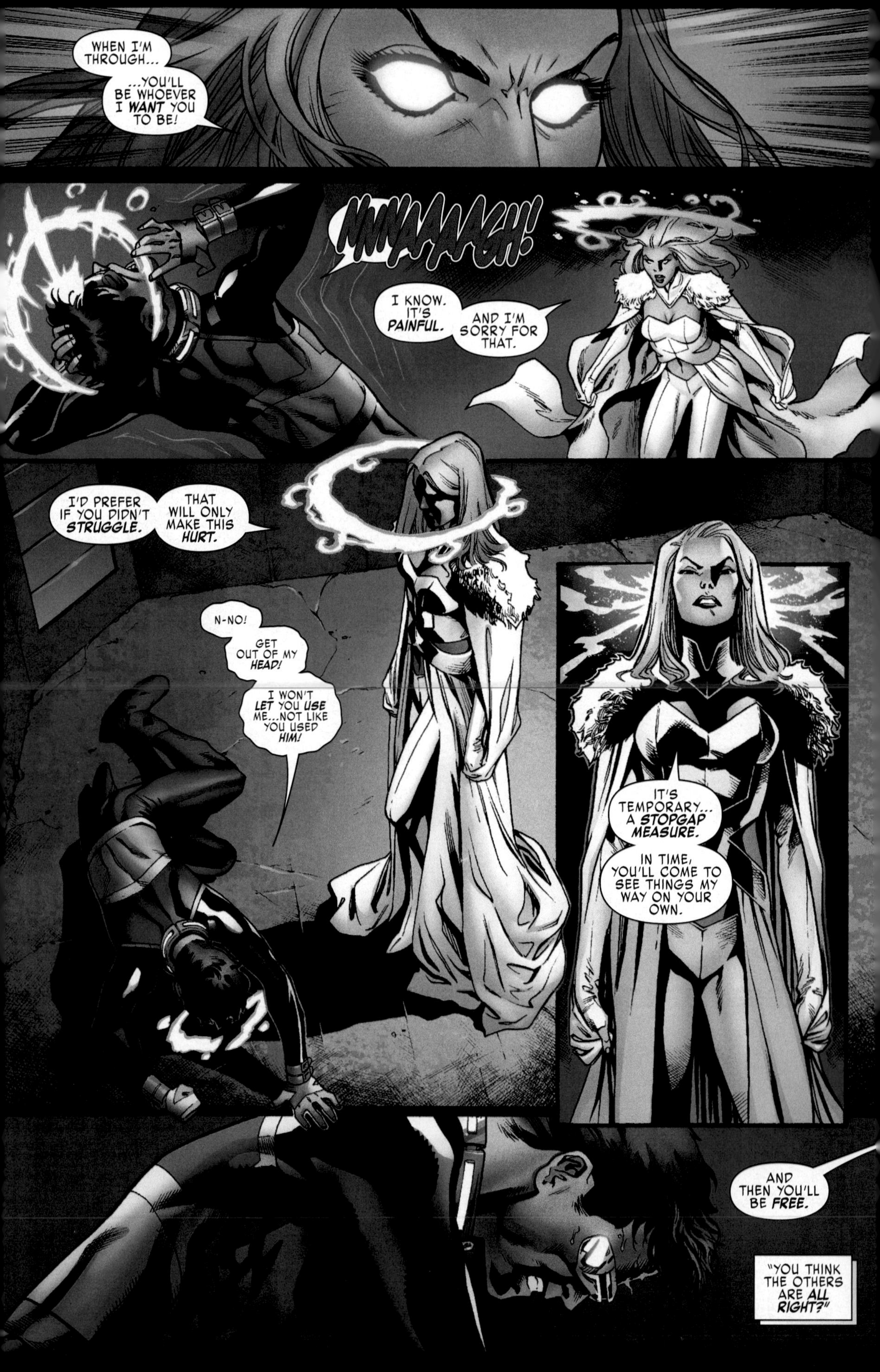
WHEN I'M THROUGH...
...YOU'LL BE WHOEVER I WANT YOU TO BE!
NNNAAAAGH!
I KNOW. IT'S PAINFUL.
AND I'M SORRY FOR THAT.
I'D PREFER IF YOU DIDN'T STRUGGLE.
THAT WILL ONLY MAKE THIS HURT.
N-NO!
GET OUT OF MY HEAD!
I WON'T LET YOU USE ME...NOT LIKE YOU USED HIM!
IT'S TEMPORARY... A STOPGAP MEASURE.
IN TIME, YOU'LL COME TO SEE THINGS MY WAY ON YOUR OWN.
AND THEN YOU'LL BE FREE.
"YOU THINK THE OTHERS ARE ALL RIGHT?"

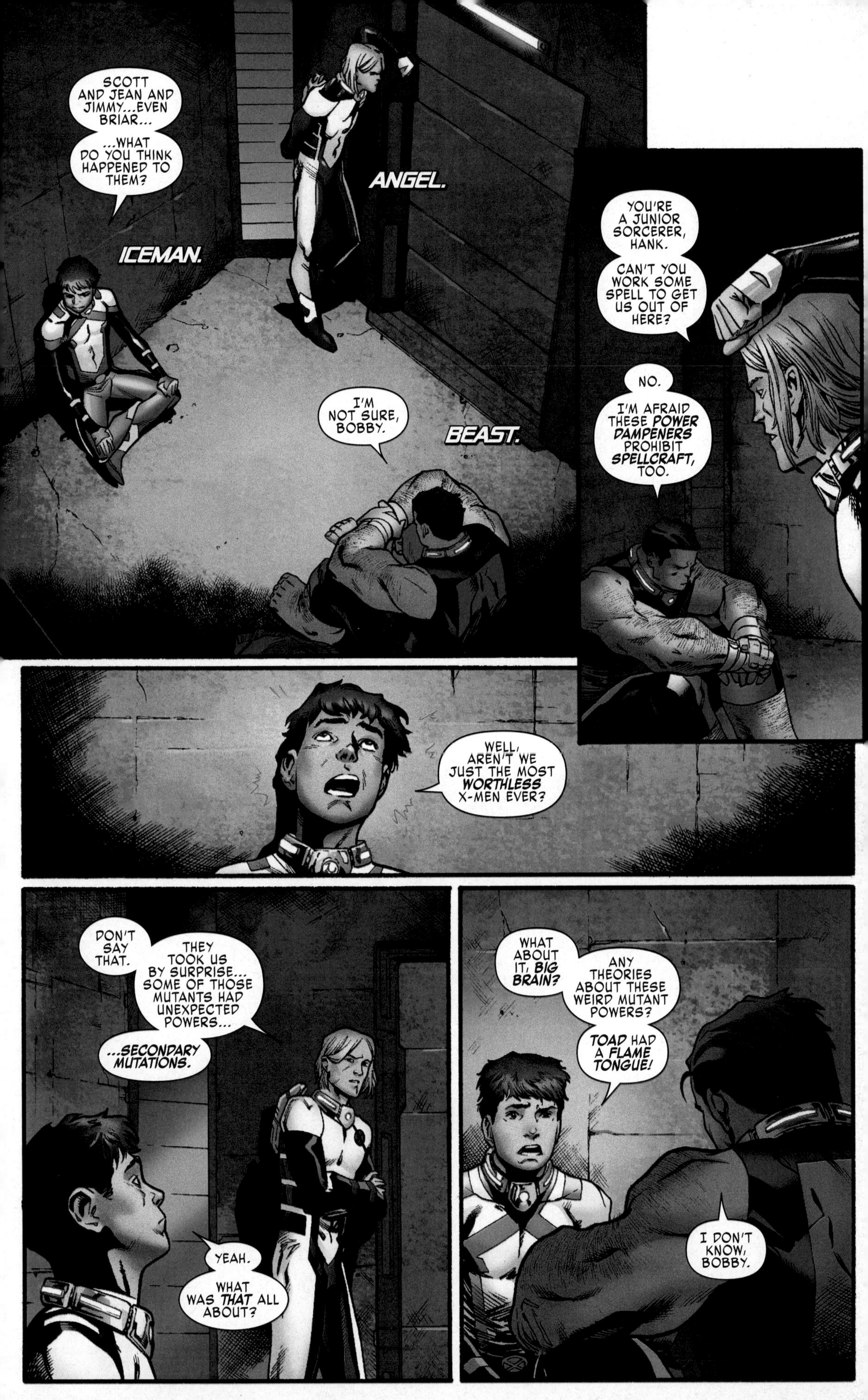
SCOTT AND JEAN AND JIMMY...EVEN BRIAR...
...WHAT DO YOU THINK HAPPENED TO THEM?
ICEMAN.
ANGEL.
I'M NOT SURE, BOBBY.
BEAST.
YOU'RE A JUNIOR SORCERER, HANK.
CAN'T YOU WORK SOME SPELL TO GET US OUT OF HERE?
NO.
I'M AFRAID THESE POWER DAMPENERS PROHIBIT SPELLCRAFT, TOO.
WELL, AREN'T WE JUST THE MOST WORTHLESS X-MEN EVER?
DON'T SAY THAT.
THEY TOOK US BY SURPRISE... SOME OF THOSE MUTANTS HAD UNEXPECTED POWERS...
...SECONDARY MUTATIONS.
YEAH.
WHAT WAS THAT ALL ABOUT?
WHAT ABOUT IT, BIG BRAIN?
ANY THEORIES ABOUT THESE WEIRD MUTANT POWERS?
TOAD HAD A FLAME TONGUE!
I DON'T KNOW, BOBBY.

WE'LL BE OKAY.

SOMEONE IS GOING TO COME LOOKING FOR US.

MAGNETO WILL COME LOOKING FOR US.

YOU DON'T REALLY BELIEVE THAT, DO YOU, WARREN?

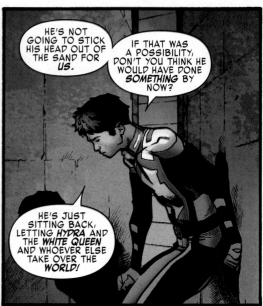

HE'S NOT GOING TO STICK HIS HEAD OUT OF THE SAND FOR US.

IF THAT WAS A POSSIBILITY, DON'T YOU THINK HE WOULD HAVE DONE SOMETHING BY NOW?

HE'S JUST SITTING BACK, LETTING HYDRA AND THE WHITE QUEEN AND WHOEVER ELSE TAKE OVER THE WORLD!

FACE IT, FLY-BOY.

EVERYBODY HAS PRIORITIES... AND THAT MEANS SOMETIMES THEY PRIORITIZE RELATIONSHIPS, TOO.

AND SOMETIMES, YOU JUST DON'T RANK.

HANK? YOU WANT TO HELP ME OUT HERE?

WHAT ARE YOU DOING?

WHAT ARE YOU LOOKING AT?

I'M THINKING.

I'M MENTALLY CATALOGUING ALL THE MEANEST SPELLS I KNOW.

BECAUSE WHEN WE GET LOOSE, I'M CASTING EVERY ONE OF THEM ON THE PEOPLE WHO PUT US HERE.

"I TRUST YOU FIND THE ACCOMMODATIONS COMFORTABLE?"

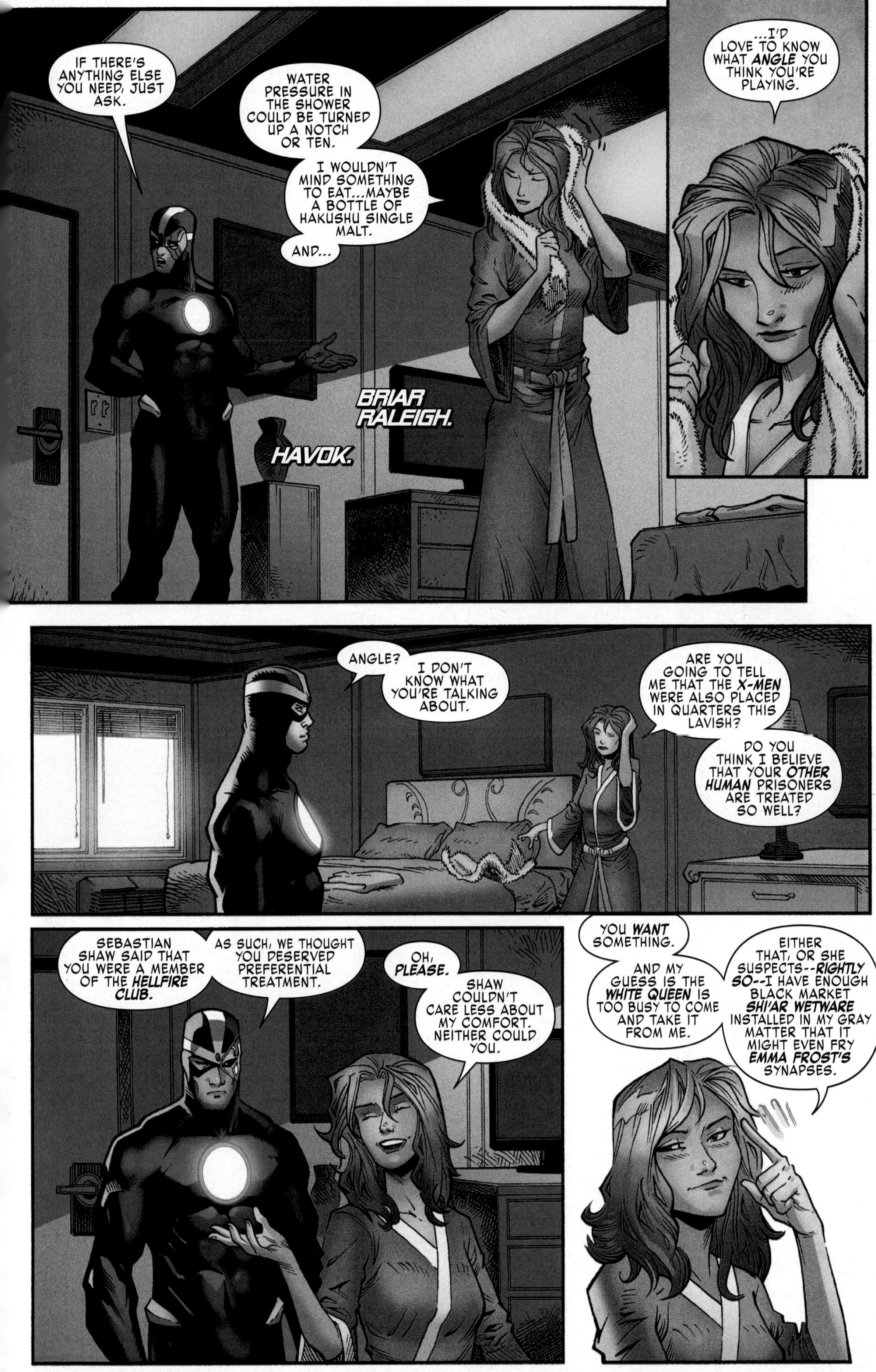
IF THERE'S ANYTHING ELSE YOU NEED, JUST ASK.
WATER PRESSURE IN THE SHOWER COULD BE TURNED UP A NOTCH OR TEN.
I WOULDN'T MIND SOMETHING TO EAT...MAYBE A BOTTLE OF HAKUSHU SINGLE MALT.
AND...
BRIAR RALEIGH.
HAVOK.
...I'D LOVE TO KNOW WHAT ANGLE YOU THINK YOU'RE PLAYING.
ANGLE?
I DON'T KNOW WHAT YOU'RE TALKING ABOUT.
ARE YOU GOING TO TELL ME THAT THE X-MEN WERE ALSO PLACED IN QUARTERS THIS LAVISH?
DO YOU THINK I BELIEVE THAT YOUR OTHER HUMAN PRISONERS ARE TREATED SO WELL?
SEBASTIAN SHAW SAID THAT YOU WERE A MEMBER OF THE HELLFIRE CLUB.
AS SUCH, WE THOUGHT YOU DESERVED PREFERENTIAL TREATMENT.
OH, PLEASE.
SHAW COULDN'T CARE LESS ABOUT MY COMFORT. NEITHER COULD YOU.
YOU WANT SOMETHING.
AND MY GUESS IS THE WHITE QUEEN IS TOO BUSY TO COME AND TAKE IT FROM ME.
EITHER THAT, OR SHE SUSPECTS--RIGHTLY SO--I HAVE ENOUGH BLACK MARKET SHI'AR WETWARE INSTALLED IN MY GRAY MATTER THAT IT MIGHT EVEN FRY EMMA FROST'S SYNAPSES.

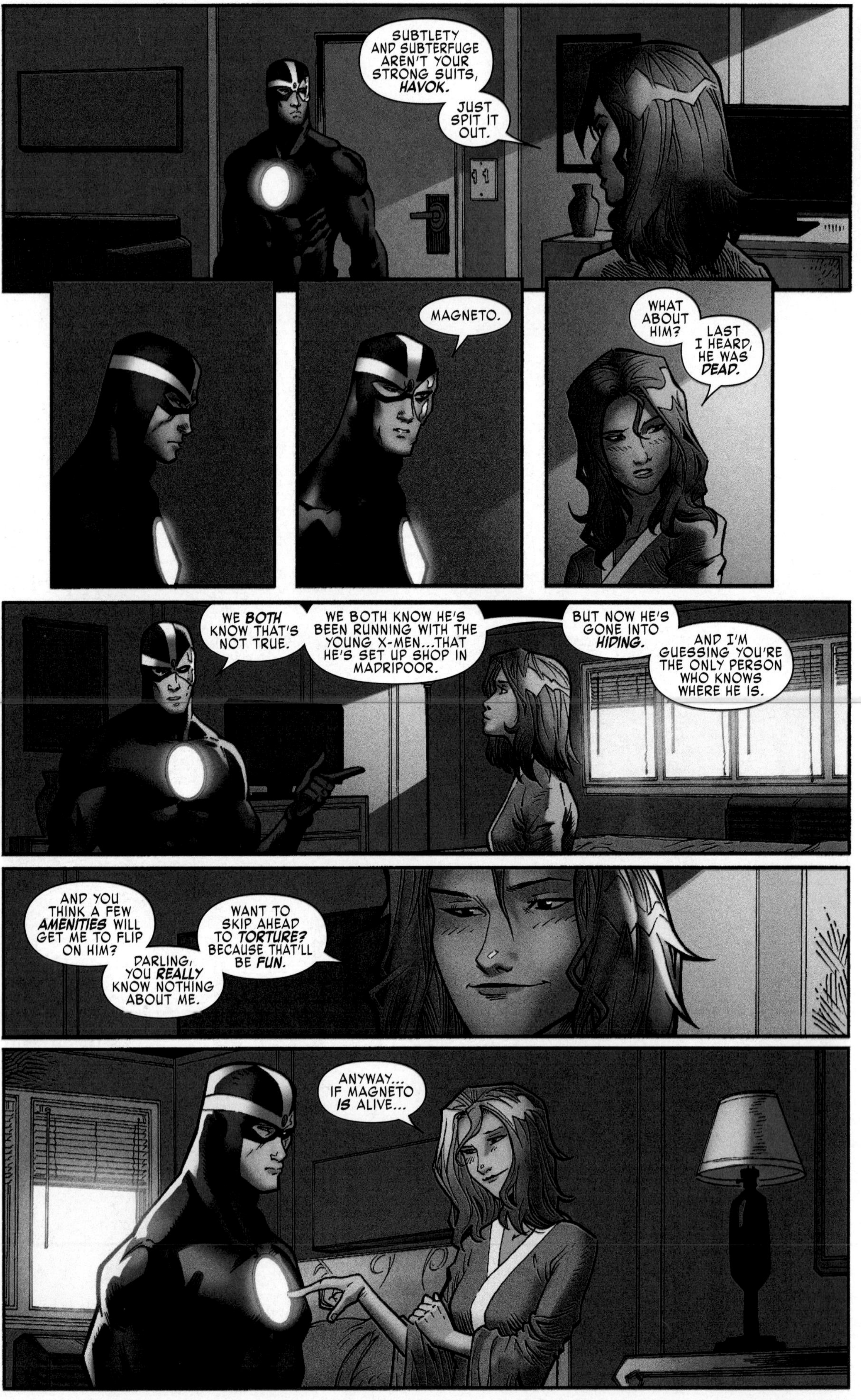
SUBTLETY AND SUBTERFUGE AREN'T YOUR STRONG SUITS, HAVOK.
JUST SPIT IT OUT.
MAGNETO.
WHAT ABOUT HIM?
LAST I HEARD, HE WAS DEAD.
WE BOTH KNOW THAT'S NOT TRUE.
WE BOTH KNOW HE'S BEEN RUNNING WITH THE YOUNG X-MEN...THAT HE'S SET UP SHOP IN MADRIPOOR.
BUT NOW HE'S GONE INTO HIDING.
AND I'M GUESSING YOU'RE THE ONLY PERSON WHO KNOWS WHERE HE IS.
AND YOU THINK A FEW AMENITIES WILL GET ME TO FLIP ON HIM?
DARLING, YOU REALLY KNOW NOTHING ABOUT ME.
WANT TO SKIP AHEAD TO TORTURE? BECAUSE THAT'LL BE FUN.
ANYWAY... IF MAGNETO IS ALIVE...

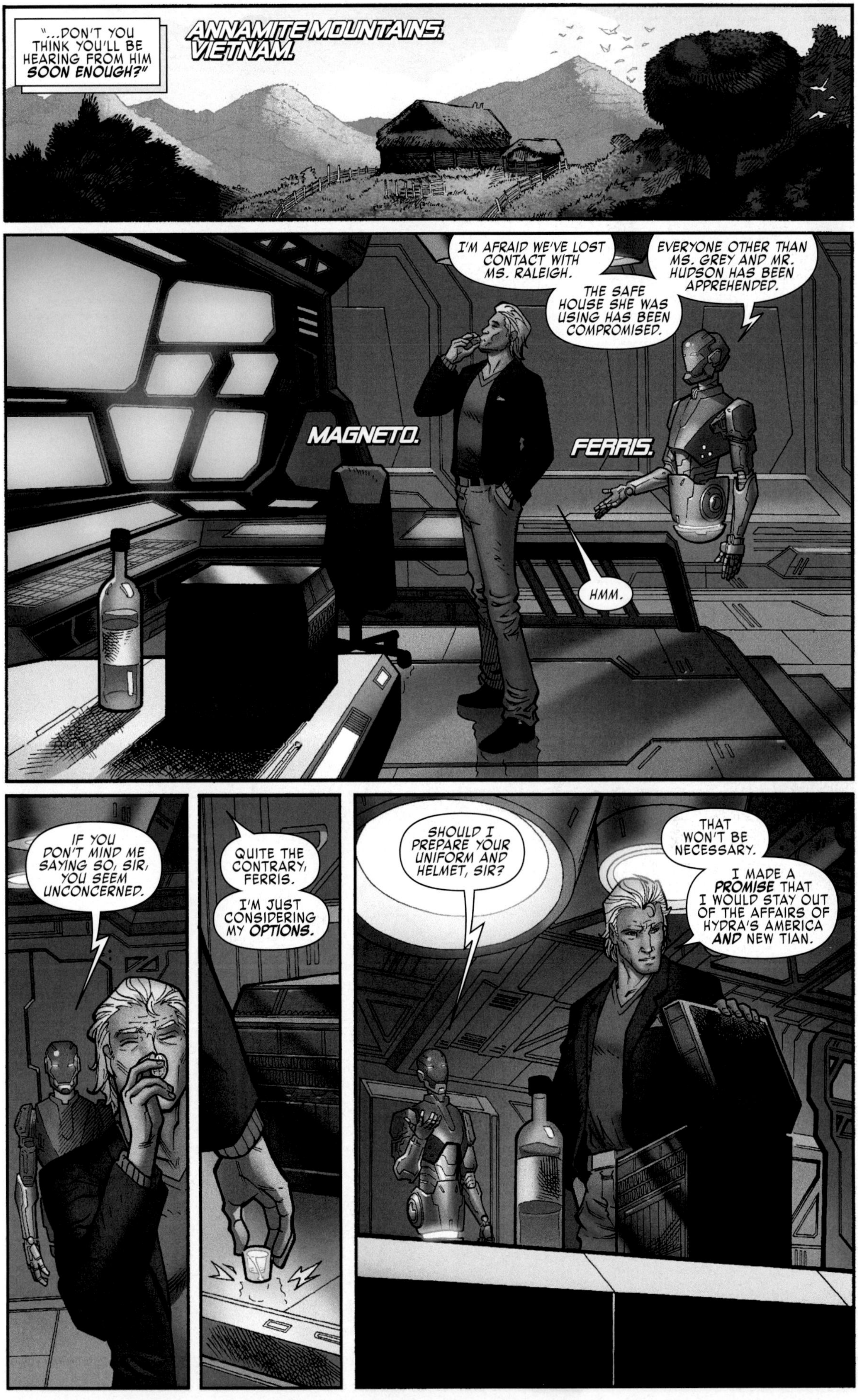
"...DON'T YOU THINK YOU'LL BE HEARING FROM HIM SOON ENOUGH?"
ANNAMITE MOUNTAINS. VIETNAM.
I'M AFRAID WE'VE LOST CONTACT WITH MS. RALEIGH.
THE SAFE HOUSE SHE WAS USING HAS BEEN COMPROMISED.
EVERYONE OTHER THAN MS. GREY AND MR. HUDSON HAS BEEN APPREHENDED.
MAGNETO.
FERRIS.
HMM.
IF YOU DON'T MIND ME SAYING SO, SIR, YOU SEEM UNCONCERNED.
QUITE THE CONTRARY, FERRIS.
I'M JUST CONSIDERING MY OPTIONS.
SHOULD I PREPARE YOUR UNIFORM AND HELMET, SIR?
THAT WON'T BE NECESSARY.
I MADE A PROMISE THAT I WOULD STAY OUT OF THE AFFAIRS OF HYDRA'S AMERICA AND NEW TIAN.

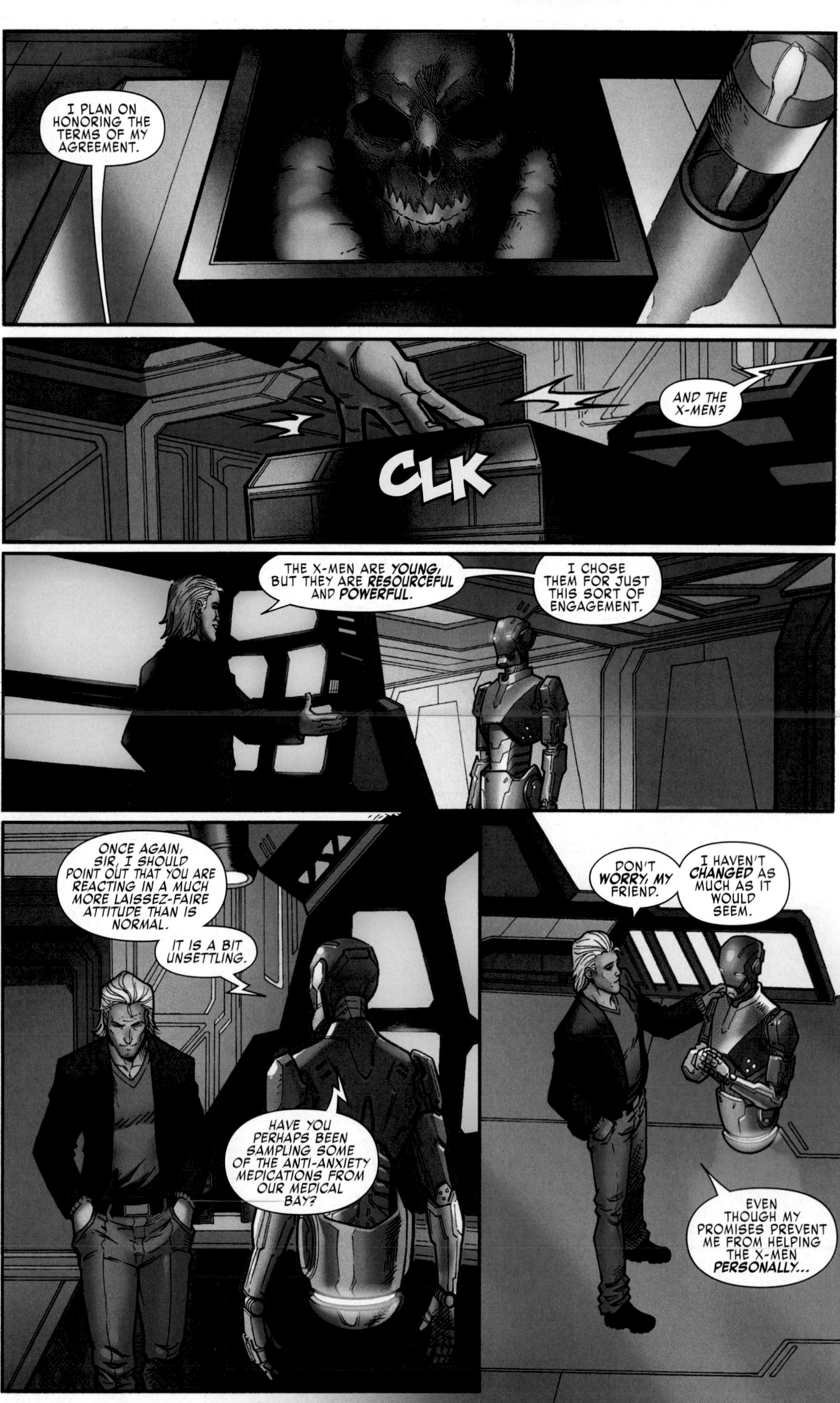

I PLAN ON HONORING THE TERMS OF MY AGREEMENT.
AND THE X-MEN?
CLK
THE X-MEN ARE YOUNG, BUT THEY ARE RESOURCEFUL AND POWERFUL.
I CHOSE THEM FOR JUST THIS SORT OF ENGAGEMENT.
ONCE AGAIN, SIR, I SHOULD POINT OUT THAT YOU ARE REACTING IN A MUCH MORE LAISSEZ-FAIRE ATTITUDE THAN IS NORMAL.
IT IS A BIT UNSETTLING.
HAVE YOU PERHAPS BEEN SAMPLING SOME OF THE ANTI-ANXIETY MEDICATIONS FROM OUR MEDICAL BAY?
DON'T WORRY, MY FRIEND.
I HAVEN'T CHANGED AS MUCH AS IT WOULD SEEM.
EVEN THOUGH MY PROMISES PREVENT ME FROM HELPING THE X-MEN PERSONALLY...

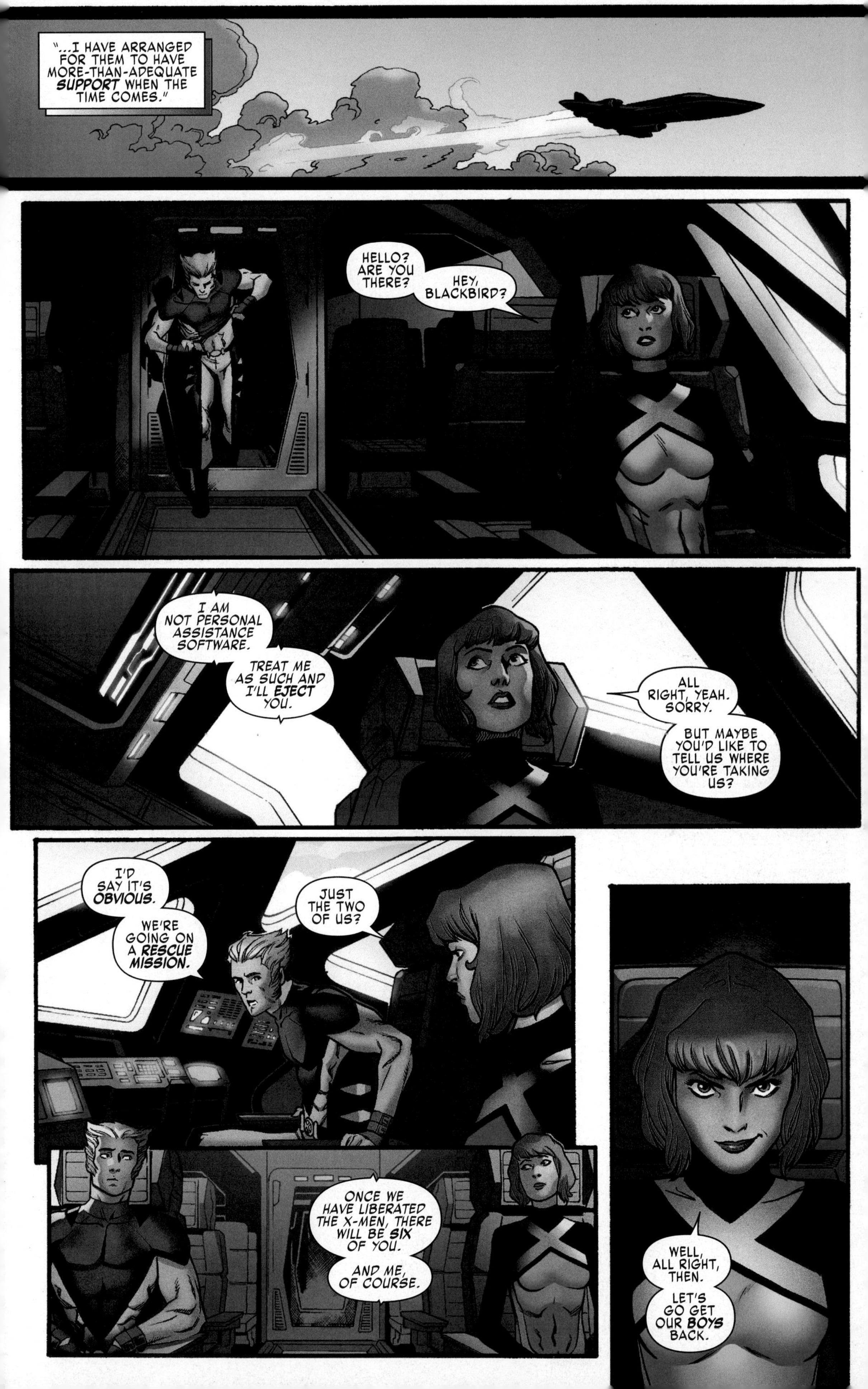
"...I HAVE ARRANGED FOR THEM TO HAVE MORE-THAN-ADEQUATE SUPPORT WHEN THE TIME COMES."
HELLO? ARE YOU THERE?
HEY, BLACKBIRD?
I AM NOT PERSONAL ASSISTANCE SOFTWARE.
TREAT ME AS SUCH AND I'LL EJECT YOU.
ALL RIGHT, YEAH. SORRY.
BUT MAYBE YOU'D LIKE TO TELL US WHERE YOU'RE TAKING US?
I'D SAY IT'S OBVIOUS.
WE'RE GOING ON A RESCUE MISSION.
JUST THE TWO OF US?
ONCE WE HAVE LIBERATED THE X-MEN, THERE WILL BE SIX OF YOU.
AND ME, OF COURSE.
WELL, ALL RIGHT, THEN.
LET'S GO GET OUR BOYS BACK.

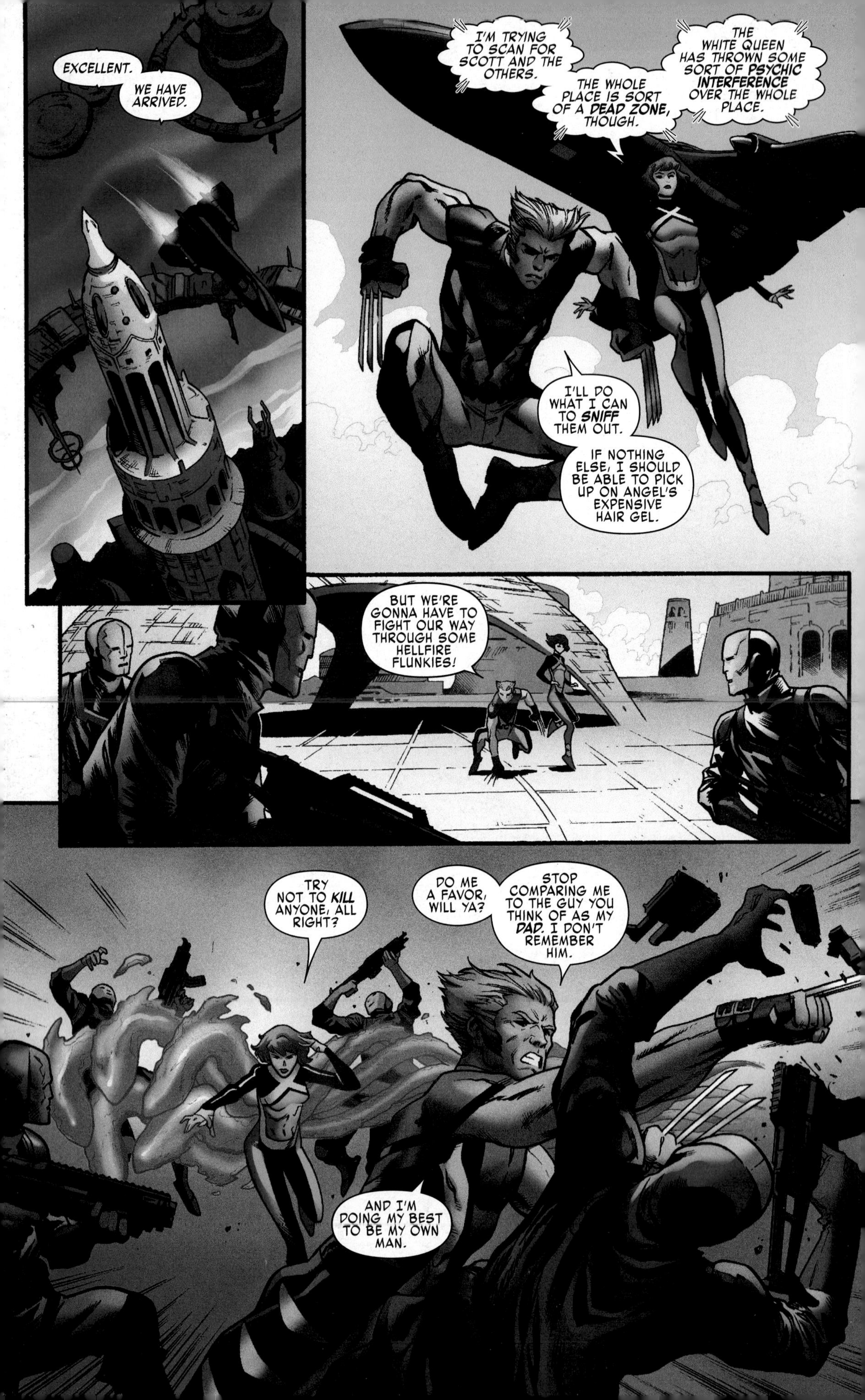
EXCELLENT.
WE HAVE ARRIVED.
I'M TRYING TO SCAN FOR SCOTT AND THE OTHERS.
THE WHOLE PLACE IS SORT OF A DEAD ZONE, THOUGH.
THE WHITE QUEEN HAS THROWN SOME SORT OF PSYCHIC INTERFERENCE OVER THE WHOLE PLACE.
I'LL DO WHAT I CAN TO SNIFF THEM OUT.
IF NOTHING ELSE, I SHOULD BE ABLE TO PICK UP ON ANGEL'S EXPENSIVE HAIR GEL.
BUT WE'RE GONNA HAVE TO FIGHT OUR WAY THROUGH SOME HELLFIRE FLUNKIES!
TRY NOT TO KILL ANYONE, ALL RIGHT?
DO ME A FAVOR, WILL YA?
STOP COMPARING ME TO THE GUY YOU THINK OF AS MY DAD. I DON'T REMEMBER HIM.
AND I'M DOING MY BEST TO BE MY OWN MAN.

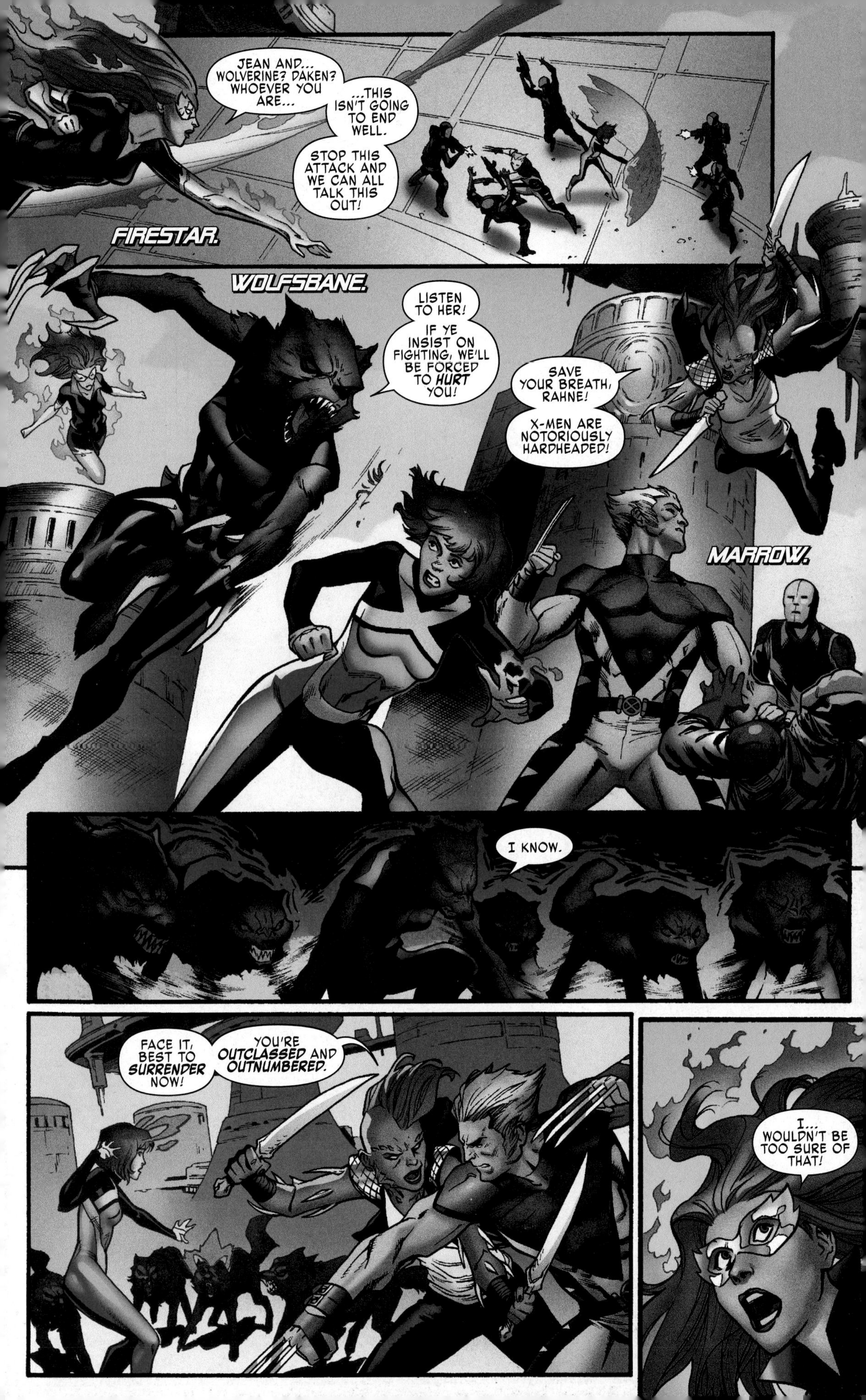
JEAN AND... WOLVERINE? DAKEN? WHOEVER YOU ARE...
...THIS ISN'T GOING TO END WELL.
STOP THIS ATTACK AND WE CAN ALL TALK THIS OUT!
FIRESTAR.
WOLFSBANE.
LISTEN TO HER!
IF YE INSIST ON FIGHTING, WE'LL BE FORCED TO HURT YOU!
SAVE YOUR BREATH, RAHNE!
X-MEN ARE NOTORIOUSLY HARDHEADED!
MARROW.
I KNOW.
FACE IT, BEST TO SURRENDER NOW!
YOU'RE OUTCLASSED AND OUTNUMBERED.
I... WOULDN'T BE TOO SURE OF THAT!

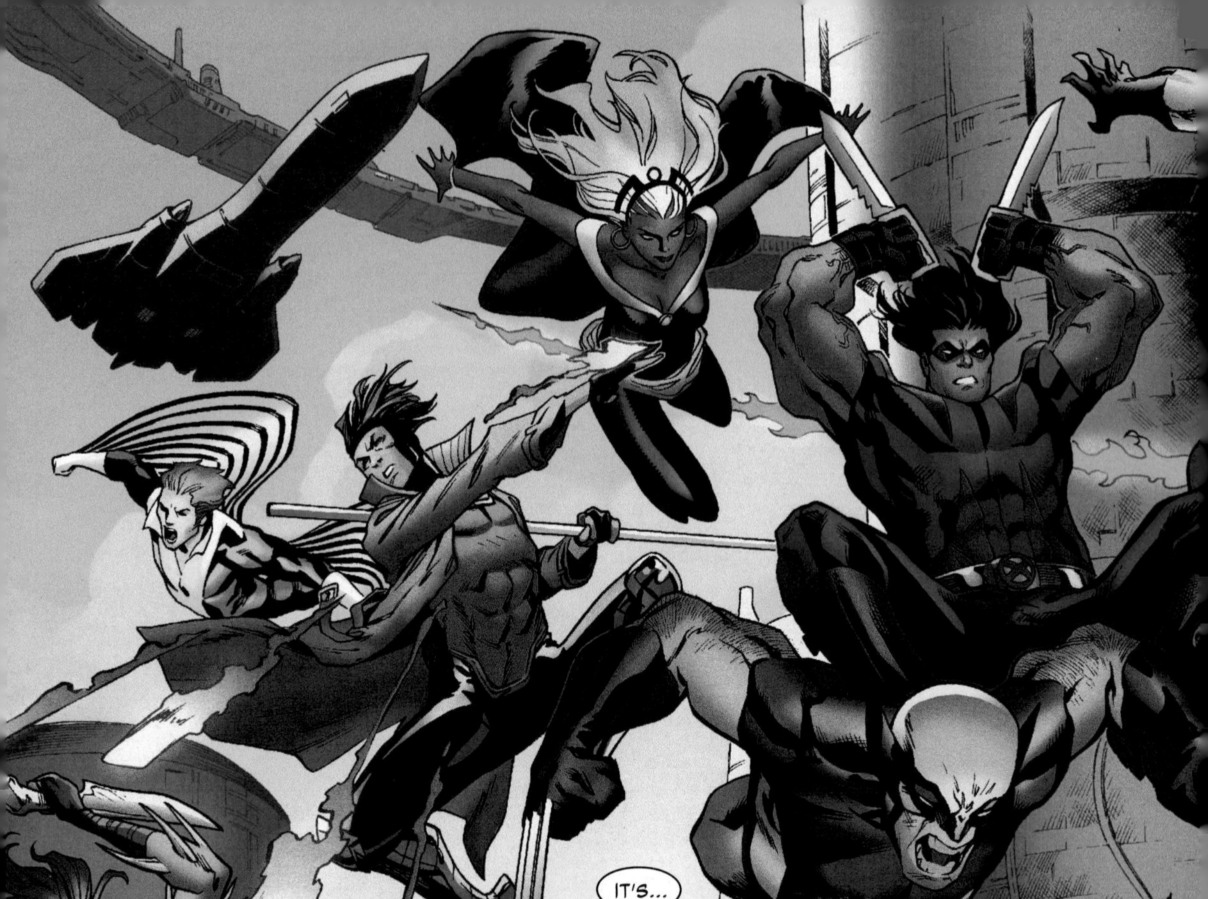
IT'S...
...IT'S THE X-MEN!

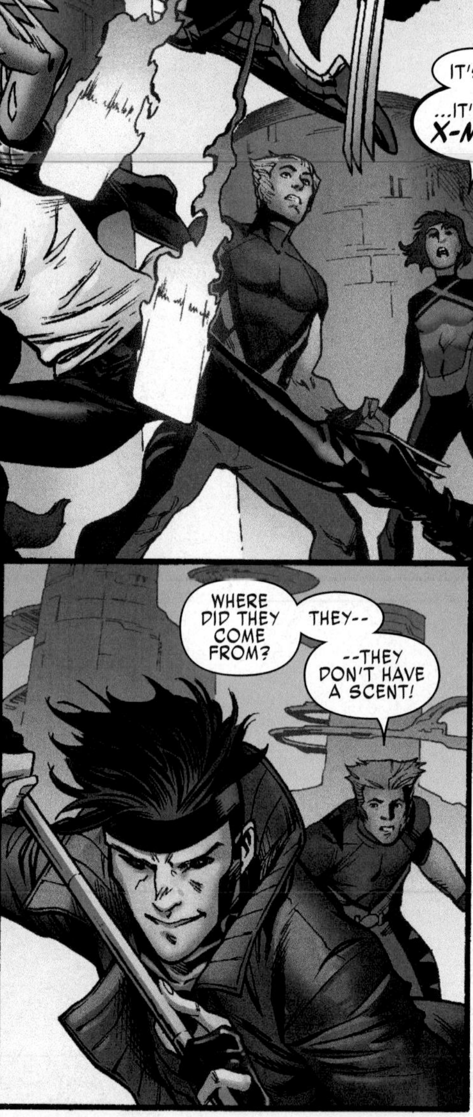
WHERE DID THEY COME FROM?
THEY--
--THEY DON'T HAVE A SCENT!

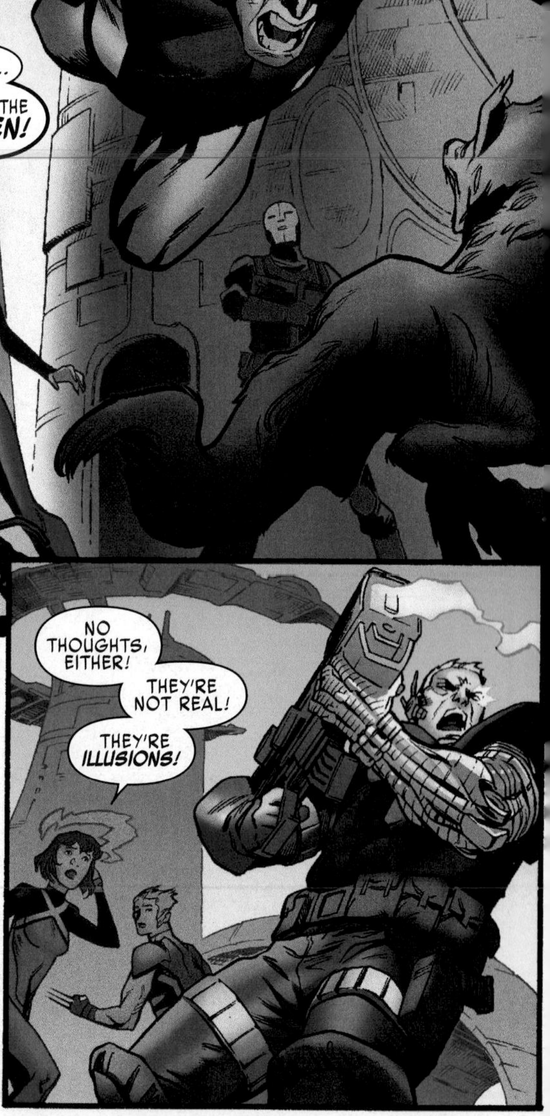
NO THOUGHTS, EITHER!
THEY'RE NOT REAL!
THEY'RE ILLUSIONS!

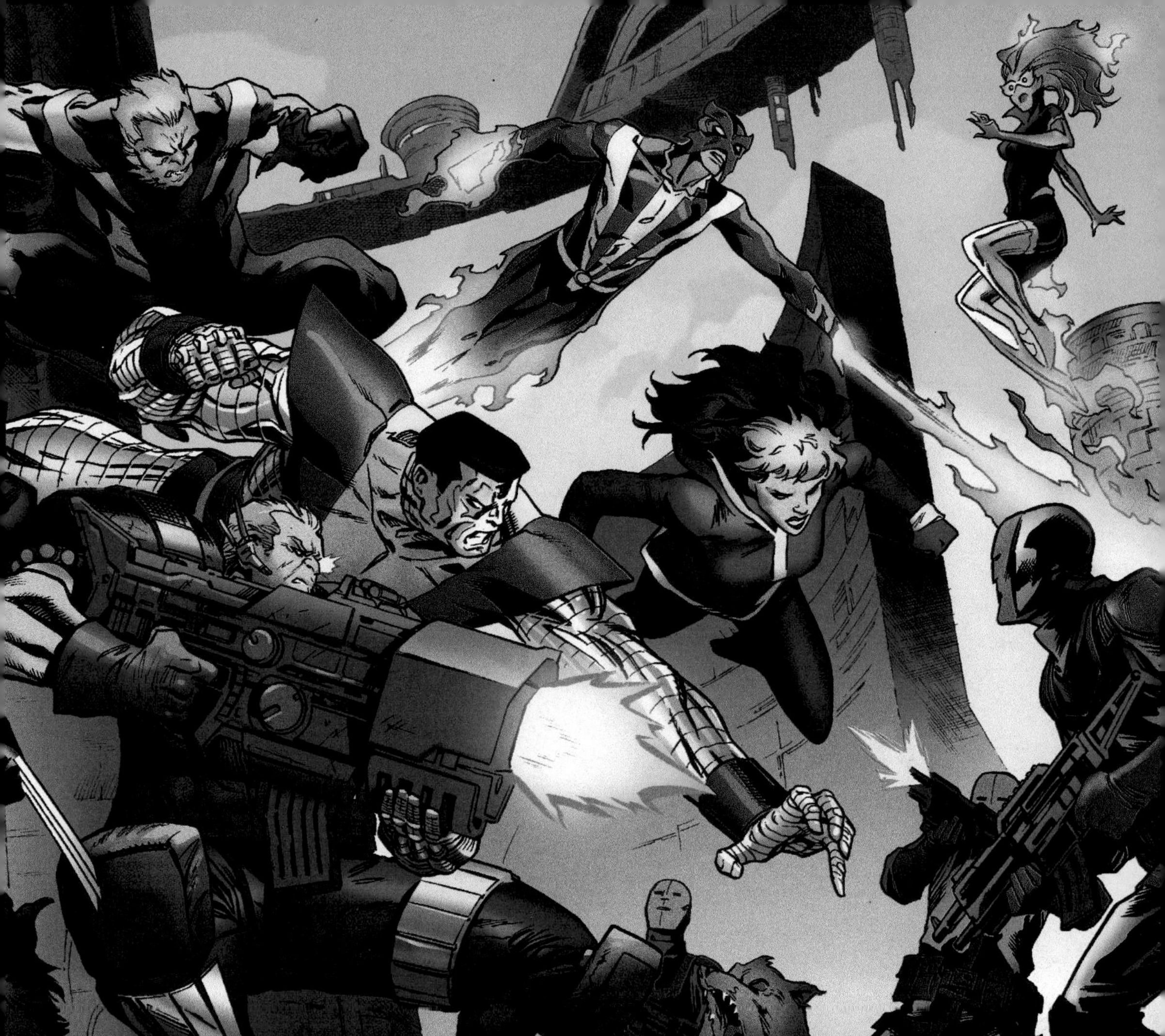

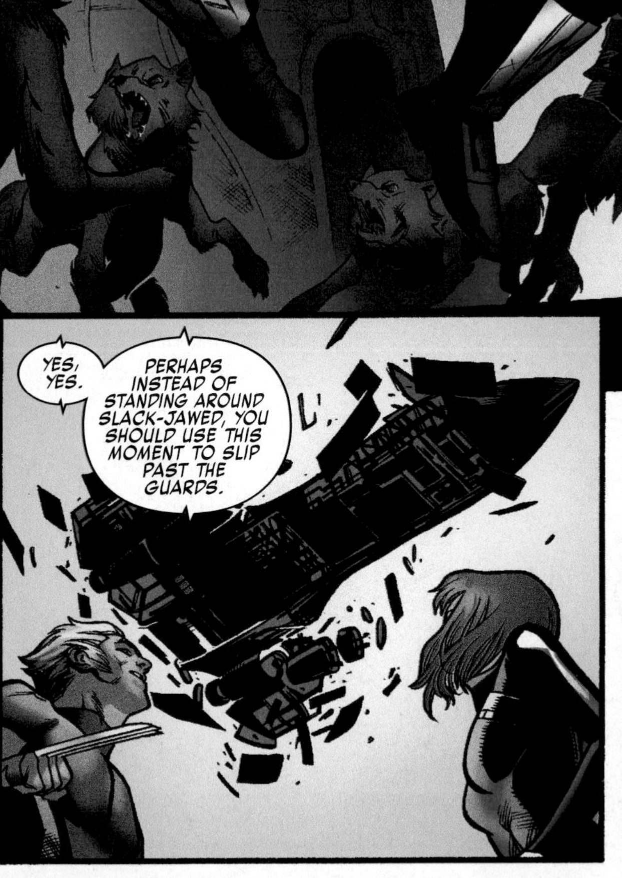
YES, YES.
PERHAPS INSTEAD OF STANDING AROUND SLACK-JAWED, YOU SHOULD USE THIS MOMENT TO SLIP PAST THE GUARDS.

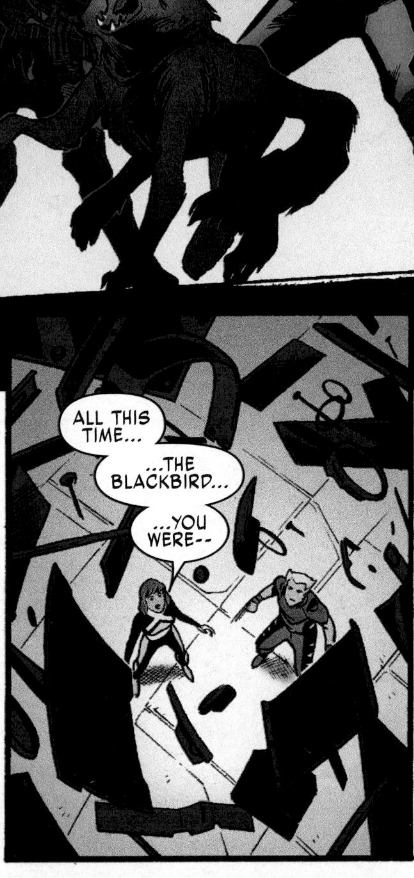
ALL THIS TIME...
...THE BLACKBIRD...
...YOU WERE--

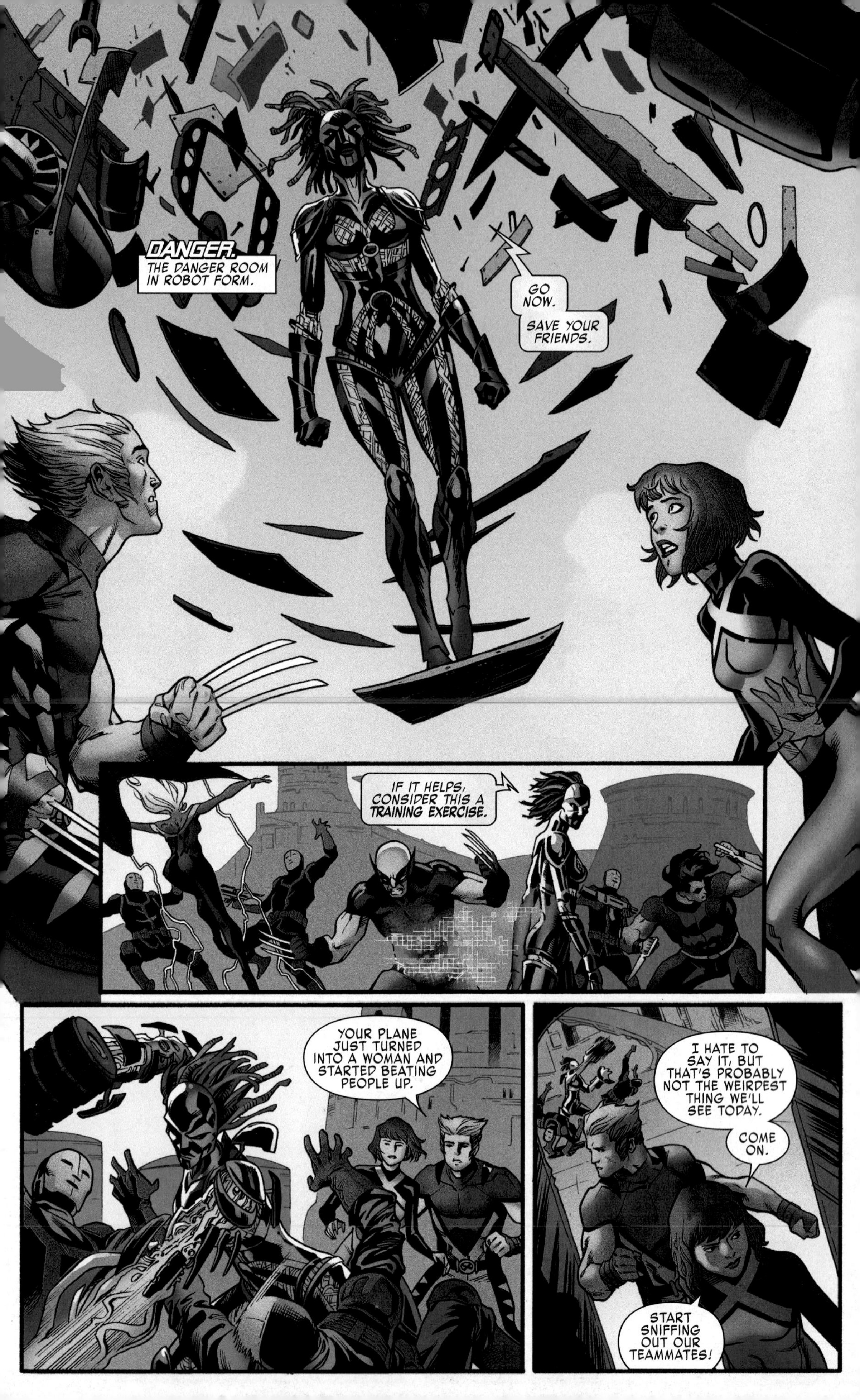

DANGER.
THE DANGER ROOM IN ROBOT FORM.
GO NOW.
SAVE YOUR FRIENDS.
IF IT HELPS, CONSIDER THIS A TRAINING EXERCISE.
YOUR PLANE JUST TURNED INTO A WOMAN AND STARTED BEATING PEOPLE UP.
I HATE TO SAY IT, BUT THAT'S PROBABLY NOT THE WEIRDEST THING WE'LL SEE TODAY.
COME ON.
START SNIFFING OUT OUR TEAMMATES!

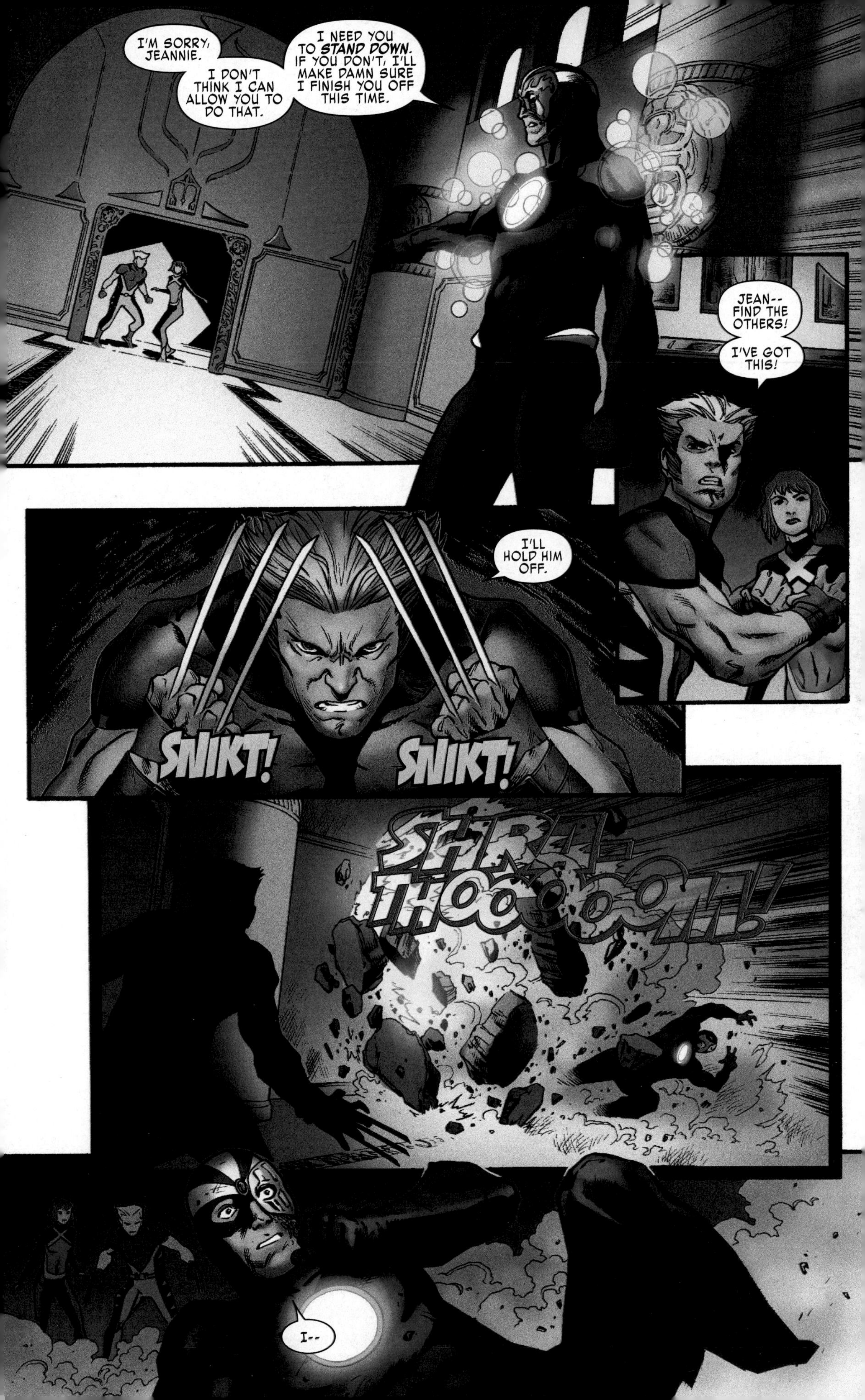
I'M SORRY, JEANNIE.
I DON'T THINK I CAN ALLOW YOU TO DO THAT.
I NEED YOU TO STAND DOWN. IF YOU DON'T, I'LL MAKE DAMN SURE I FINISH YOU OFF THIS TIME.
JEAN-- FIND THE OTHERS!
I'VE GOT THIS!
I'LL HOLD HIM OFF.
SNIKT!
SNIKT!
SHRAK THOOOOOM!
I--

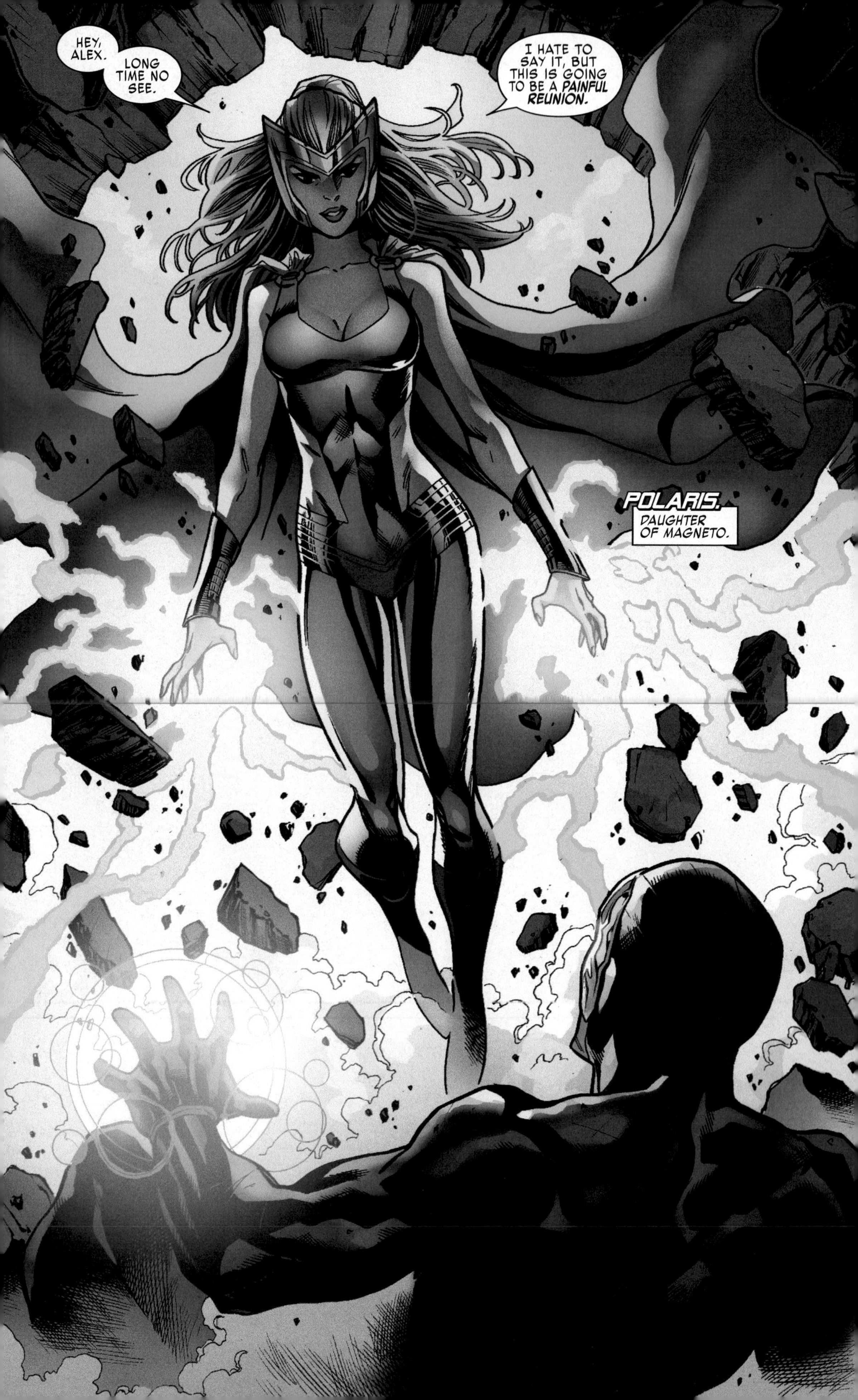
HEY, ALEX.
LONG TIME NO SEE.
I HATE TO SAY IT, BUT THIS IS GOING TO BE A PAINFUL REUNION.
POLARIS.
DAUGHTER OF MAGNETO.

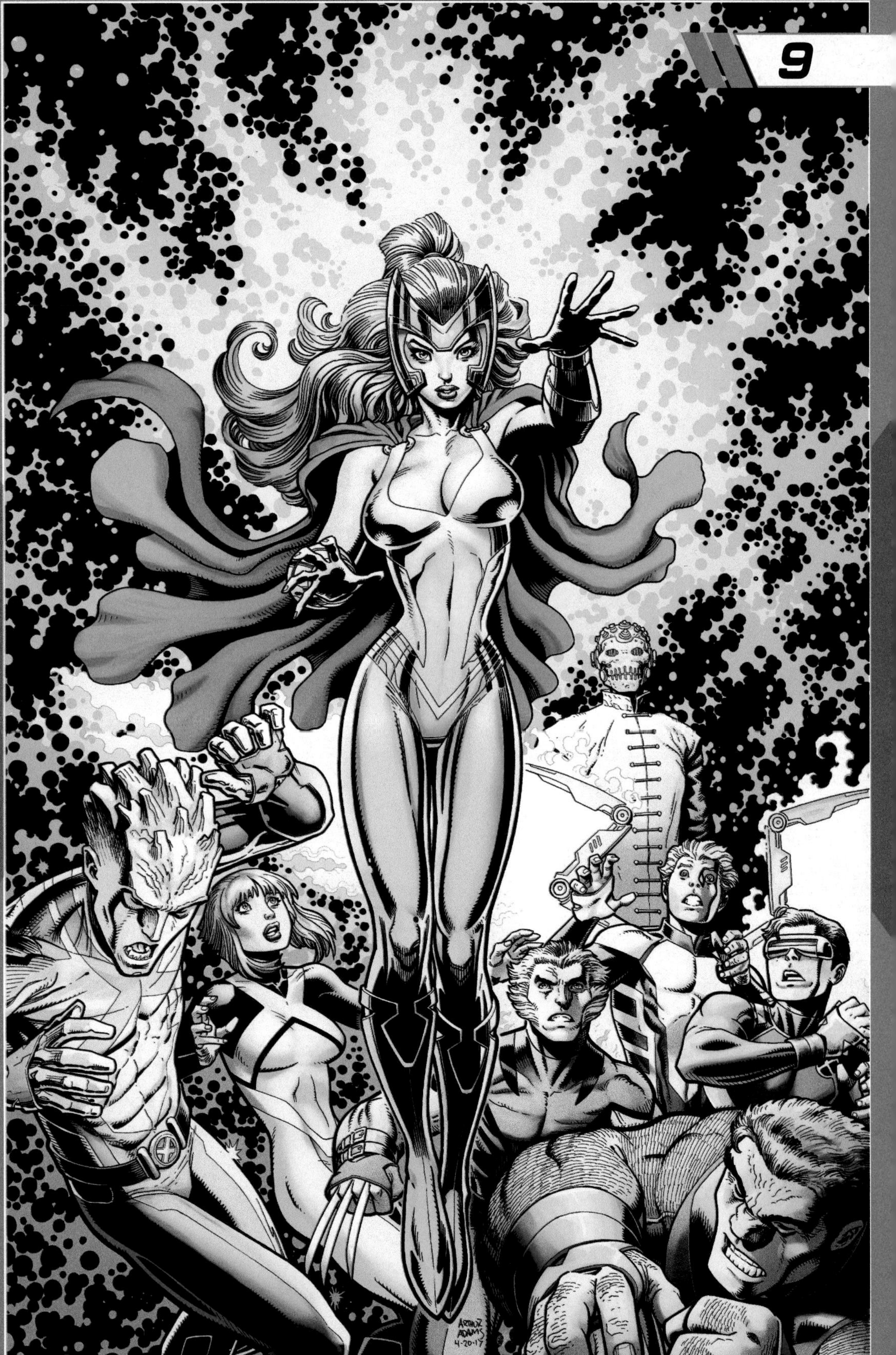
9
ARTHUR ADAMS 4-20-17

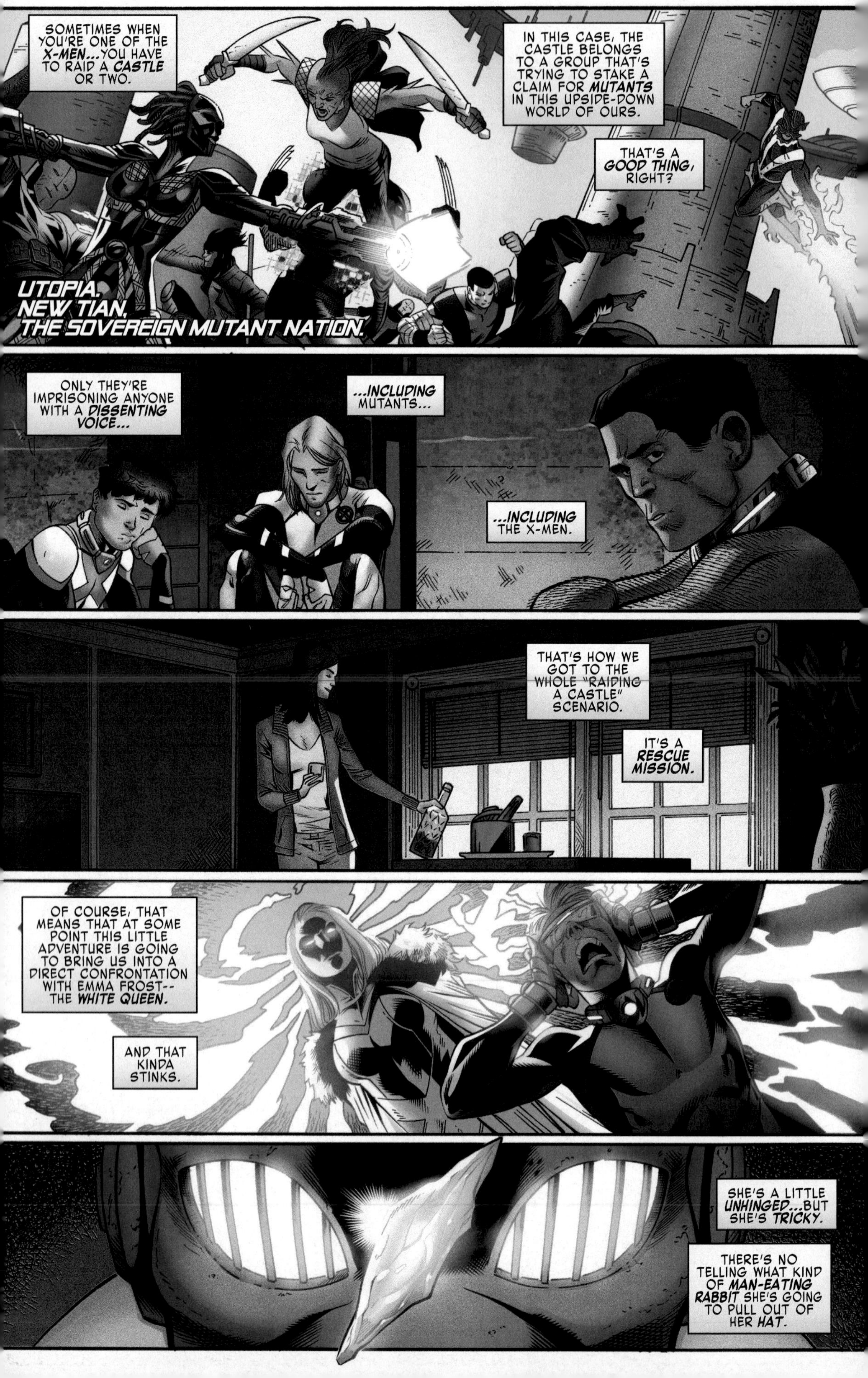
SOMETIMES WHEN YOU'RE ONE OF THE X-MEN...YOU HAVE TO RAID A CASTLE OR TWO.
IN THIS CASE, THE CASTLE BELONGS TO A GROUP THAT'S TRYING TO STAKE A CLAIM FOR MUTANTS IN THIS UPSIDE-DOWN WORLD OF OURS.
THAT'S A GOOD THING, RIGHT?
UTOPIA. NEW TIAN, THE SOVEREIGN MUTANT NATION.
ONLY THEY'RE IMPRISONING ANYONE WITH A DISSENTING VOICE...
...INCLUDING MUTANTS...
...INCLUDING THE X-MEN.
THAT'S HOW WE GOT TO THE WHOLE "RAIDING A CASTLE" SCENARIO.
IT'S A RESCUE MISSION.
OF COURSE, THAT MEANS THAT AT SOME POINT THIS LITTLE ADVENTURE IS GOING TO BRING US INTO A DIRECT CONFRONTATION WITH EMMA FROST--THE WHITE QUEEN.
AND THAT KINDA STINKS.
SHE'S A LITTLE UNHINGED...BUT SHE'S TRICKY.
THERE'S NO TELLING WHAT KIND OF MAN-EATING RABBIT SHE'S GOING TO PULL OUT OF HER HAT.

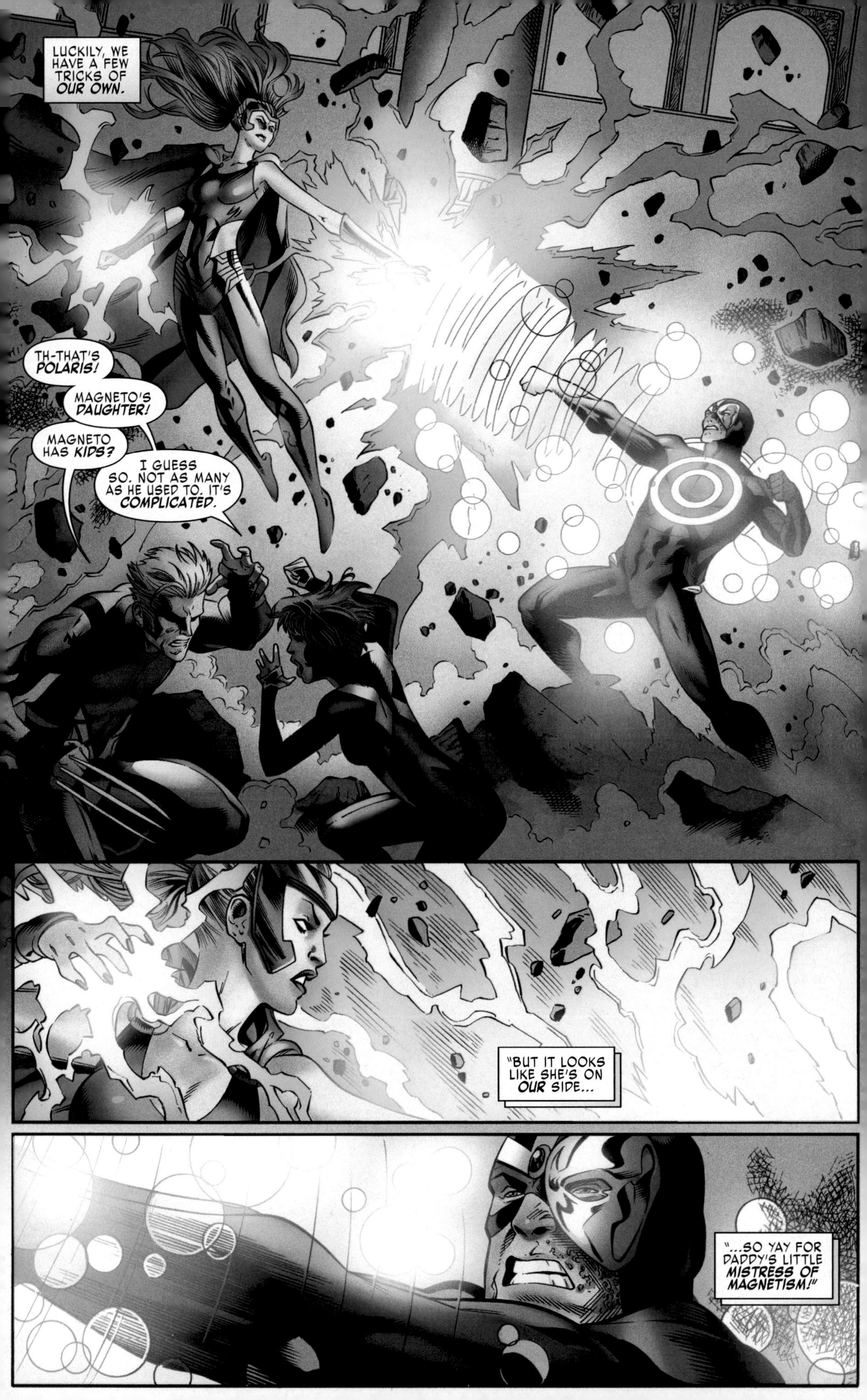
LUCKILY, WE HAVE A FEW TRICKS OF OUR OWN.
TH-THAT'S POLARIS!
MAGNETO'S DAUGHTER!
MAGNETO HAS KIDS?
I GUESS SO. NOT AS MANY AS HE USED TO. IT'S COMPLICATED.
"BUT IT LOOKS LIKE SHE'S ON OUR SIDE...
"...SO YAY FOR DADDY'S LITTLE MISTRESS OF MAGNETISM!"

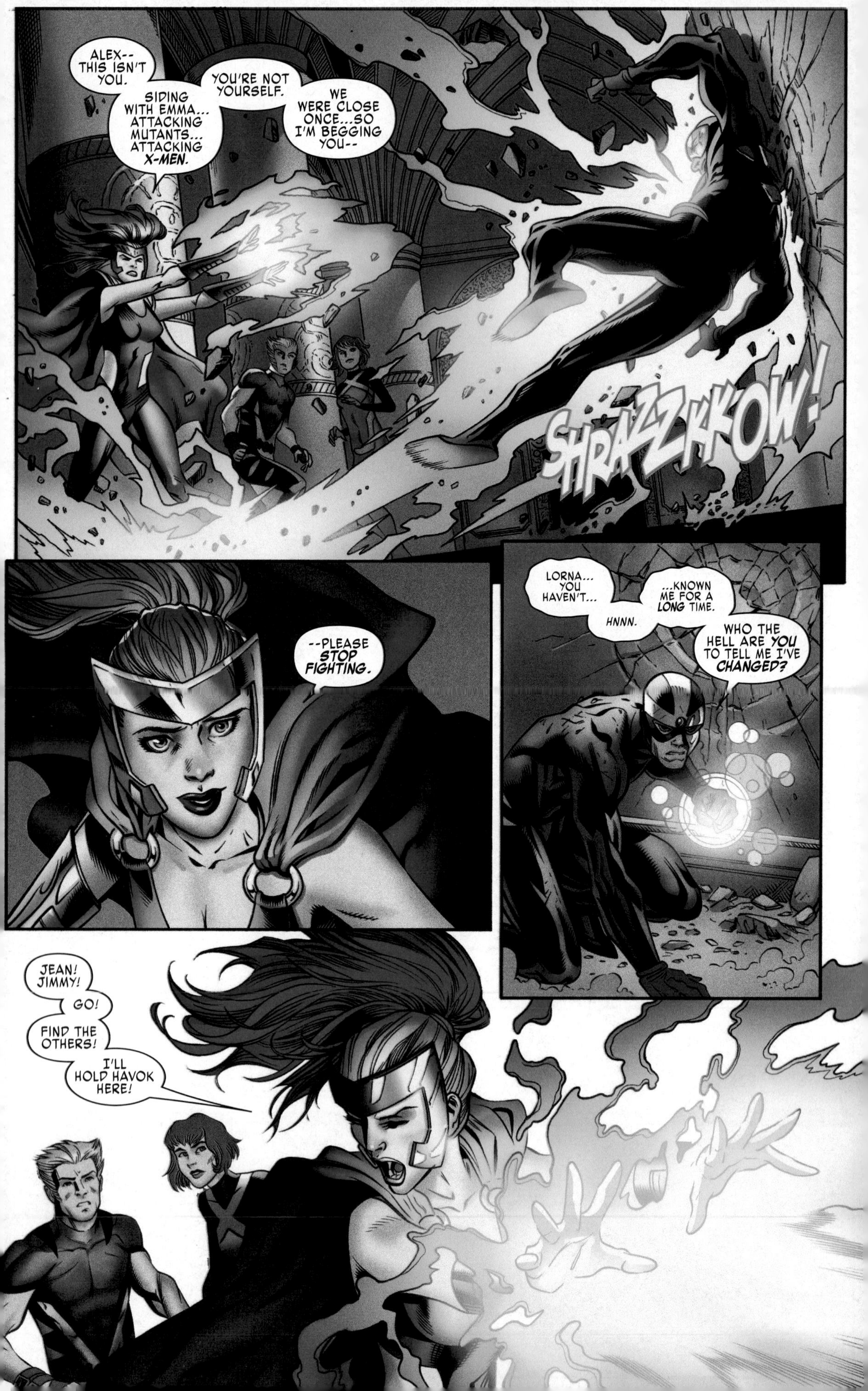
ALEX-- THIS ISN'T YOU.
SIDING WITH EMMA... ATTACKING MUTANTS... ATTACKING X-MEN.
YOU'RE NOT YOURSELF.
WE WERE CLOSE ONCE...SO I'M BEGGING YOU--
SHRAZZKKOW!
--PLEASE STOP FIGHTING.
LORNA... YOU HAVEN'T...
HNNN.
...KNOWN ME FOR A LONG TIME.
WHO THE HELL ARE YOU TO TELL ME I'VE CHANGED?
JEAN! JIMMY!
GO!
FIND THE OTHERS!
I'LL HOLD HAVOK HERE!

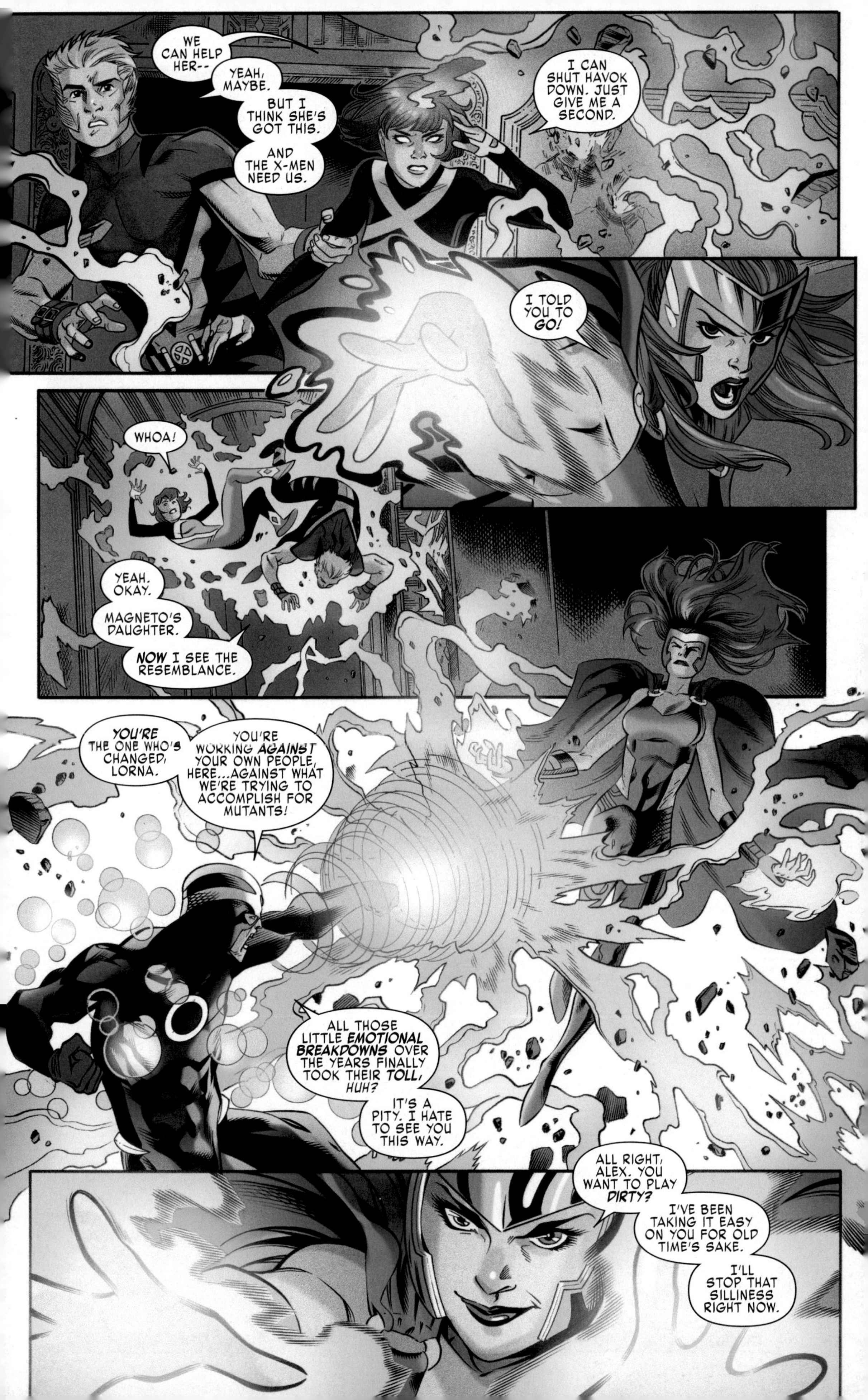

WE CAN HELP HER--
YEAH, MAYBE.
BUT I THINK SHE'S GOT THIS.
AND THE X-MEN NEED US.
I CAN SHUT HAVOK DOWN. JUST GIVE ME A SECOND.
I TOLD YOU TO GO!
WHOA!
YEAH. OKAY.
MAGNETO'S DAUGHTER.
NOW I SEE THE RESEMBLANCE.
YOU'RE THE ONE WHO'S CHANGED, LORNA.
YOU'RE WORKING AGAINST YOUR OWN PEOPLE, HERE...AGAINST WHAT WE'RE TRYING TO ACCOMPLISH FOR MUTANTS!
ALL THOSE LITTLE EMOTIONAL BREAKDOWNS OVER THE YEARS FINALLY TOOK THEIR TOLL, HUH?
IT'S A PITY. I HATE TO SEE YOU THIS WAY.
ALL RIGHT, ALEX. YOU WANT TO PLAY DIRTY?
I'VE BEEN TAKING IT EASY ON YOU FOR OLD TIME'S SAKE.
I'LL STOP THAT SILLINESS RIGHT NOW.

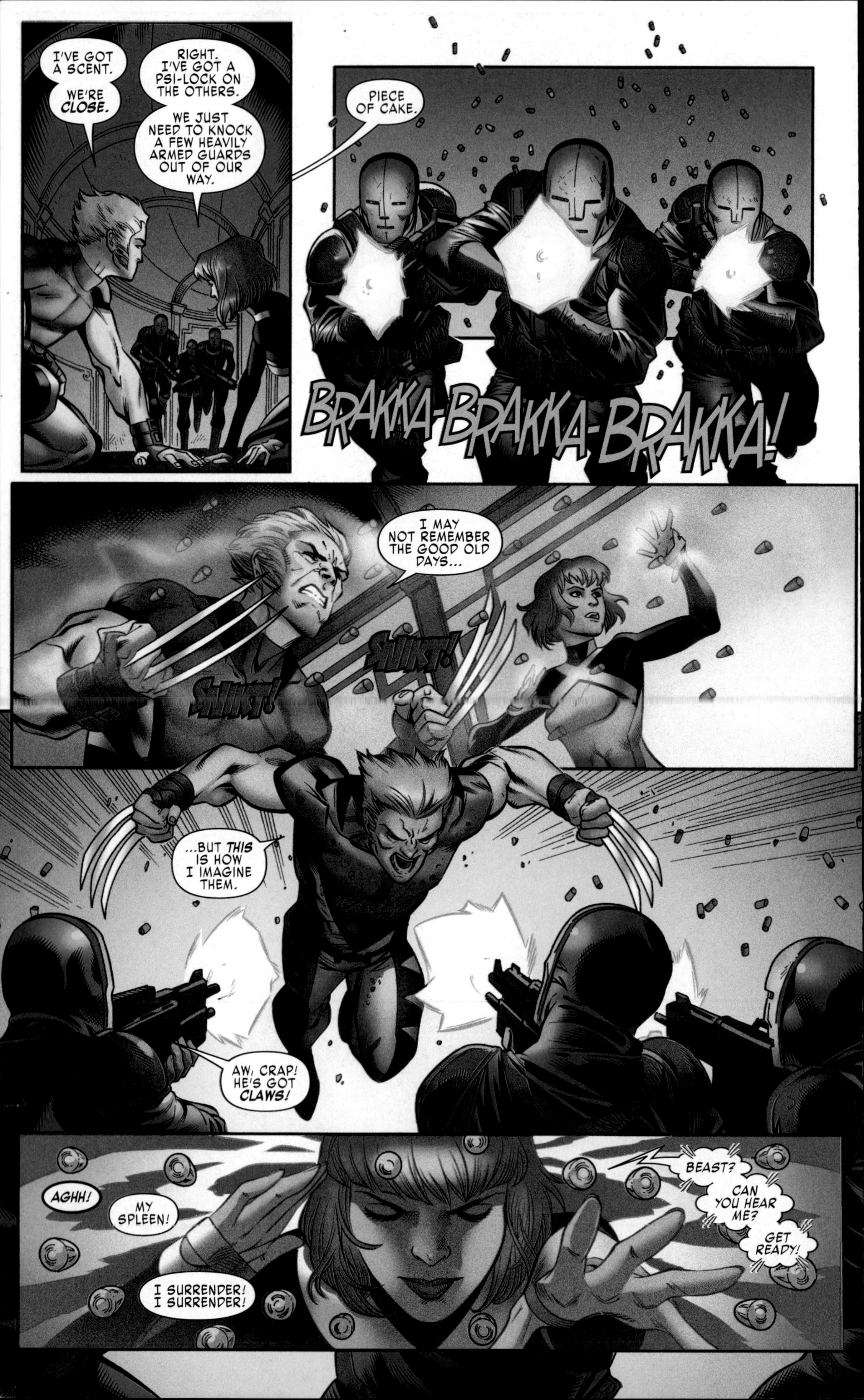
I'VE GOT A SCENT.
WE'RE CLOSE.
RIGHT. I'VE GOT A PSI-LOCK ON THE OTHERS.
WE JUST NEED TO KNOCK A FEW HEAVILY ARMED GUARDS OUT OF OUR WAY.
PIECE OF CAKE.
BRAKKA-BRAKKA-BRAKKA!
I MAY NOT REMEMBER THE GOOD OLD DAYS...
SNIKT!
SNIKT!
...BUT THIS IS HOW I IMAGINE THEM.
AW, CRAP! HE'S GOT CLAWS!
AGHH!
MY SPLEEN!
I SURRENDER! I SURRENDER!
BEAST?
CAN YOU HEAR ME?
GET READY!

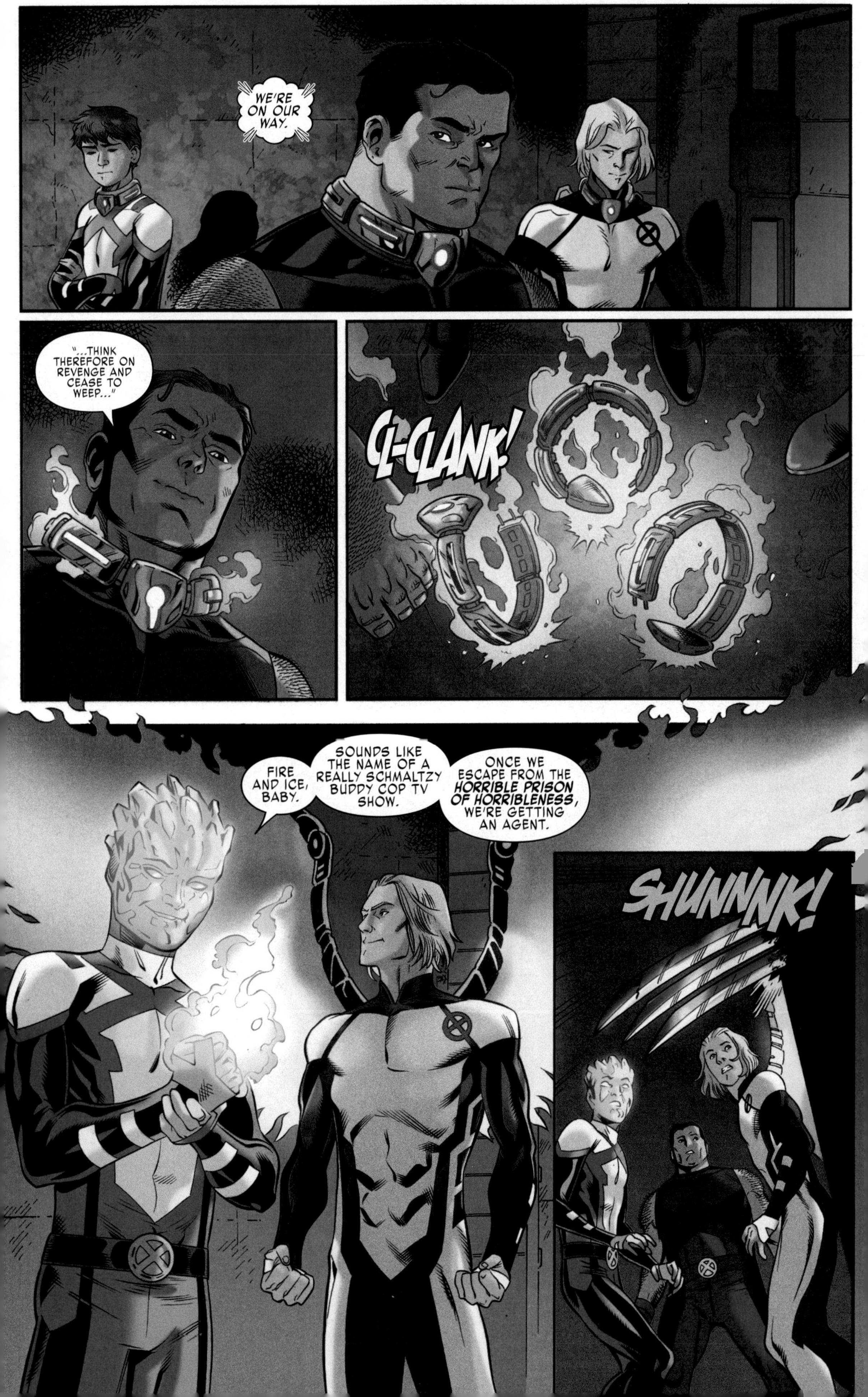
WE'RE ON OUR WAY.
"...THINK THEREFORE ON REVENGE AND CEASE TO WEEP..."
CL-CLANK!
FIRE AND ICE, BABY.
SOUNDS LIKE THE NAME OF A REALLY SCHMALTZY BUDDY COP TV SHOW.
ONCE WE ESCAPE FROM THE *HORRIBLE PRISON OF HORRIBLENESS,* WE'RE GETTING AN AGENT.
SHUNNNK!

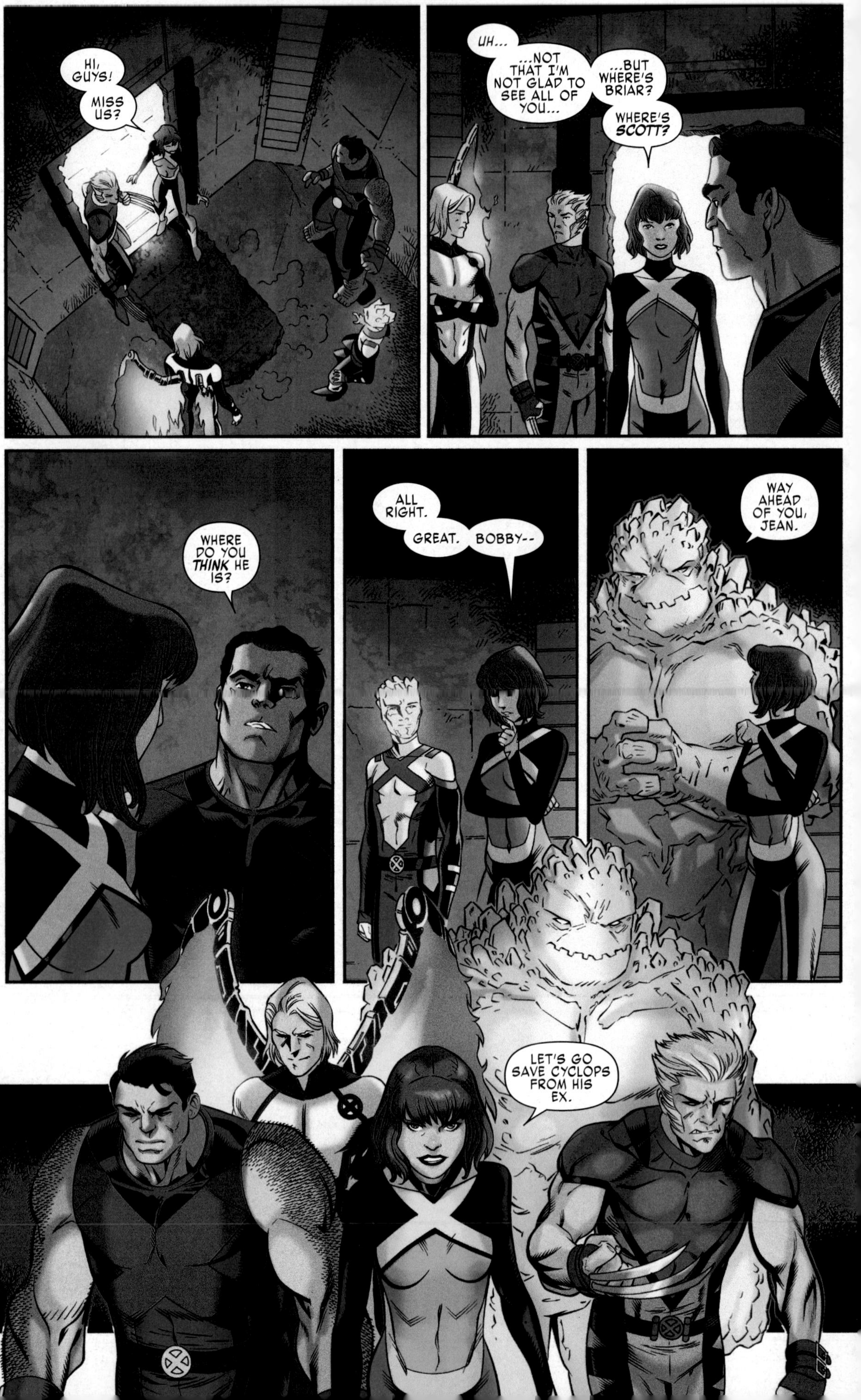
HI, GUYS!
MISS US?
UH...
...NOT THAT I'M NOT GLAD TO SEE ALL OF YOU...
...BUT WHERE'S BRIAR?
WHERE'S SCOTT?
WHERE DO YOU THINK HE IS?
ALL RIGHT.
GREAT.
BOBBY--
WAY AHEAD OF YOU, JEAN.
LET'S GO SAVE CYCLOPS FROM HIS EX.

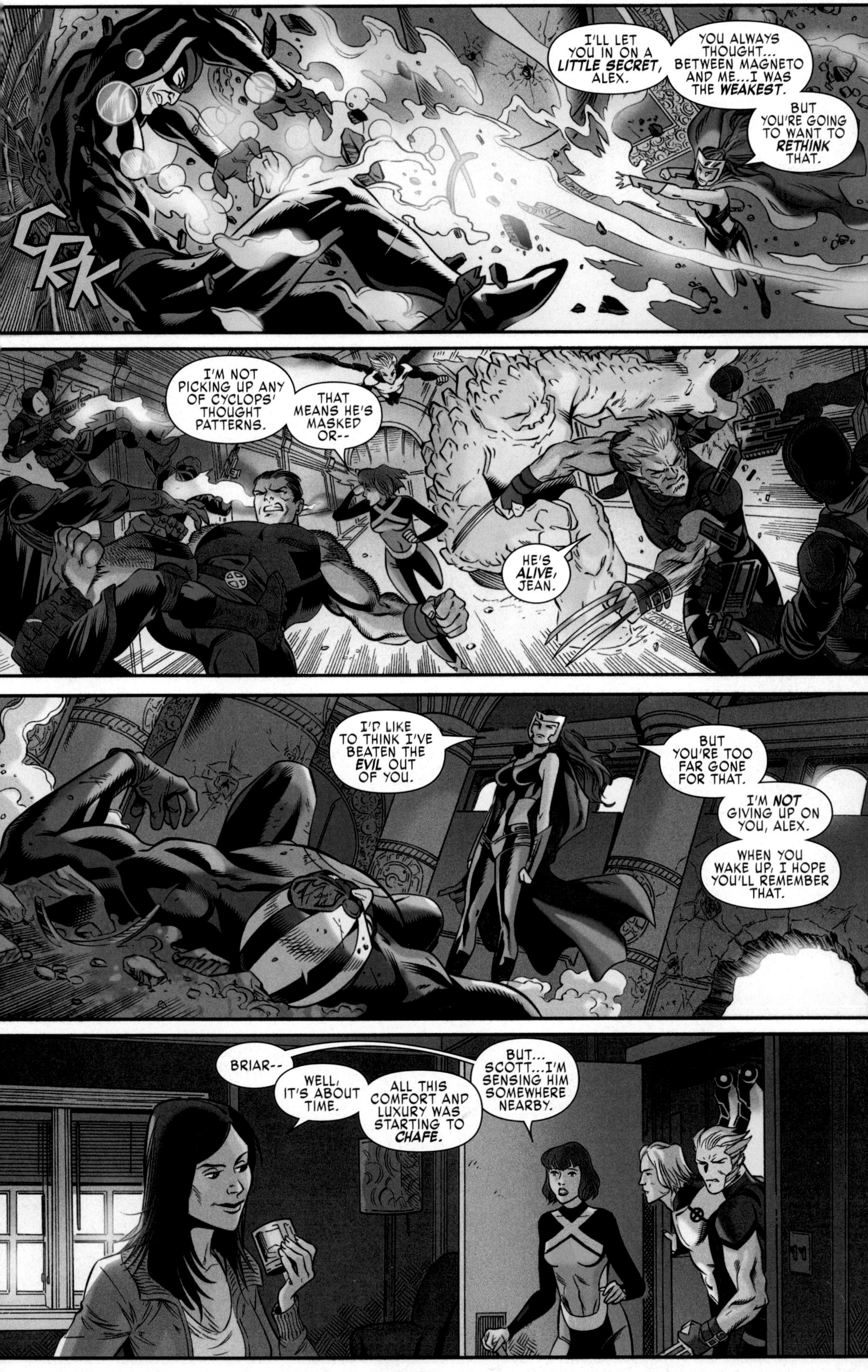
CRK
I'LL LET YOU IN ON A LITTLE SECRET, ALEX.
YOU ALWAYS THOUGHT... BETWEEN MAGNETO AND ME...I WAS THE WEAKEST.
BUT YOU'RE GOING TO WANT TO RETHINK THAT.
I'M NOT PICKING UP ANY OF CYCLOPS' THOUGHT PATTERNS.
THAT MEANS HE'S MASKED OR--
HE'S ALIVE, JEAN.
I'D LIKE TO THINK I'VE BEATEN THE EVIL OUT OF YOU.
BUT YOU'RE TOO FAR GONE FOR THAT.
I'M NOT GIVING UP ON YOU, ALEX.
WHEN YOU WAKE UP, I HOPE YOU'LL REMEMBER THAT.
BRIAR--
BUT... SCOTT...I'M SENSING HIM SOMEWHERE NEARBY.
WELL, IT'S ABOUT TIME.
ALL THIS COMFORT AND LUXURY WAS STARTING TO CHAFE.

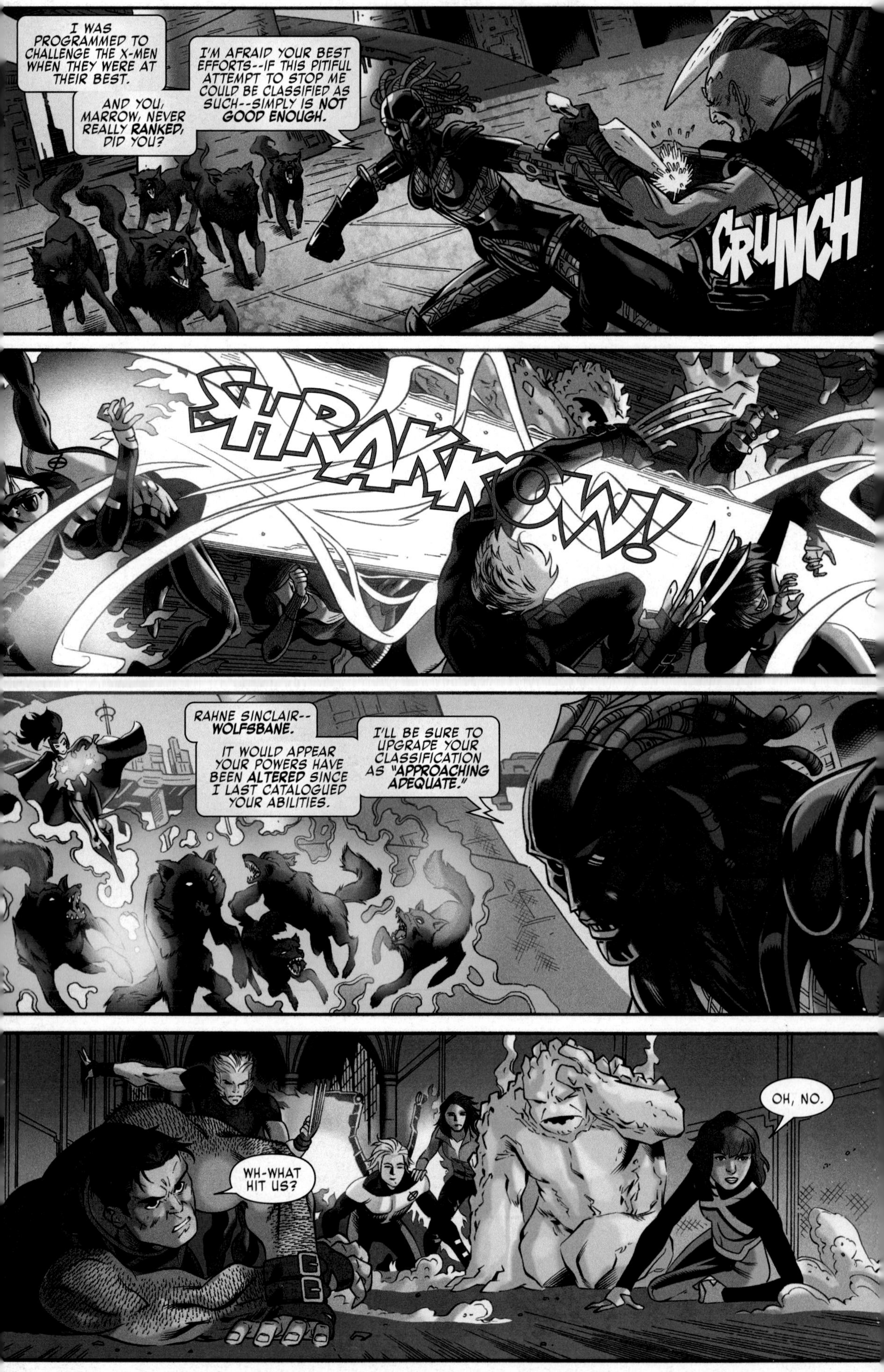
I WAS PROGRAMMED TO CHALLENGE THE X-MEN WHEN THEY WERE AT THEIR BEST.
AND YOU, MARROW, NEVER REALLY RANKED, DID YOU?
I'M AFRAID YOUR BEST EFFORTS--IF THIS PITIFUL ATTEMPT TO STOP ME COULD BE CLASSIFIED AS SUCH--SIMPLY IS NOT GOOD ENOUGH.
CRUNCH
SHRAKKOOW!
RAHNE SINCLAIR--WOLFSBANE.
IT WOULD APPEAR YOUR POWERS HAVE BEEN ALTERED SINCE I LAST CATALOGUED YOUR ABILITIES.
I'LL BE SURE TO UPGRADE YOUR CLASSIFICATION AS "APPROACHING ADEQUATE."
WH-WHAT HIT US?
OH, NO.

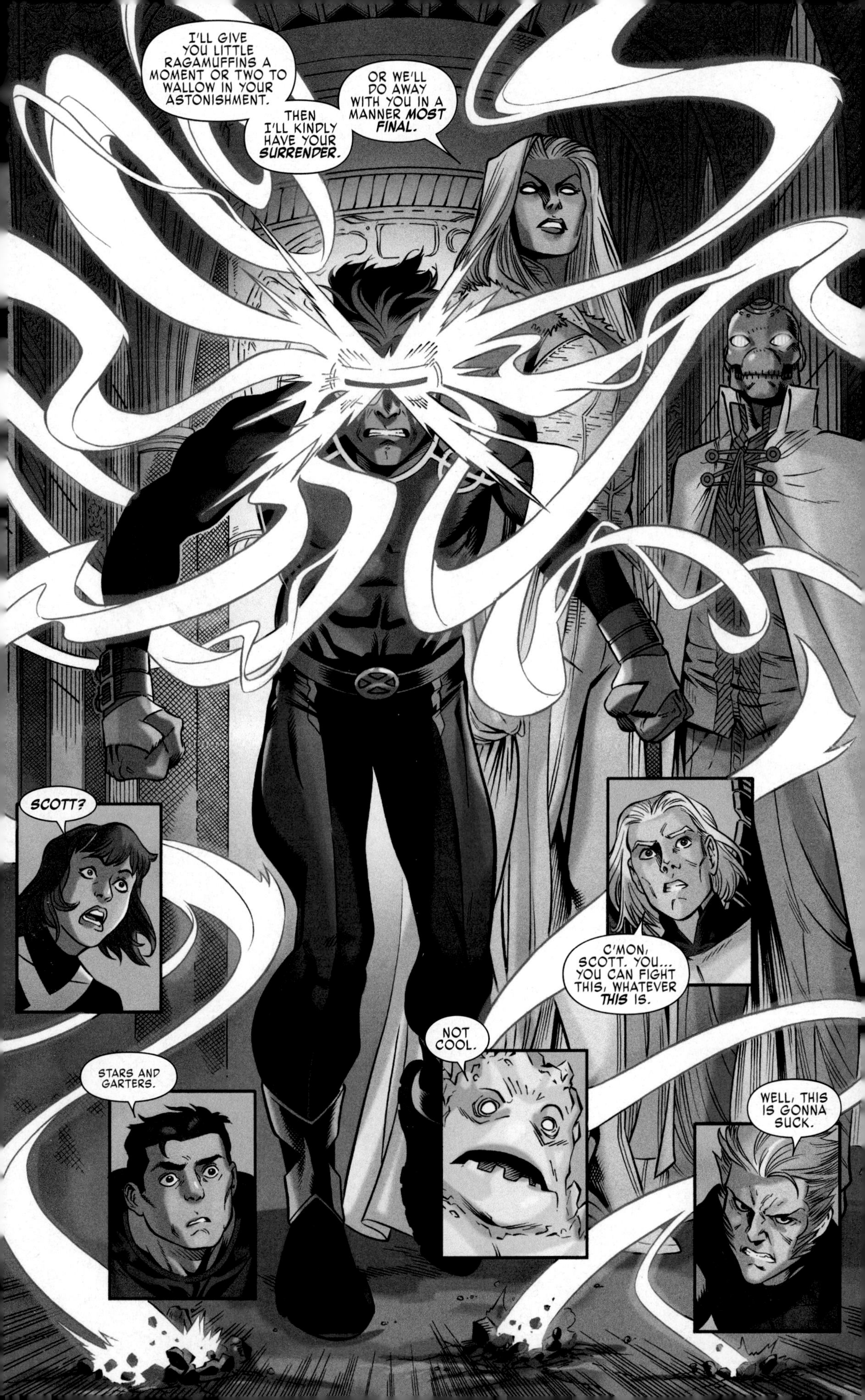
I'LL GIVE YOU LITTLE RAGAMUFFINS A MOMENT OR TWO TO WALLOW IN YOUR ASTONISHMENT.
THEN I'LL KINDLY HAVE YOUR SURRENDER.
OR WE'LL DO AWAY WITH YOU IN A MANNER MOST FINAL.
SCOTT?
C'MON, SCOTT. YOU... YOU CAN FIGHT THIS, WHATEVER THIS IS.
STARS AND GARTERS.
NOT COOL.
WELL, THIS IS GONNA SUCK.

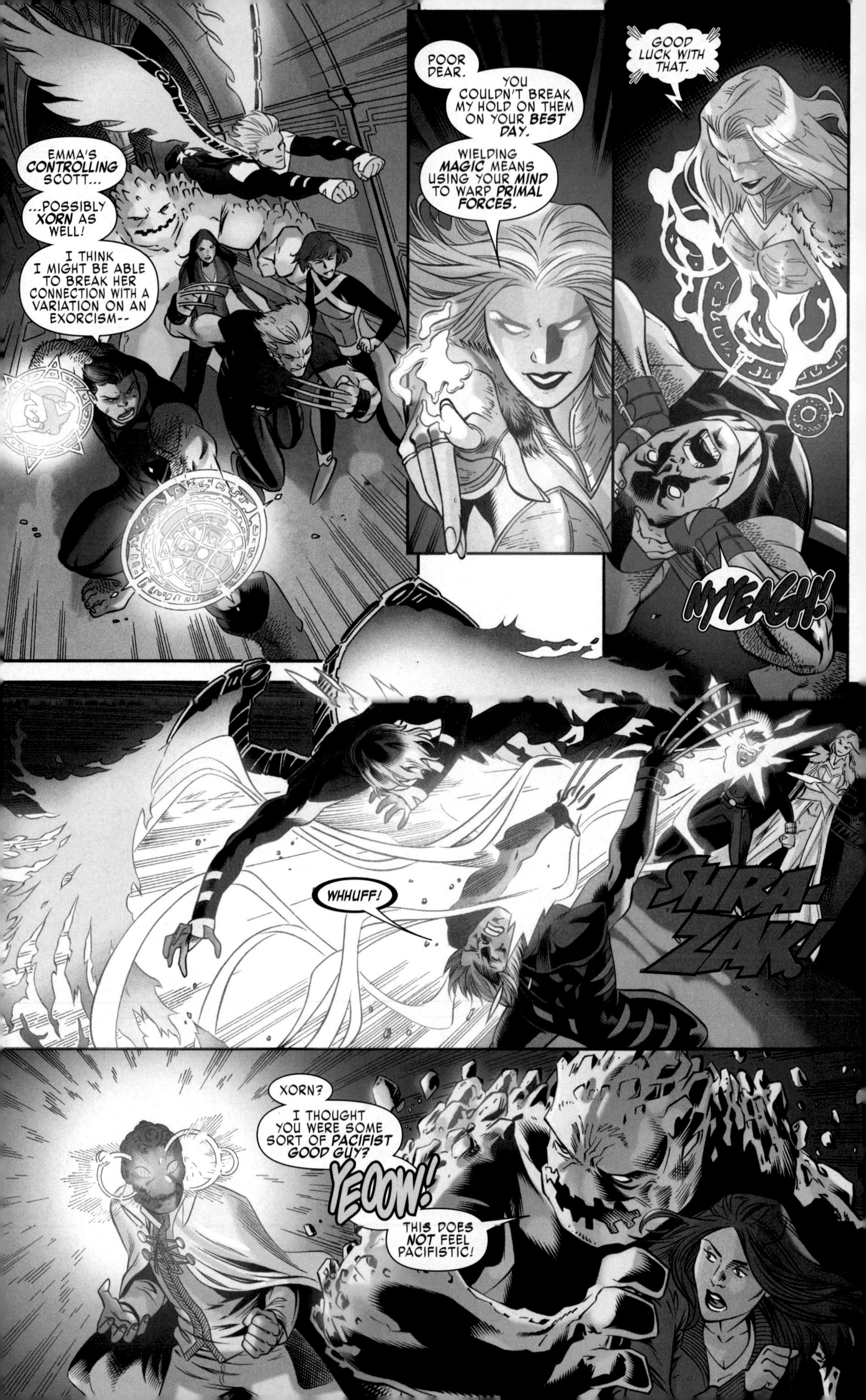
EMMA'S CONTROLLING SCOTT...
...POSSIBLY XORN AS WELL!
I THINK I MIGHT BE ABLE TO BREAK HER CONNECTION WITH A VARIATION ON AN EXORCISM--
POOR DEAR.
YOU COULDN'T BREAK MY HOLD ON THEM ON YOUR BEST DAY.
WIELDING MAGIC MEANS USING YOUR MIND TO WARP PRIMAL FORCES.
GOOD LUCK WITH THAT.
NYYEAGH!
WHHUFF!
SHRA-ZAK!
XORN?
I THOUGHT YOU WERE SOME SORT OF PACIFIST GOOD GUY?
YEOOW!
THIS DOES NOT FEEL PACIFISTIC!

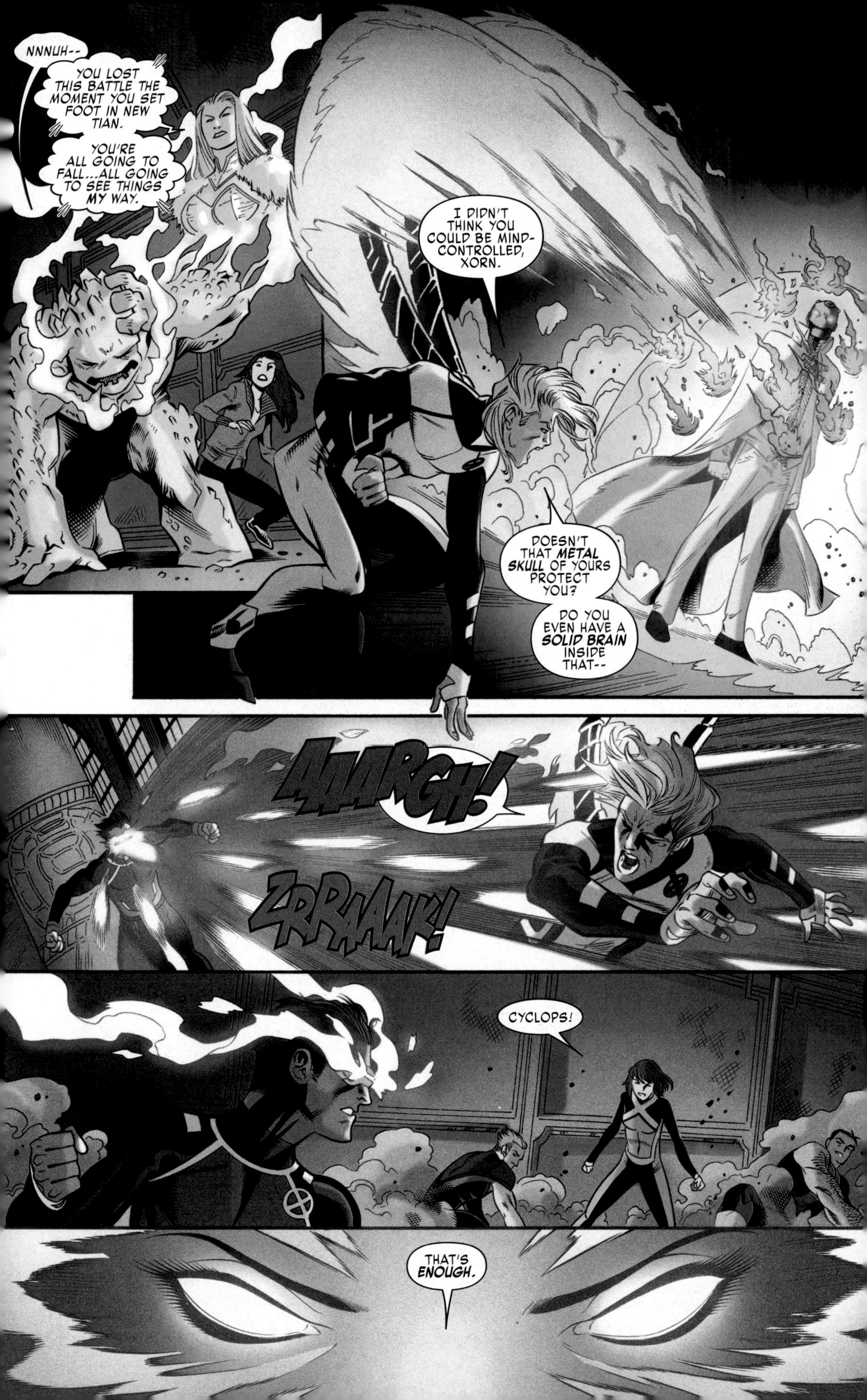
NNNUH--
YOU LOST THIS BATTLE THE MOMENT YOU SET FOOT IN NEW TIAN.
YOU'RE ALL GOING TO FALL...ALL GOING TO SEE THINGS MY WAY.
I DIDN'T THINK YOU COULD BE MIND-CONTROLLED, XORN.
DOESN'T THAT METAL SKULL OF YOURS PROTECT YOU?
DO YOU EVEN HAVE A SOLID BRAIN INSIDE THAT--
AAARGH!
ZRRAAAK!
CYCLOPS!
THAT'S ENOUGH.

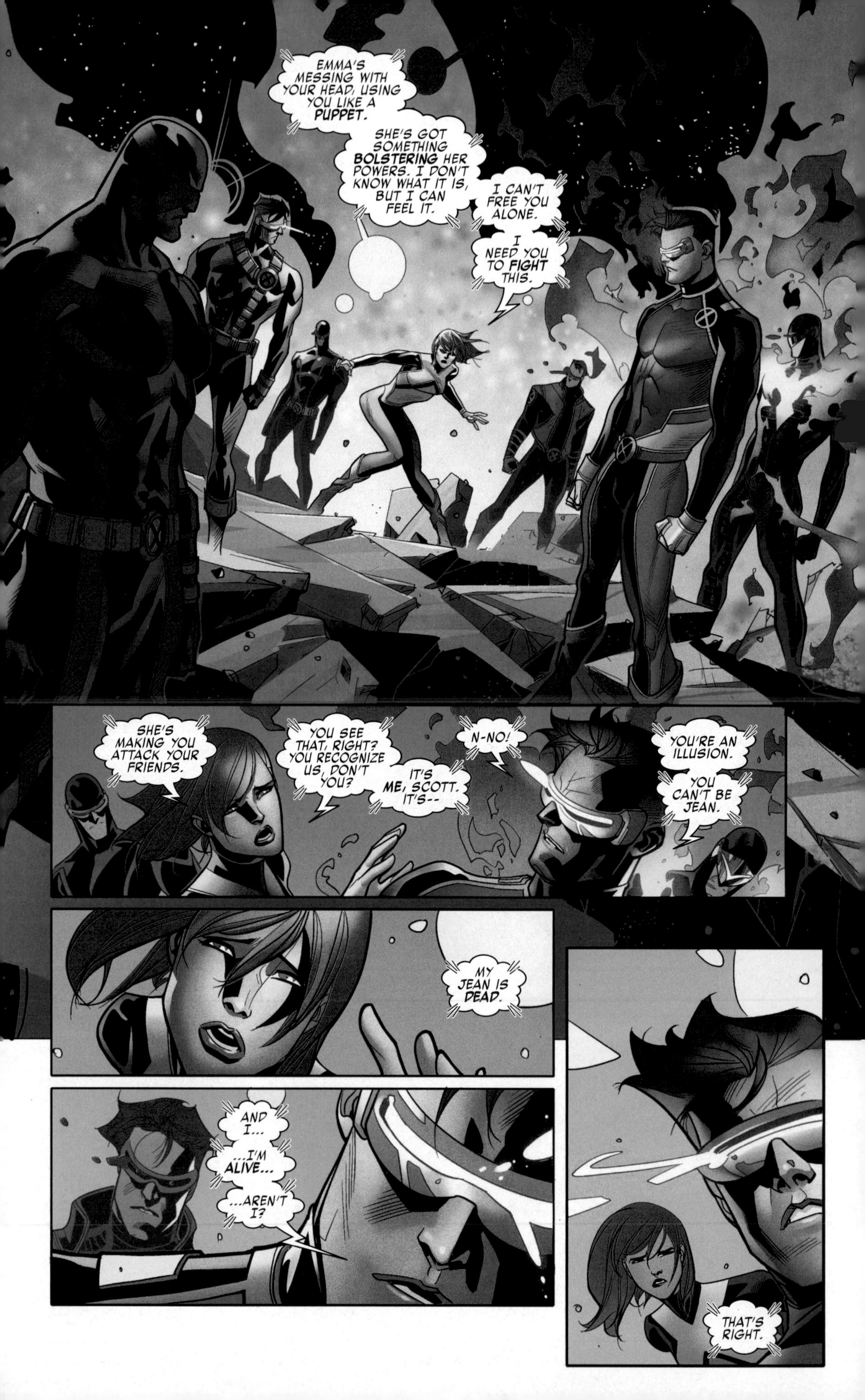
EMMA'S MESSING WITH YOUR HEAD, USING YOU LIKE A PUPPET.
SHE'S GOT SOMETHING BOLSTERING HER POWERS. I DON'T KNOW WHAT IT IS, BUT I CAN FEEL IT.
I CAN'T FREE YOU ALONE.
I NEED YOU TO FIGHT THIS.
SHE'S MAKING YOU ATTACK YOUR FRIENDS.
YOU SEE THAT, RIGHT? YOU RECOGNIZE US, DON'T YOU?
N-NO!
IT'S ME, SCOTT. IT'S--
YOU'RE AN ILLUSION.
YOU CAN'T BE JEAN.
MY JEAN IS DEAD.
AND I...
...I'M ALIVE...
...AREN'T I?
THAT'S RIGHT.

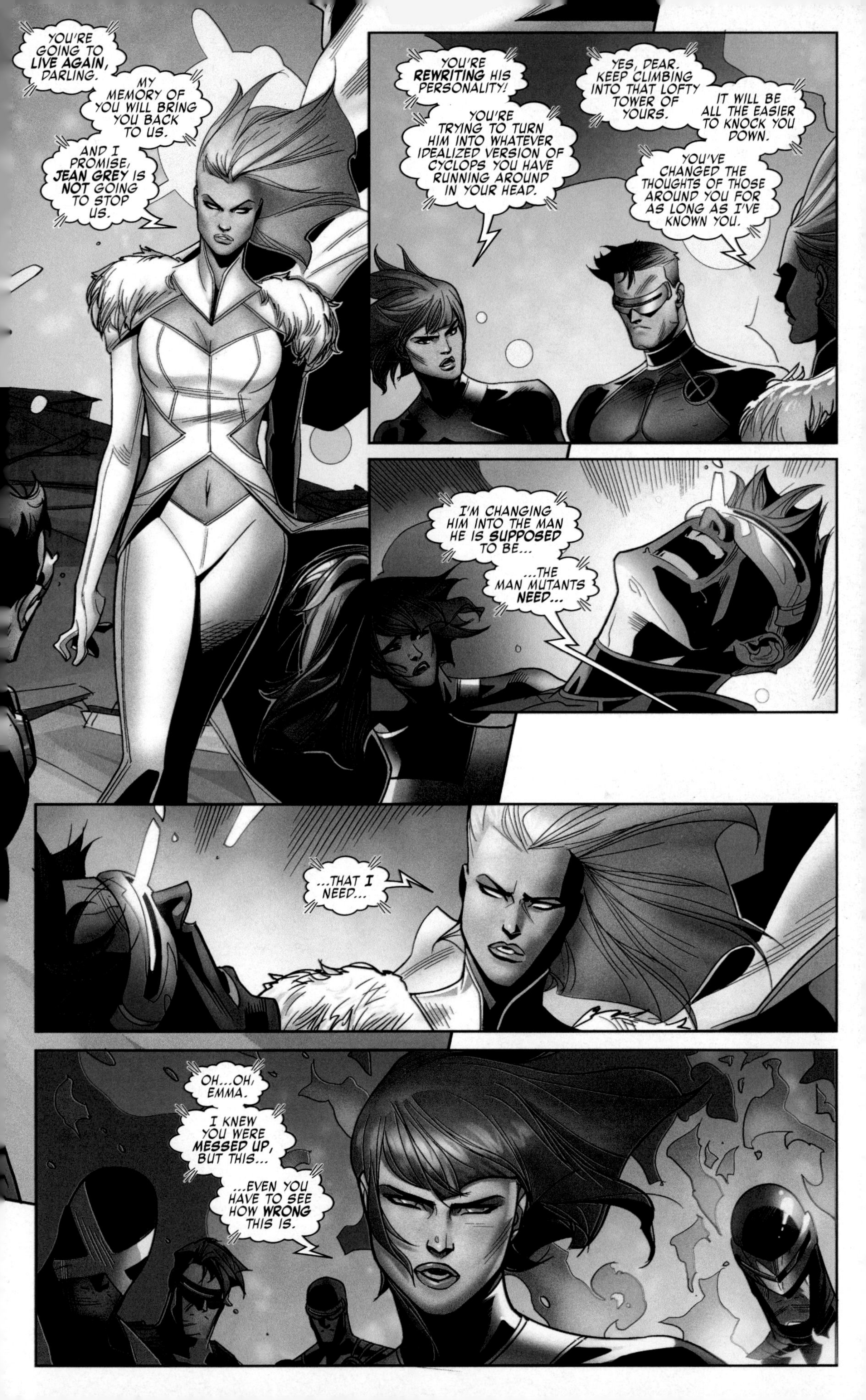

YOU'RE GOING TO LIVE AGAIN, DARLING.
MY MEMORY OF YOU WILL BRING YOU BACK TO US.
AND I PROMISE, JEAN GREY IS NOT GOING TO STOP US.
YOU'RE REWRITING HIS PERSONALITY!
YOU'RE TRYING TO TURN HIM INTO WHATEVER IDEALIZED VERSION OF CYCLOPS YOU HAVE RUNNING AROUND IN YOUR HEAD.
YES, DEAR. KEEP CLIMBING INTO THAT LOFTY TOWER OF YOURS.
IT WILL BE ALL THE EASIER TO KNOCK YOU DOWN.
YOU'VE CHANGED THE THOUGHTS OF THOSE AROUND YOU FOR AS LONG AS I'VE KNOWN YOU.
I'M CHANGING HIM INTO THE MAN HE IS SUPPOSED TO BE...
...THE MAN MUTANTS NEED...
...THAT I NEED...
OH...OH, EMMA.
I KNEW YOU WERE MESSED UP, BUT THIS...
...EVEN YOU HAVE TO SEE HOW WRONG THIS IS.

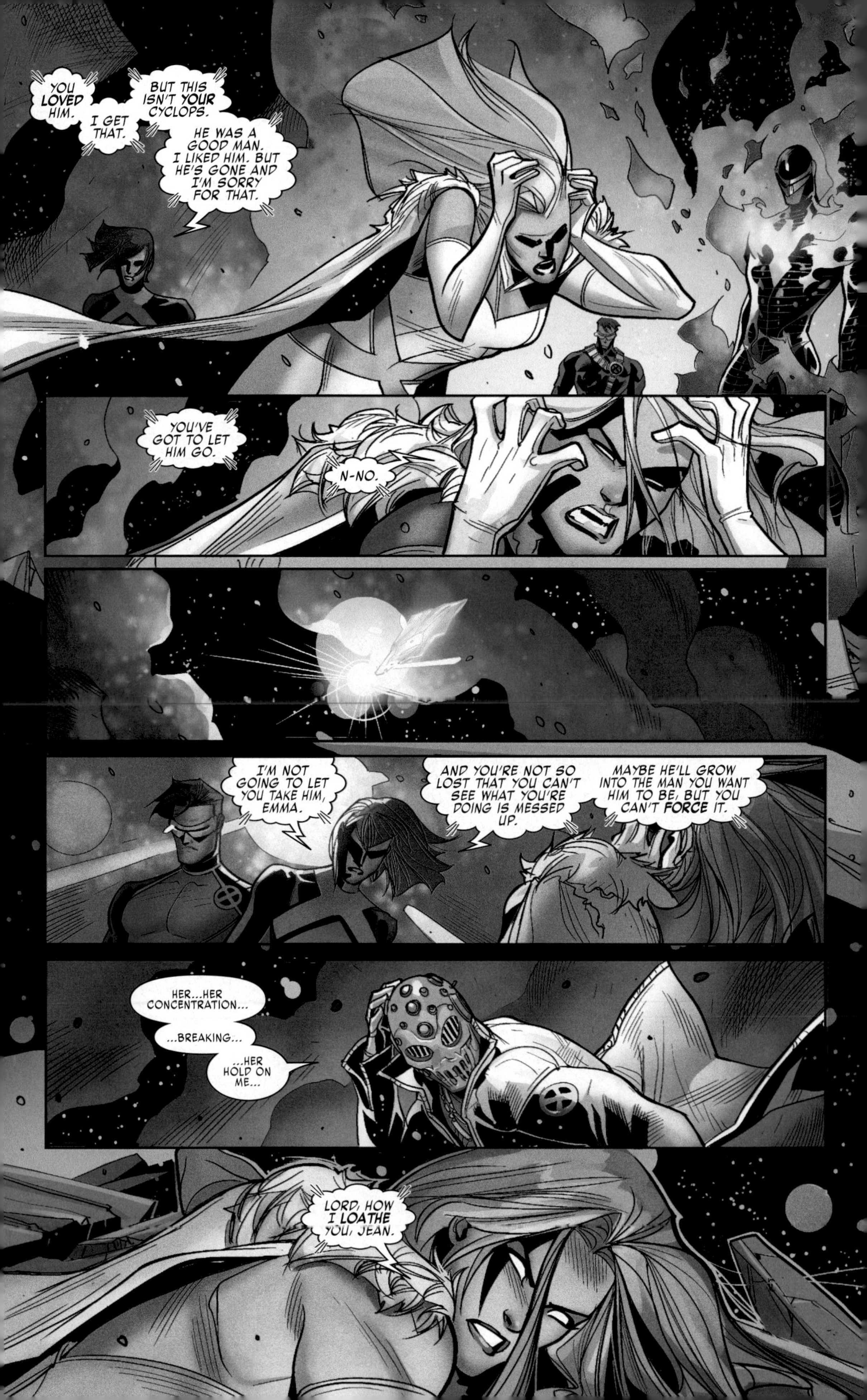
YOU LOVED HIM.
I GET THAT.
BUT THIS ISN'T YOUR CYCLOPS.
HE WAS A GOOD MAN. I LIKED HIM. BUT HE'S GONE AND I'M SORRY FOR THAT.
YOU'VE GOT TO LET HIM GO.
N-NO.
I'M NOT GOING TO LET YOU TAKE HIM, EMMA.
AND YOU'RE NOT SO LOST THAT YOU CAN'T SEE WHAT YOU'RE DOING IS MESSED UP.
MAYBE HE'LL GROW INTO THE MAN YOU WANT HIM TO BE, BUT YOU CAN'T FORCE IT.
HER...HER CONCENTRATION...
...BREAKING...
...HER HOLD ON ME...
LORD, HOW I LOATHE YOU, JEAN.

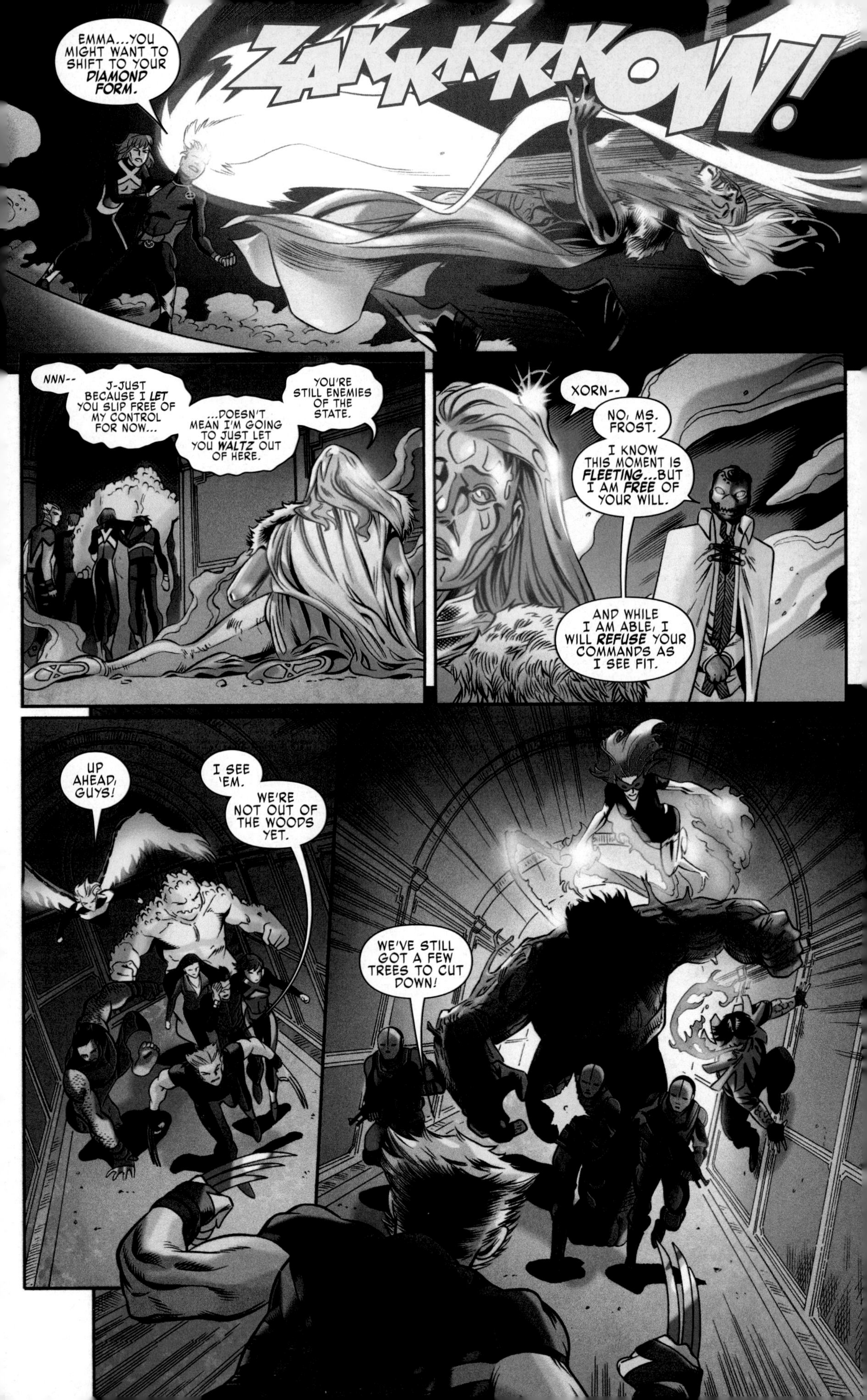
EMMA...YOU MIGHT WANT TO SHIFT TO YOUR DIAMOND FORM.
ZAKKKKKKOW!
NNN--
J-JUST BECAUSE I LET YOU SLIP FREE OF MY CONTROL FOR NOW...
...DOESN'T MEAN I'M GOING TO JUST LET YOU WALTZ OUT OF HERE.
YOU'RE STILL ENEMIES OF THE STATE.
XORN--
NO, MS. FROST.
I KNOW THIS MOMENT IS FLEETING...BUT I AM FREE OF YOUR WILL.
AND WHILE I AM ABLE, I WILL REFUSE YOUR COMMANDS AS I SEE FIT.
UP AHEAD, GUYS!
I SEE 'EM.
WE'RE NOT OUT OF THE WOODS YET.
WE'VE STILL GOT A FEW TREES TO CUT DOWN!

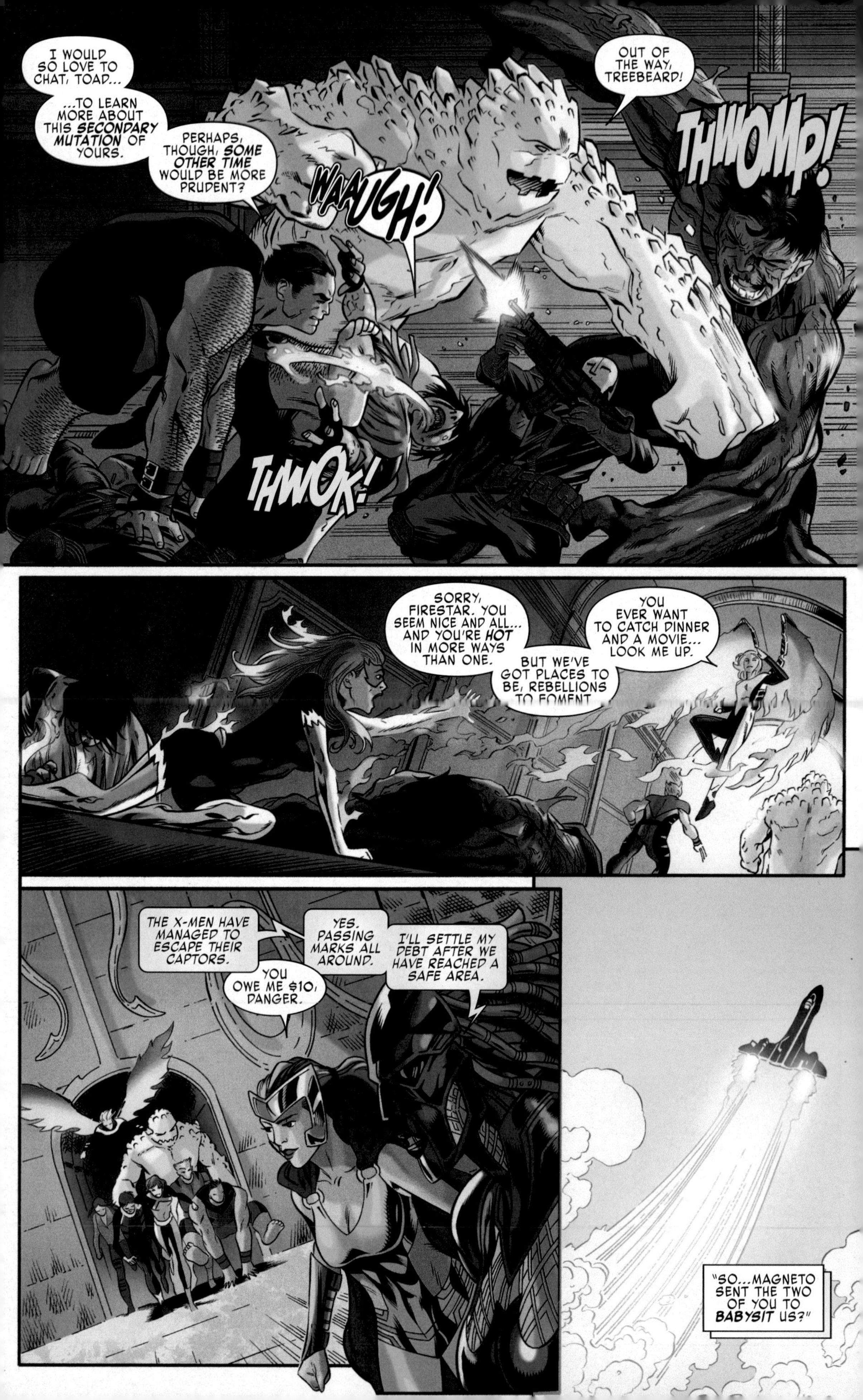
I WOULD SO LOVE TO CHAT, TOAD...
...TO LEARN MORE ABOUT THIS SECONDARY MUTATION OF YOURS.
PERHAPS, THOUGH, SOME OTHER TIME WOULD BE MORE PRUDENT?
WAAUGH!
OUT OF THE WAY, TREEBEARD!
THWOMP!
THWOK!
SORRY, FIRESTAR. YOU SEEM NICE AND ALL... AND YOU'RE HOT IN MORE WAYS THAN ONE.
BUT WE'VE GOT PLACES TO BE, REBELLIONS TO FOMENT.
YOU EVER WANT TO CATCH DINNER AND A MOVIE... LOOK ME UP.
THE X-MEN HAVE MANAGED TO ESCAPE THEIR CAPTORS.
YES. PASSING MARKS ALL AROUND.
YOU OWE ME $10, DANGER.
I'LL SETTLE MY DEBT AFTER WE HAVE REACHED A SAFE AREA.
"SO...MAGNETO SENT THE TWO OF YOU TO BABYSIT US?"

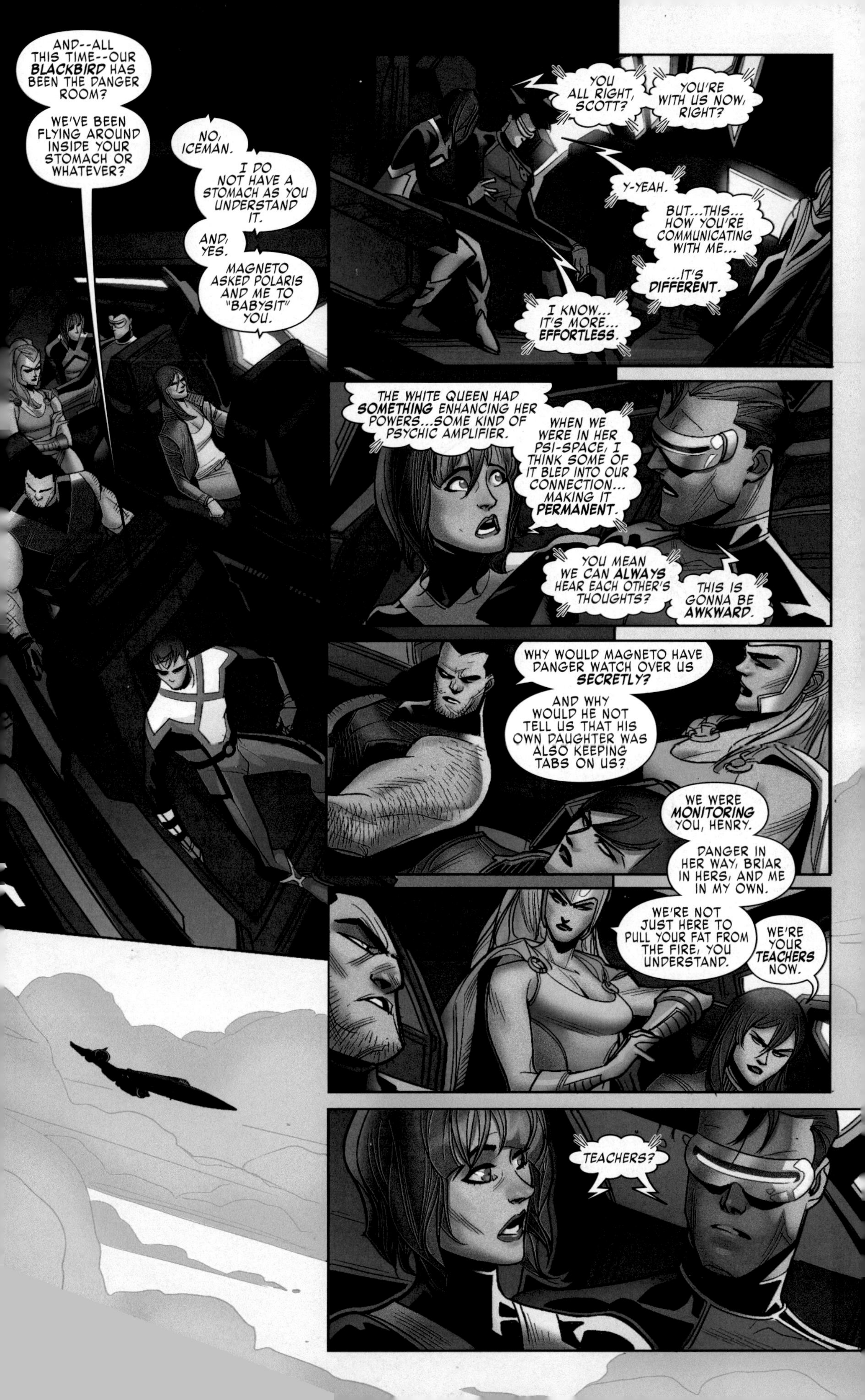

AND--ALL THIS TIME--OUR BLACKBIRD HAS BEEN THE DANGER ROOM?
WE'VE BEEN FLYING AROUND INSIDE YOUR STOMACH OR WHATEVER?
NO, ICEMAN.
I DO NOT HAVE A STOMACH AS YOU UNDERSTAND IT.
AND, YES.
MAGNETO ASKED POLARIS AND ME TO "BABYSIT" YOU.
YOU ALL RIGHT, SCOTT?
YOU'RE WITH US NOW, RIGHT?
Y-YEAH.
BUT...THIS... HOW YOU'RE COMMUNICATING WITH ME...
...IT'S DIFFERENT.
I KNOW... IT'S MORE... EFFORTLESS.
THE WHITE QUEEN HAD SOMETHING ENHANCING HER POWERS...SOME KIND OF PSYCHIC AMPLIFIER.
WHEN WE WERE IN HER PSI-SPACE, I THINK SOME OF IT BLED INTO OUR CONNECTION... MAKING IT PERMANENT.
YOU MEAN WE CAN ALWAYS HEAR EACH OTHER'S THOUGHTS?
THIS IS GONNA BE AWKWARD.
WHY WOULD MAGNETO HAVE DANGER WATCH OVER US SECRETLY?
AND WHY WOULD HE NOT TELL US THAT HIS OWN DAUGHTER WAS ALSO KEEPING TABS ON US?
WE WERE MONITORING YOU, HENRY.
DANGER IN HER WAY, BRIAR IN HERS, AND ME IN MY OWN.
WE'RE NOT JUST HERE TO PULL YOUR FAT FROM THE FIRE, YOU UNDERSTAND.
WE'RE YOUR TEACHERS NOW.
TEACHERS?

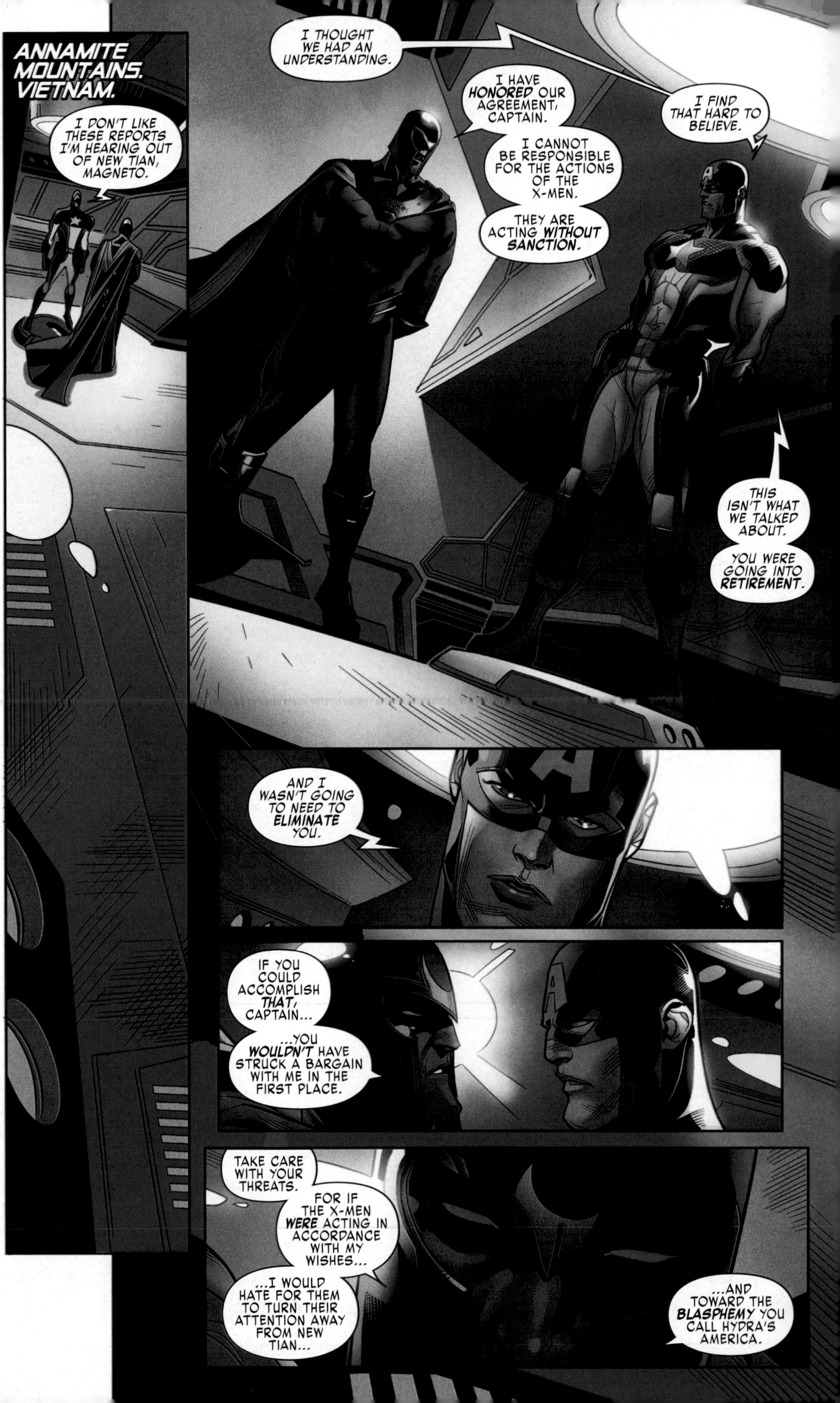
ANNAMITE MOUNTAINS. VIETNAM.
I DON'T LIKE THESE REPORTS I'M HEARING OUT OF NEW TIAN, MAGNETO.
I THOUGHT WE HAD AN UNDERSTANDING.
I HAVE HONORED OUR AGREEMENT, CAPTAIN.
I CANNOT BE RESPONSIBLE FOR THE ACTIONS OF THE X-MEN.
THEY ARE ACTING WITHOUT SANCTION.
I FIND THAT HARD TO BELIEVE.
THIS ISN'T WHAT WE TALKED ABOUT.
YOU WERE GOING INTO RETIREMENT.
AND I WASN'T GOING TO NEED TO ELIMINATE YOU.
IF YOU COULD ACCOMPLISH THAT, CAPTAIN...
...YOU WOULDN'T HAVE STRUCK A BARGAIN WITH ME IN THE FIRST PLACE.
TAKE CARE WITH YOUR THREATS.
FOR IF THE X-MEN WERE ACTING IN ACCORDANCE WITH MY WISHES...
...I WOULD HATE FOR THEM TO TURN THEIR ATTENTION AWAY FROM NEW TIAN...
...AND TOWARD THE BLASPHEMY YOU CALL HYDRA'S AMERICA.

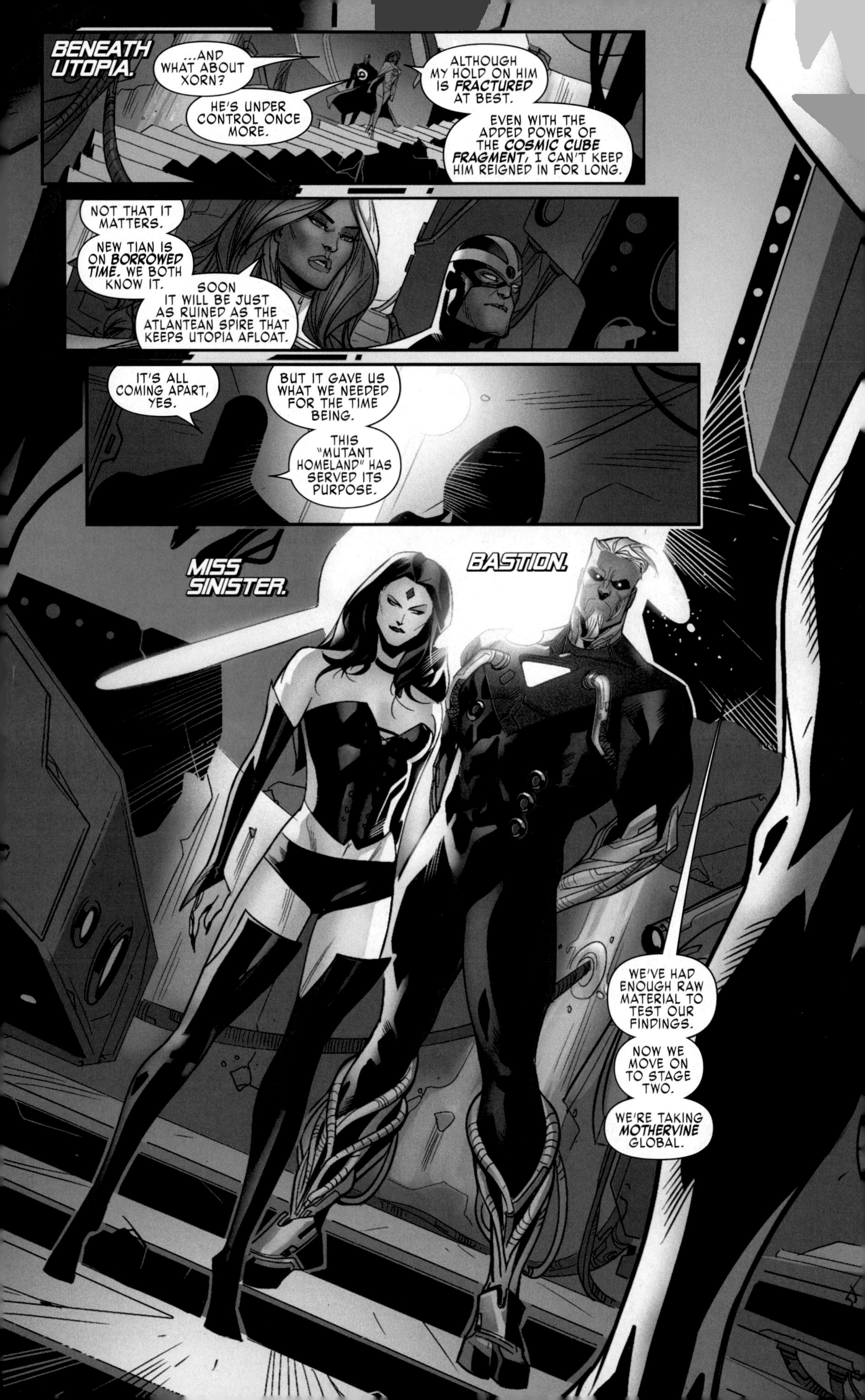
BENEATH UTOPIA.
...AND WHAT ABOUT XORN?
HE'S UNDER CONTROL ONCE MORE.
ALTHOUGH MY HOLD ON HIM IS FRACTURED AT BEST.
EVEN WITH THE ADDED POWER OF THE COSMIC CUBE FRAGMENT, I CAN'T KEEP HIM REIGNED IN FOR LONG.
NOT THAT IT MATTERS.
NEW TIAN IS ON BORROWED TIME. WE BOTH KNOW IT.
SOON IT WILL BE JUST AS RUINED AS THE ATLANTEAN SPIRE THAT KEEPS UTOPIA AFLOAT.
IT'S ALL COMING APART, YES.
BUT IT GAVE US WHAT WE NEEDED FOR THE TIME BEING.
THIS "MUTANT HOMELAND" HAS SERVED ITS PURPOSE.
MISS SINISTER.
BASTION.
WE'VE HAD ENOUGH RAW MATERIAL TO TEST OUR FINDINGS.
NOW WE MOVE ON TO STAGE TWO.
WE'RE TAKING MOTHERVINE GLOBAL.

10

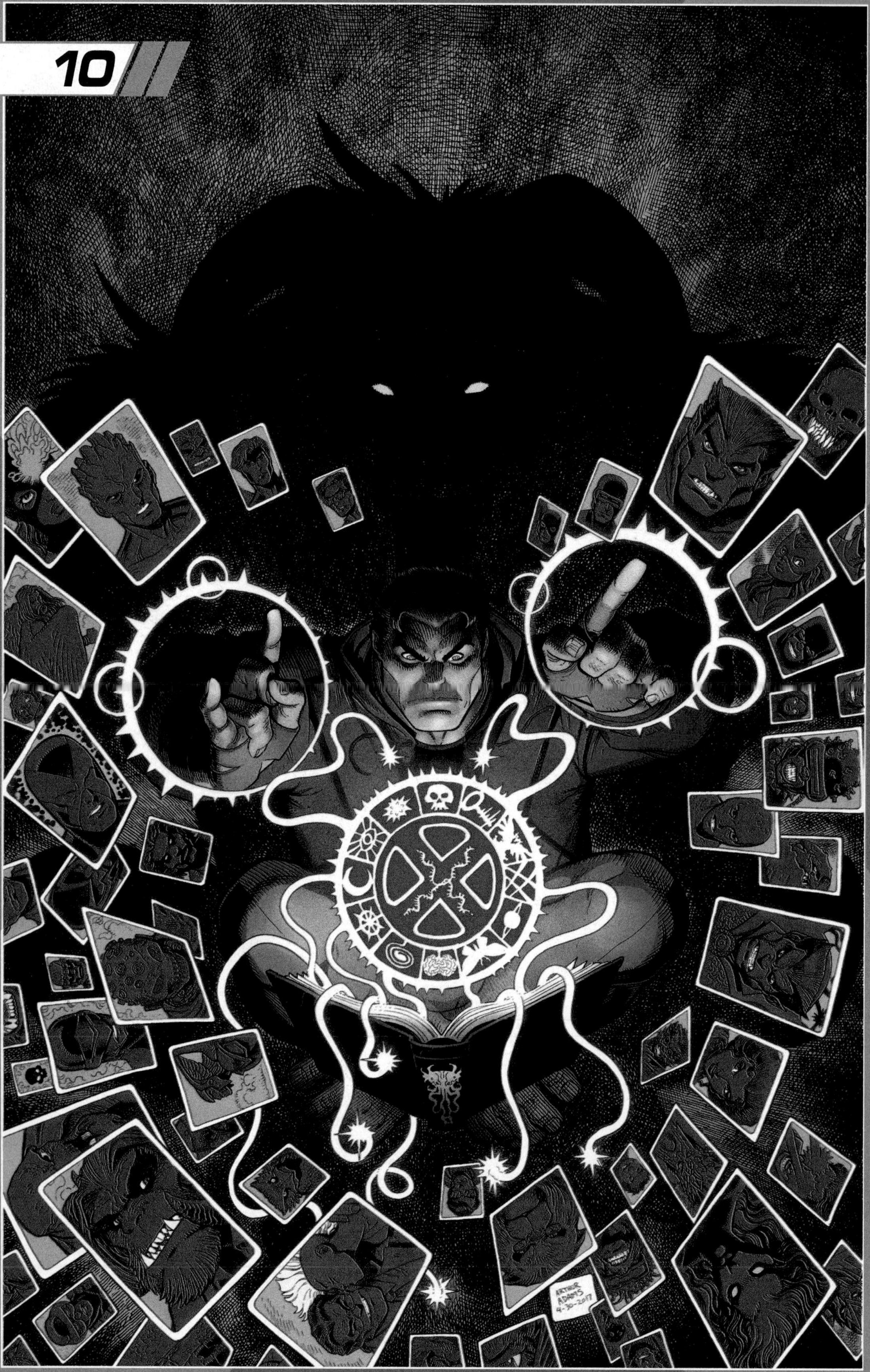
ARTHUR ADAMS
4-30-2017

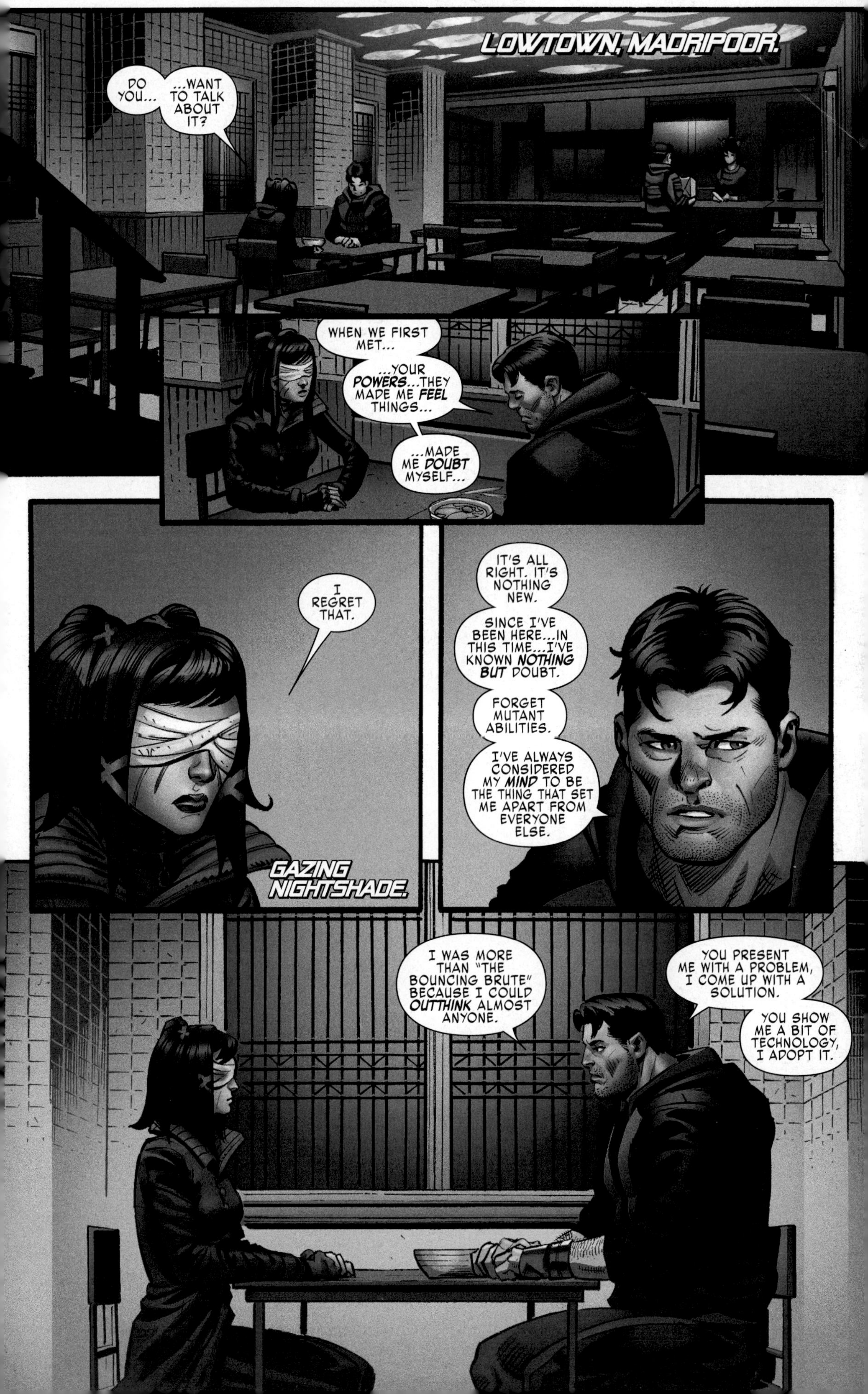
LOWTOWN, MADRIPOOR.
DO YOU...
...WANT TO TALK ABOUT IT?
WHEN WE FIRST MET...
...YOUR POWERS...THEY MADE ME FEEL THINGS...
...MADE ME DOUBT MYSELF...
I REGRET THAT.
GAZING NIGHTSHADE.
IT'S ALL RIGHT. IT'S NOTHING NEW.
SINCE I'VE BEEN HERE...IN THIS TIME...I'VE KNOWN NOTHING BUT DOUBT.
FORGET MUTANT ABILITIES.
I'VE ALWAYS CONSIDERED MY MIND TO BE THE THING THAT SET ME APART FROM EVERYONE ELSE.
I WAS MORE THAN "THE BOUNCING BRUTE" BECAUSE I COULD OUTTHINK ALMOST ANYONE.
YOU PRESENT ME WITH A PROBLEM, I COME UP WITH A SOLUTION.
YOU SHOW ME A BIT OF TECHNOLOGY, I ADOPT IT.

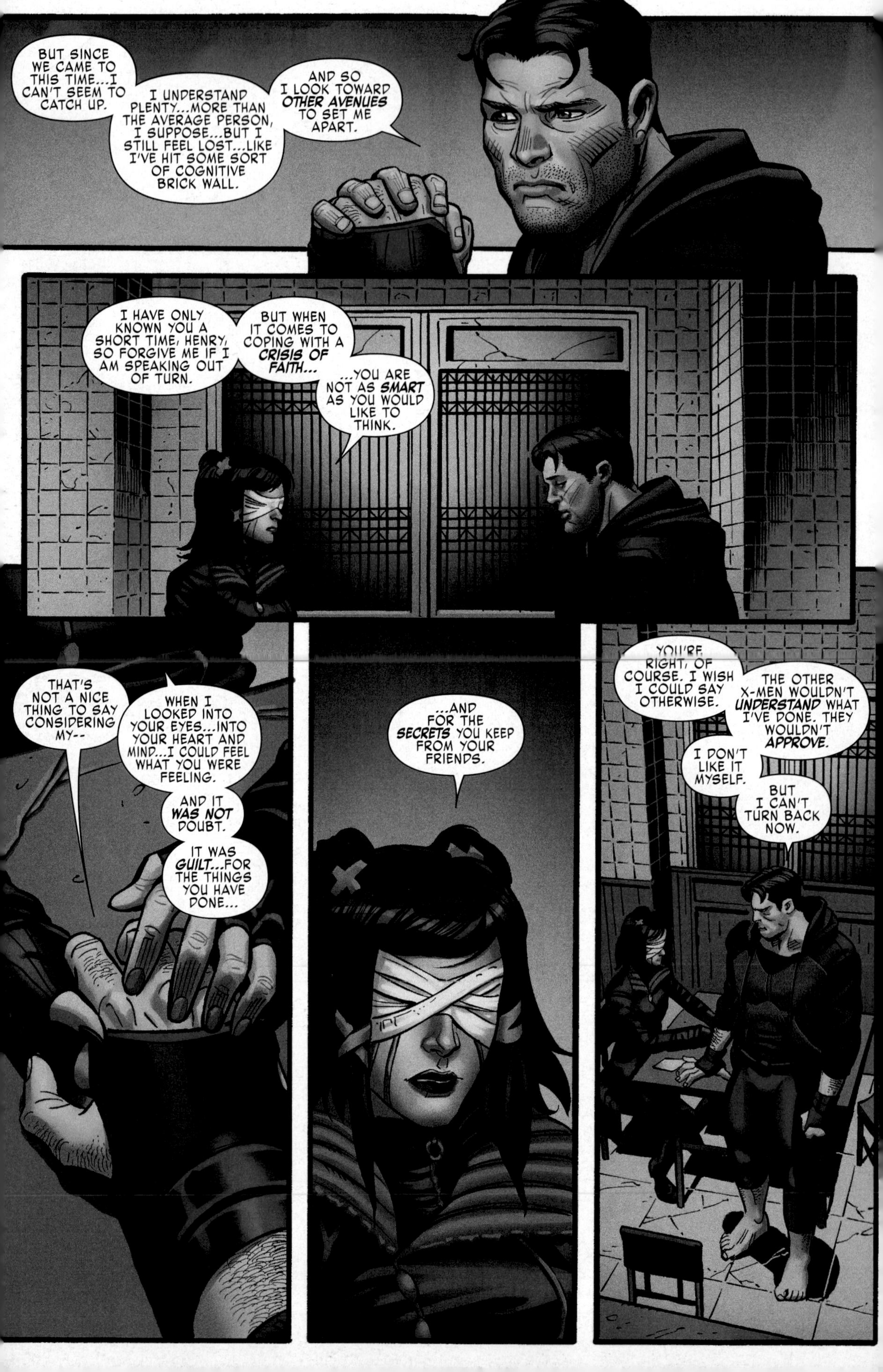
BUT SINCE WE CAME TO THIS TIME...I CAN'T SEEM TO CATCH UP.
I UNDERSTAND PLENTY...MORE THAN THE AVERAGE PERSON, I SUPPOSE...BUT I STILL FEEL LOST...LIKE I'VE HIT SOME SORT OF COGNITIVE BRICK WALL.
AND SO I LOOK TOWARD OTHER AVENUES TO SET ME APART.
I HAVE ONLY KNOWN YOU A SHORT TIME, HENRY, SO FORGIVE ME IF I AM SPEAKING OUT OF TURN.
BUT WHEN IT COMES TO COPING WITH A CRISIS OF FAITH...
...YOU ARE NOT AS SMART AS YOU WOULD LIKE TO THINK.
THAT'S NOT A NICE THING TO SAY CONSIDERING MY--
WHEN I LOOKED INTO YOUR EYES...INTO YOUR HEART AND MIND...I COULD FEEL WHAT YOU WERE FEELING.
AND IT WAS NOT DOUBT.
IT WAS GUILT...FOR THE THINGS YOU HAVE DONE...
...AND FOR THE SECRETS YOU KEEP FROM YOUR FRIENDS.
YOU'RE RIGHT, OF COURSE. I WISH I COULD SAY OTHERWISE.
THE OTHER X-MEN WOULDN'T UNDERSTAND WHAT I'VE DONE. THEY WOULDN'T APPROVE.
I DON'T LIKE IT MYSELF.
BUT I CAN'T TURN BACK NOW.

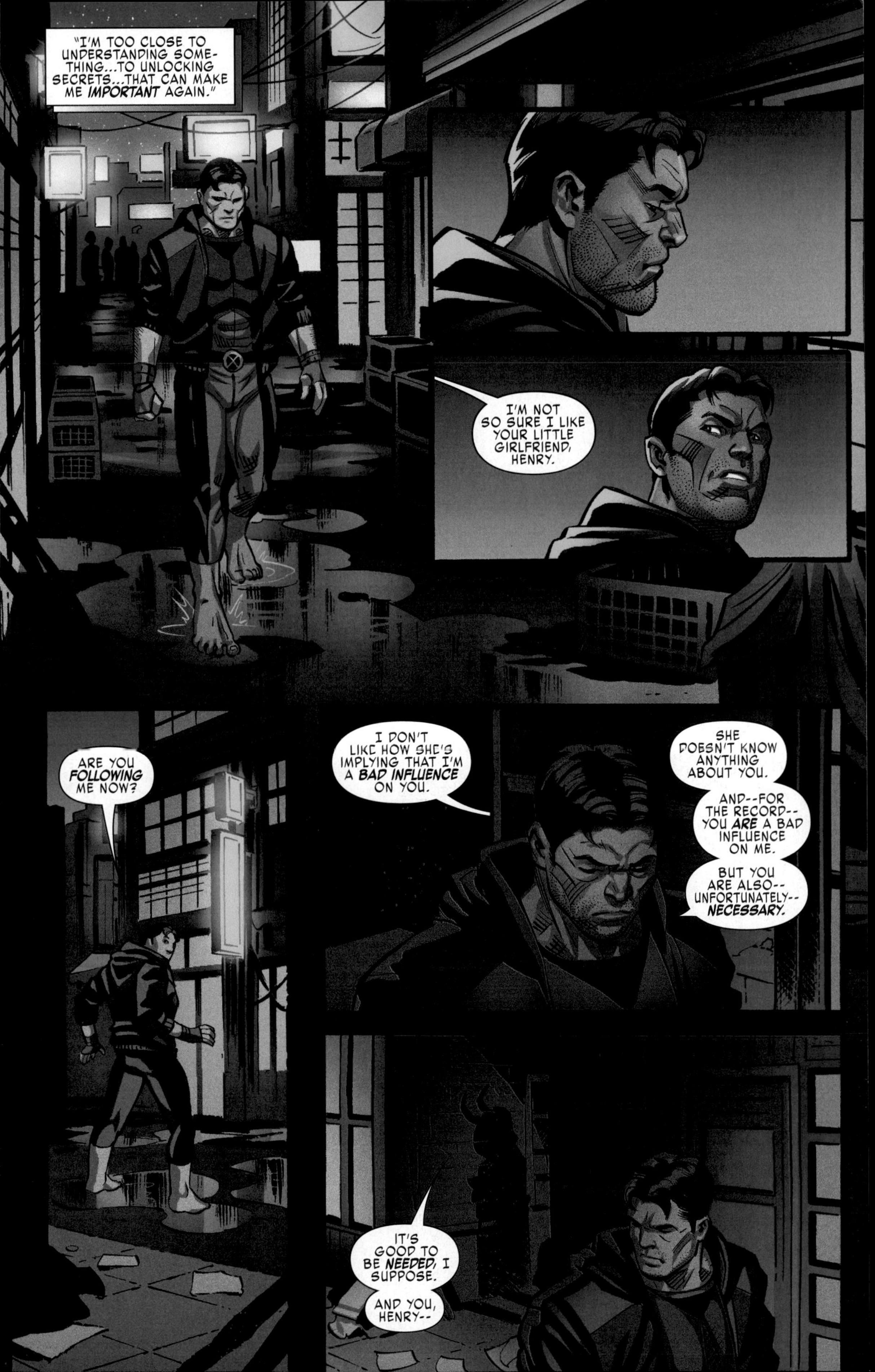
"I'M TOO CLOSE TO UNDERSTANDING SOMETHING...TO UNLOCKING SECRETS...THAT CAN MAKE ME IMPORTANT AGAIN."
I'M NOT SO SURE I LIKE YOUR LITTLE GIRLFRIEND, HENRY.
ARE YOU FOLLOWING ME NOW?
I DON'T LIKE HOW SHE'S IMPLYING THAT I'M A BAD INFLUENCE ON YOU.
SHE DOESN'T KNOW ANYTHING ABOUT YOU.
AND--FOR THE RECORD--YOU ARE A BAD INFLUENCE ON ME.
BUT YOU ARE ALSO--UNFORTUNATELY--NECESSARY.
IT'S GOOD TO BE NEEDED, I SUPPOSE.
AND YOU, HENRY--

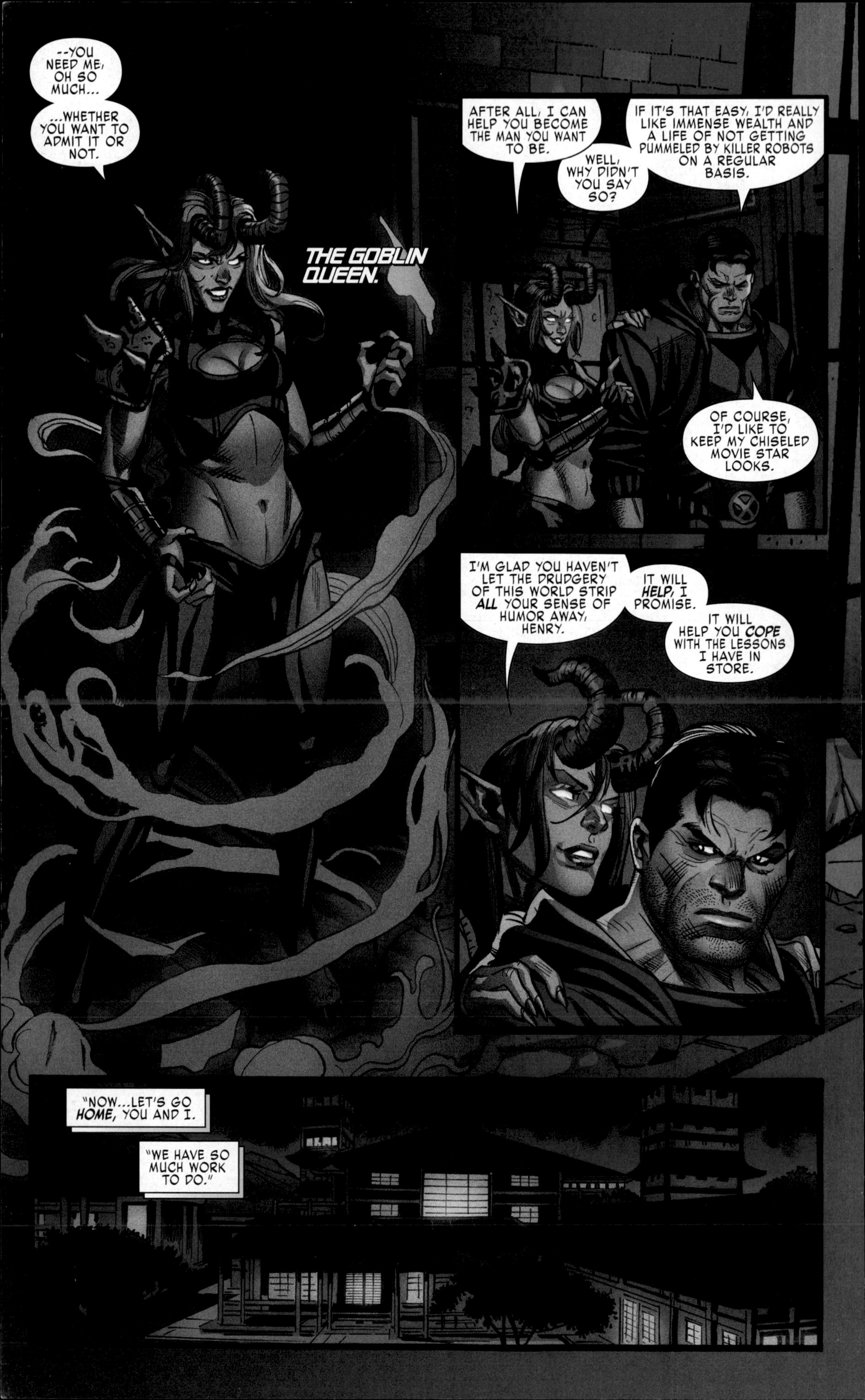
--YOU NEED ME, OH SO MUCH...
...WHETHER YOU WANT TO ADMIT IT OR NOT.
THE GOBLIN QUEEN.
AFTER ALL, I CAN HELP YOU BECOME THE MAN YOU WANT TO BE.
WELL, WHY DIDN'T YOU SAY SO?
IF IT'S THAT EASY, I'D REALLY LIKE IMMENSE WEALTH AND A LIFE OF NOT GETTING PUMMELED BY KILLER ROBOTS ON A REGULAR BASIS.
OF COURSE, I'D LIKE TO KEEP MY CHISELED MOVIE STAR LOOKS.
I'M GLAD YOU HAVEN'T LET THE DRUDGERY OF THIS WORLD STRIP ALL YOUR SENSE OF HUMOR AWAY, HENRY.
IT WILL HELP, I PROMISE.
IT WILL HELP YOU COPE WITH THE LESSONS I HAVE IN STORE.
"NOW...LET'S GO HOME, YOU AND I.
"WE HAVE SO MUCH WORK TO DO."

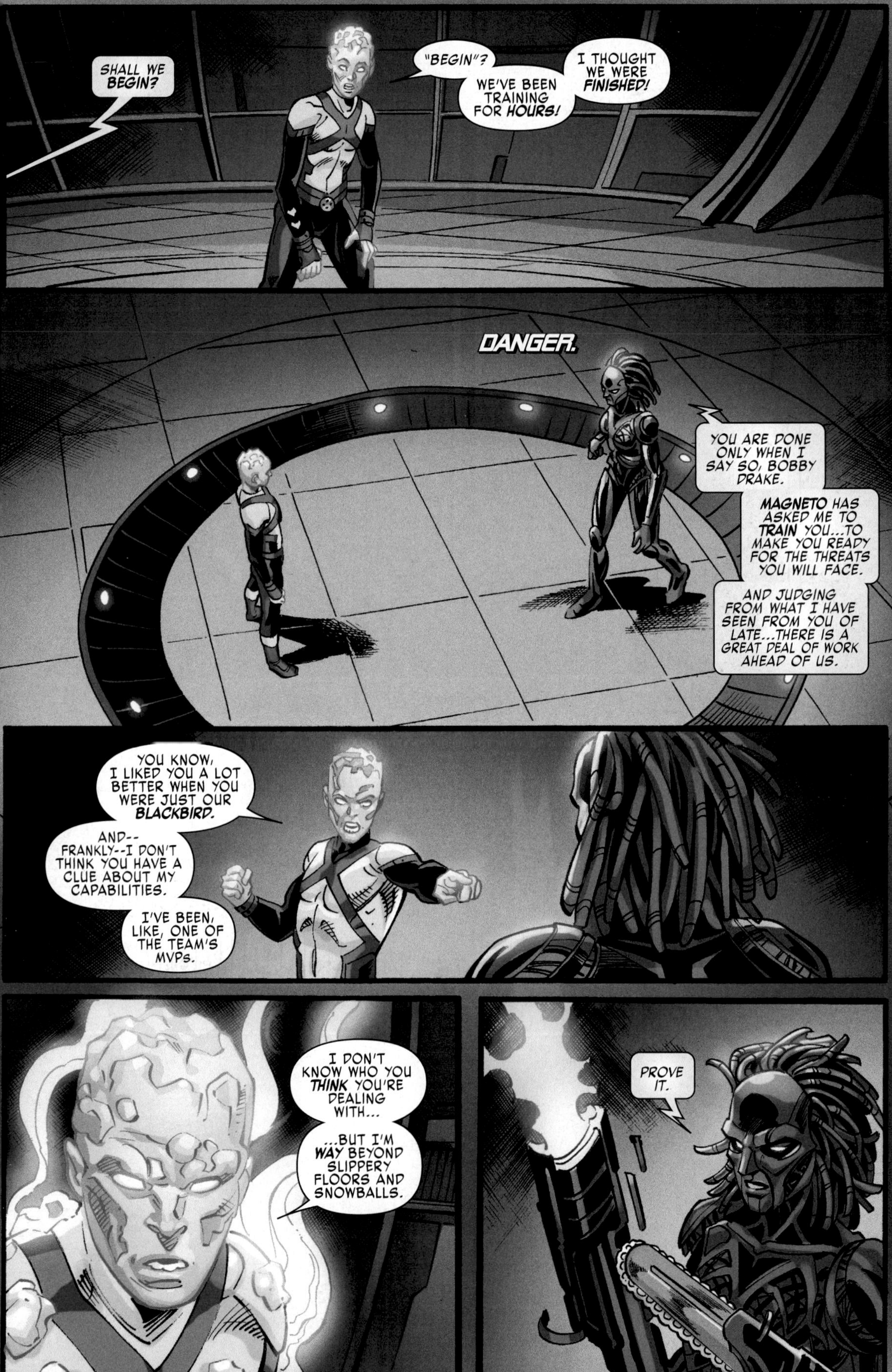
SHALL WE BEGIN?
"BEGIN"? WE'VE BEEN TRAINING FOR HOURS!
I THOUGHT WE WERE FINISHED!
DANGER.
YOU ARE DONE ONLY WHEN I SAY SO, BOBBY DRAKE.
MAGNETO HAS ASKED ME TO TRAIN YOU...TO MAKE YOU READY FOR THE THREATS YOU WILL FACE.
AND JUDGING FROM WHAT I HAVE SEEN FROM YOU OF LATE...THERE IS A GREAT DEAL OF WORK AHEAD OF US.
YOU KNOW, I LIKED YOU A LOT BETTER WHEN YOU WERE JUST OUR BLACKBIRD.
AND--FRANKLY--I DON'T THINK YOU HAVE A CLUE ABOUT MY CAPABILITIES.
I'VE BEEN, LIKE, ONE OF THE TEAM'S MVPs.
I DON'T KNOW WHO YOU THINK YOU'RE DEALING WITH...
...BUT I'M WAY BEYOND SLIPPERY FLOORS AND SNOWBALLS.
PROVE IT.

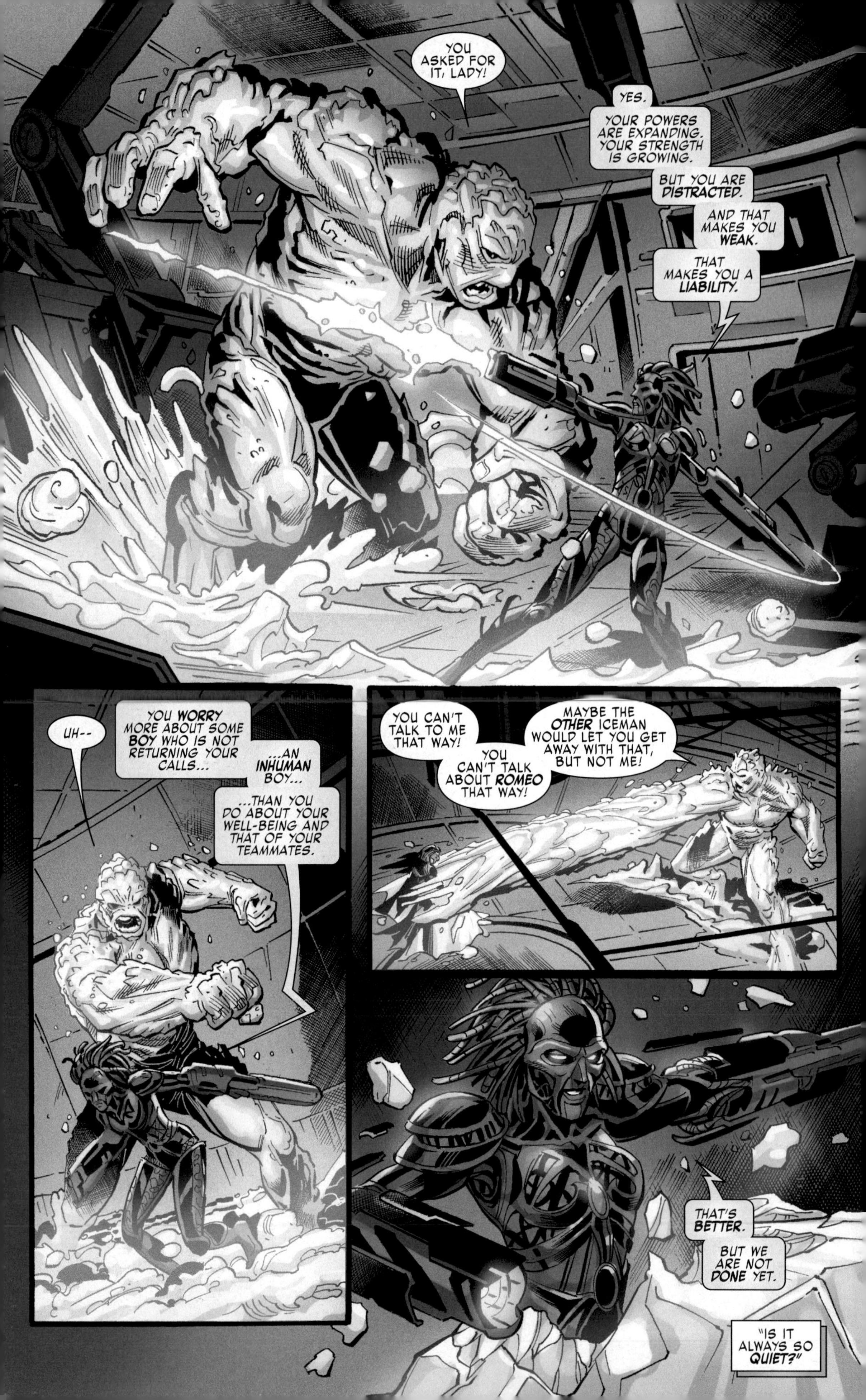
YOU ASKED FOR IT, LADY!
YES.
YOUR POWERS ARE EXPANDING. YOUR STRENGTH IS GROWING.
BUT YOU ARE DISTRACTED.
AND THAT MAKES YOU WEAK.
THAT MAKES YOU A LIABILITY.
YOU WORRY MORE ABOUT SOME BOY WHO IS NOT RETURNING YOUR CALLS...
...AN INHUMAN BOY...
...THAN YOU DO ABOUT YOUR WELL-BEING AND THAT OF YOUR TEAMMATES.
UH--
YOU CAN'T TALK TO ME THAT WAY!
YOU CAN'T TALK ABOUT ROMEO THAT WAY!
MAYBE THE OTHER ICEMAN WOULD LET YOU GET AWAY WITH THAT, BUT NOT ME!
THAT'S BETTER.
BUT WE ARE NOT DONE YET.
"IS IT ALWAYS SO QUIET?"

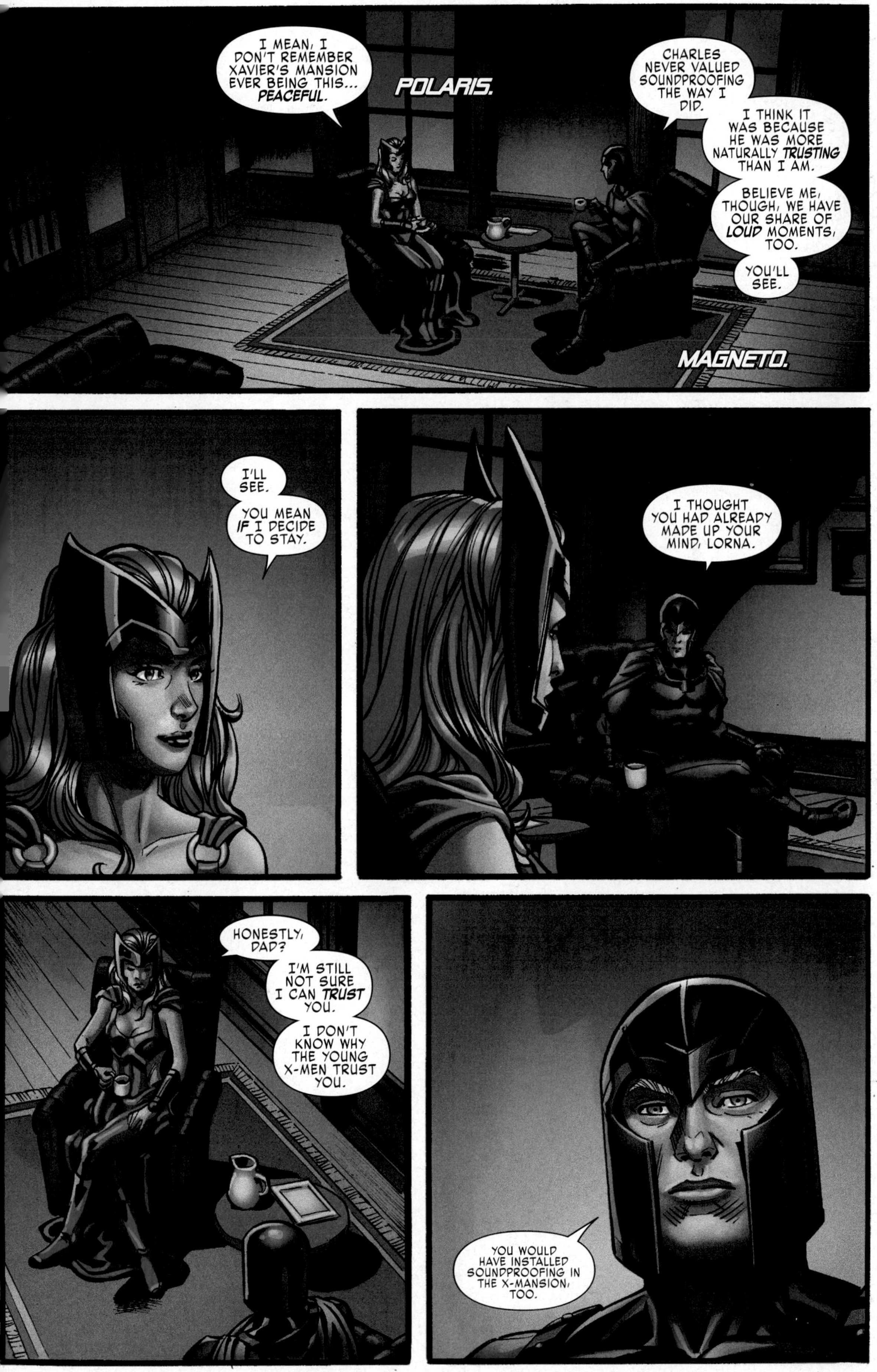
I MEAN, I DON'T REMEMBER XAVIER'S MANSION EVER BEING THIS... PEACEFUL.
POLARIS.
CHARLES NEVER VALUED SOUNDPROOFING THE WAY I DID.
I THINK IT WAS BECAUSE HE WAS MORE NATURALLY TRUSTING THAN I AM.
BELIEVE ME, THOUGH, WE HAVE OUR SHARE OF LOUD MOMENTS, TOO.
YOU'LL SEE.
MAGNETO.
I'LL SEE.
YOU MEAN IF I DECIDE TO STAY.
I THOUGHT YOU HAD ALREADY MADE UP YOUR MIND, LORNA.
HONESTLY, DAD?
I'M STILL NOT SURE I CAN TRUST YOU.
I DON'T KNOW WHY THE YOUNG X-MEN TRUST YOU.
YOU WOULD HAVE INSTALLED SOUNDPROOFING IN THE X-MANSION, TOO.

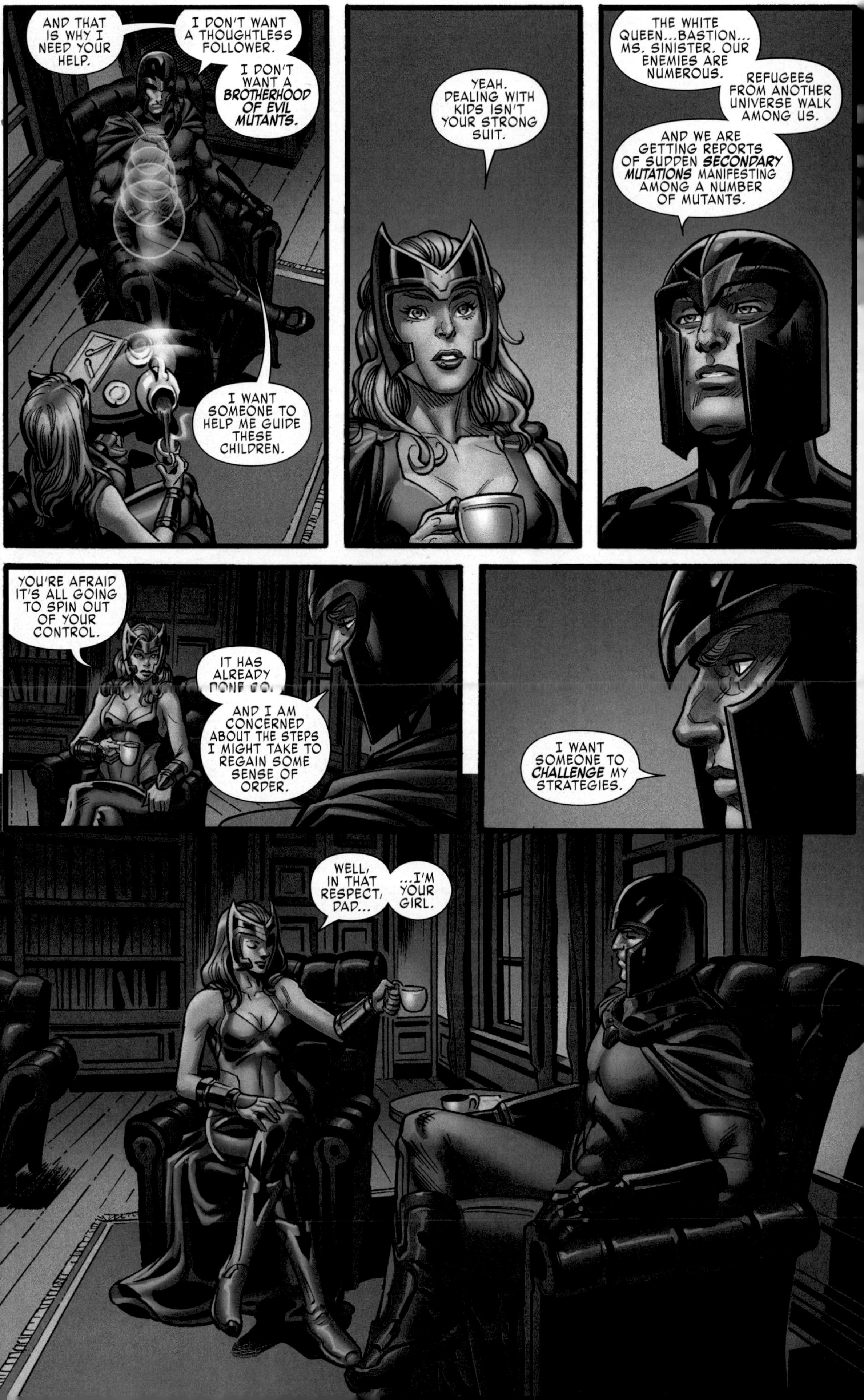

AND THAT IS WHY I NEED YOUR HELP.
I DON'T WANT A THOUGHTLESS FOLLOWER.
I DON'T WANT A BROTHERHOOD OF EVIL MUTANTS.
I WANT SOMEONE TO HELP ME GUIDE THESE CHILDREN.
YEAH. DEALING WITH KIDS ISN'T YOUR STRONG SUIT.
THE WHITE QUEEN...BASTION... MS. SINISTER. OUR ENEMIES ARE NUMEROUS.
REFUGEES FROM ANOTHER UNIVERSE WALK AMONG US.
AND WE ARE GETTING REPORTS OF SUDDEN SECONDARY MUTATIONS MANIFESTING AMONG A NUMBER OF MUTANTS.
YOU'RE AFRAID IT'S ALL GOING TO SPIN OUT OF YOUR CONTROL.
IT HAS ALREADY
AND I AM CONCERNED ABOUT THE STEPS I MIGHT TAKE TO REGAIN SOME SENSE OF ORDER.
I WANT SOMEONE TO CHALLENGE MY STRATEGIES.
WELL, IN THAT RESPECT, DAD...
...I'M YOUR GIRL.

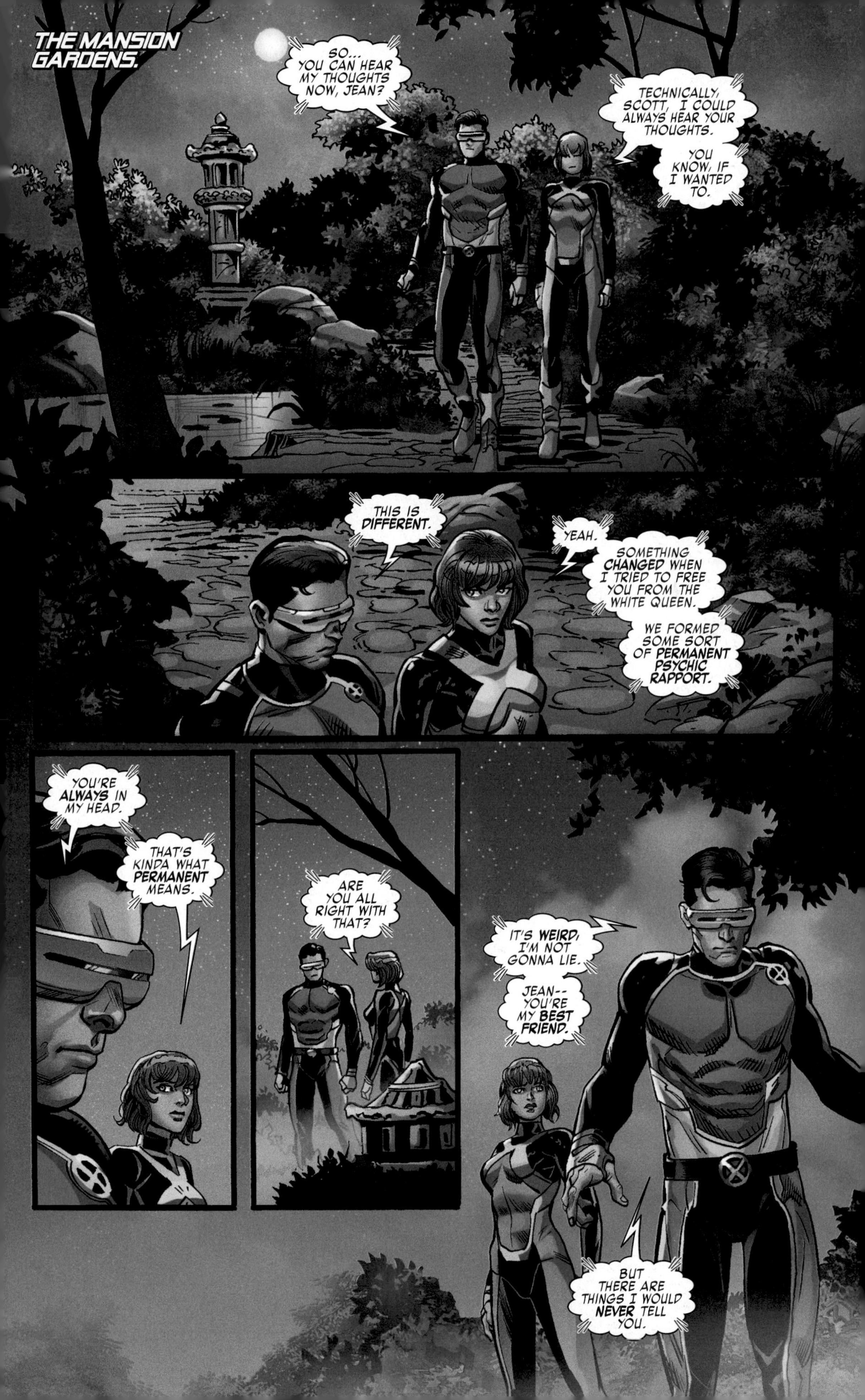
THE MANSION GARDENS.
SO... YOU CAN HEAR MY THOUGHTS NOW, JEAN?
TECHNICALLY, SCOTT, I COULD ALWAYS HEAR YOUR THOUGHTS.
YOU KNOW, IF I WANTED TO.
THIS IS DIFFERENT.
YEAH.
SOMETHING CHANGED WHEN I TRIED TO FREE YOU FROM THE WHITE QUEEN.
WE FORMED SOME SORT OF PERMANENT PSYCHIC RAPPORT.
YOU'RE ALWAYS IN MY HEAD.
THAT'S KINDA WHAT PERMANENT MEANS.
ARE YOU ALL RIGHT WITH THAT?
IT'S WEIRD, I'M NOT GONNA LIE.
JEAN-- YOU'RE MY BEST FRIEND.
BUT THERE ARE THINGS I WOULD NEVER TELL YOU.

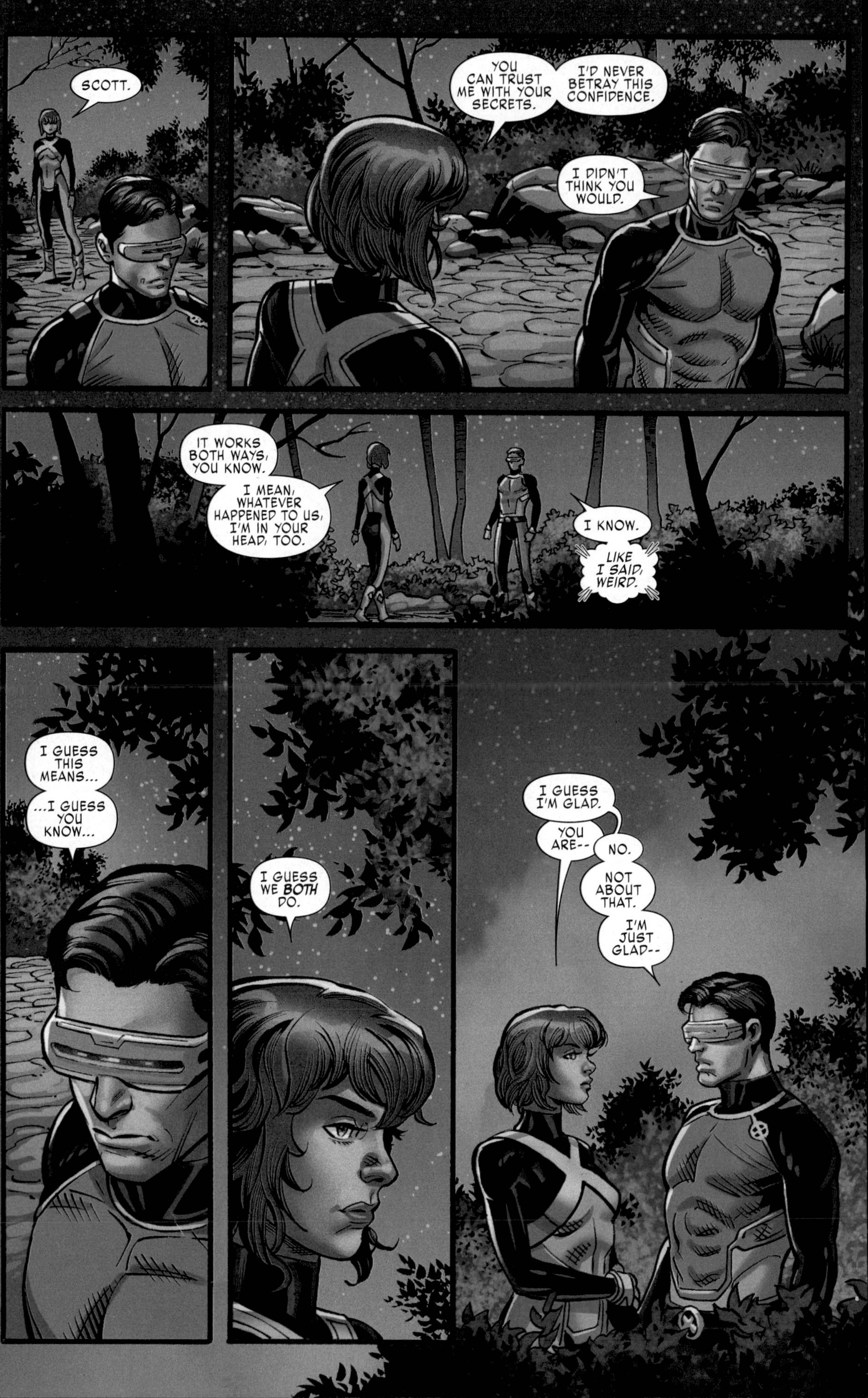
SCOTT.
YOU CAN TRUST ME WITH YOUR SECRETS.
I'D NEVER BETRAY THIS CONFIDENCE.
I DIDN'T THINK YOU WOULD.
IT WORKS BOTH WAYS, YOU KNOW.
I MEAN, WHATEVER HAPPENED TO US, I'M IN YOUR HEAD, TOO.
I KNOW.
LIKE I SAID, WEIRD.
I GUESS THIS MEANS...
...I GUESS YOU KNOW...
I GUESS WE BOTH DO.
I GUESS I'M GLAD.
YOU ARE--
NO.
NOT ABOUT THAT.
I'M JUST GLAD--

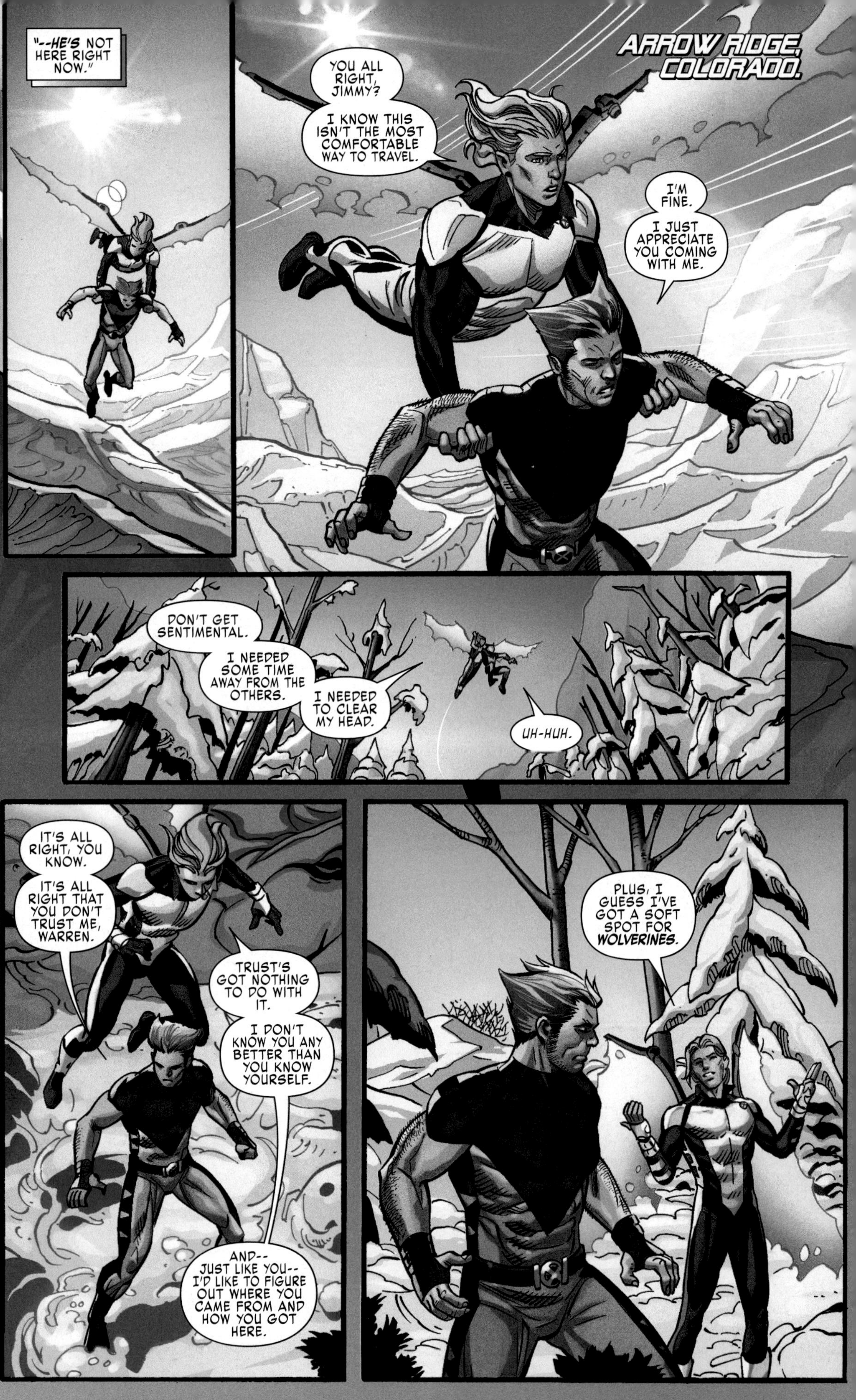
"--HE'S NOT HERE RIGHT NOW."
ARROW RIDGE, COLORADO.
YOU ALL RIGHT, JIMMY?
I KNOW THIS ISN'T THE MOST COMFORTABLE WAY TO TRAVEL.
I'M FINE.
I JUST APPRECIATE YOU COMING WITH ME.
DON'T GET SENTIMENTAL.
I NEEDED SOME TIME AWAY FROM THE OTHERS.
I NEEDED TO CLEAR MY HEAD.
UH-HUH.
IT'S ALL RIGHT, YOU KNOW.
IT'S ALL RIGHT THAT YOU DON'T TRUST ME, WARREN.
TRUST'S GOT NOTHING TO DO WITH IT.
I DON'T KNOW YOU ANY BETTER THAN YOU KNOW YOURSELF.
AND-- JUST LIKE YOU-- I'D LIKE TO FIGURE OUT WHERE YOU CAME FROM AND HOW YOU GOT HERE.
PLUS, I GUESS I'VE GOT A SOFT SPOT FOR WOLVERINES.

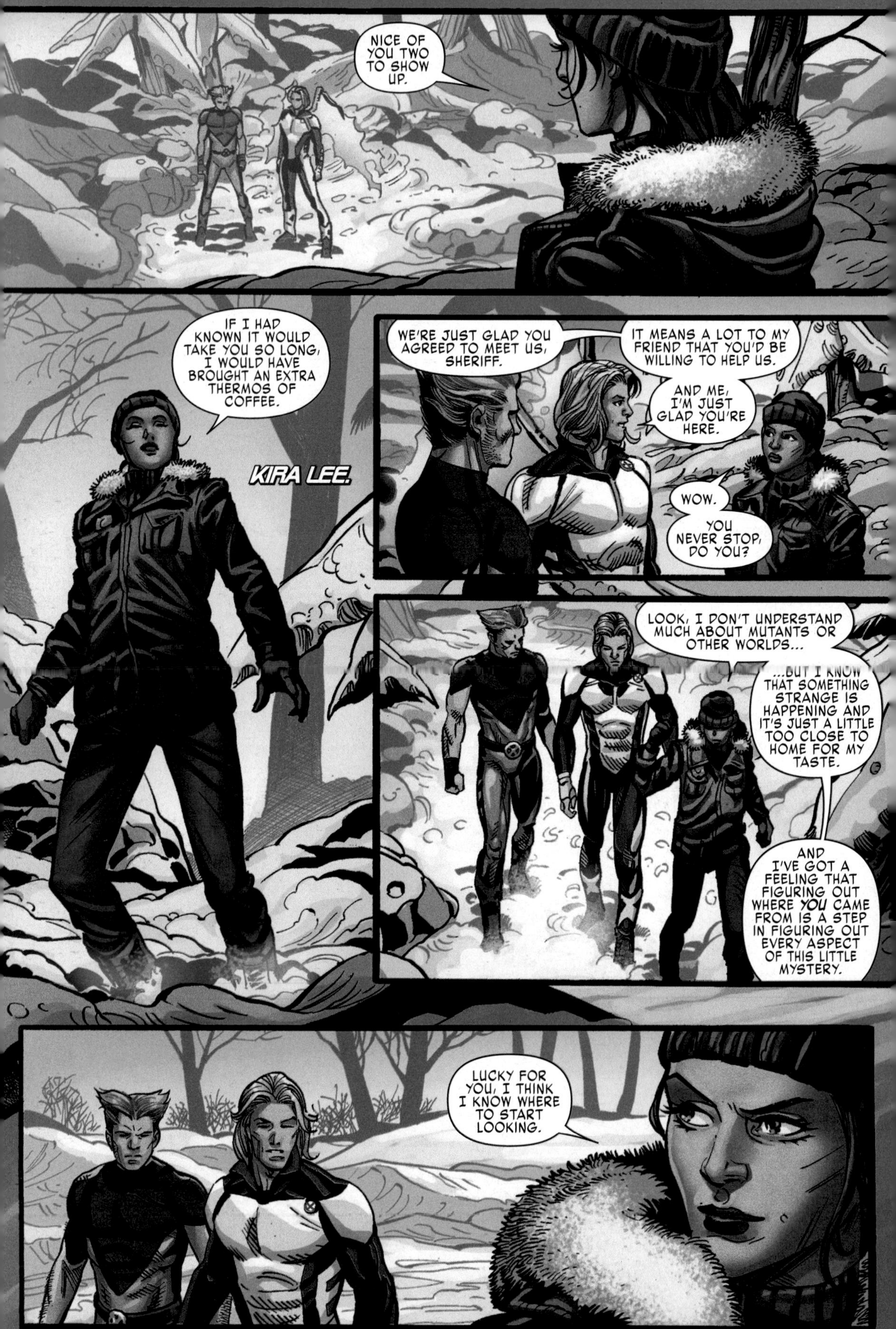
NICE OF YOU TWO TO SHOW UP.
IF I HAD KNOWN IT WOULD TAKE YOU SO LONG, I WOULD HAVE BROUGHT AN EXTRA THERMOS OF COFFEE.
KIRA LEE.
WE'RE JUST GLAD YOU AGREED TO MEET US, SHERIFF.
IT MEANS A LOT TO MY FRIEND THAT YOU'D BE WILLING TO HELP US.
AND ME, I'M JUST GLAD YOU'RE HERE.
WOW.
YOU NEVER STOP, DO YOU?
LOOK, I DON'T UNDERSTAND MUCH ABOUT MUTANTS OR OTHER WORLDS...
...BUT I KNOW THAT SOMETHING STRANGE IS HAPPENING AND IT'S JUST A LITTLE TOO CLOSE TO HOME FOR MY TASTE.
AND I'VE GOT A FEELING THAT FIGURING OUT WHERE YOU CAME FROM IS A STEP IN FIGURING OUT EVERY ASPECT OF THIS LITTLE MYSTERY.
LUCKY FOR YOU, I THINK I KNOW WHERE TO START LOOKING.

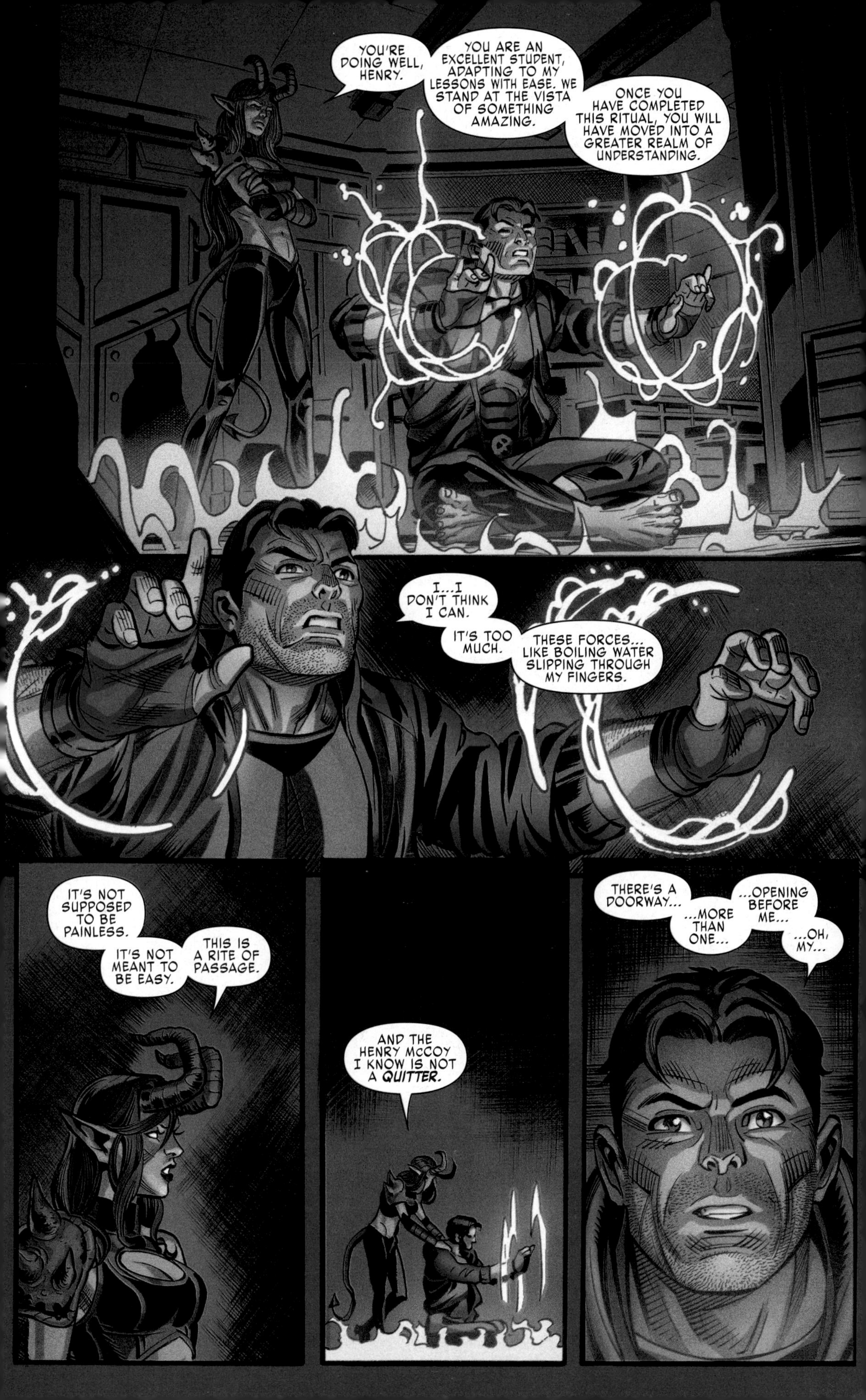
YOU'RE DOING WELL, HENRY.
YOU ARE AN EXCELLENT STUDENT, ADAPTING TO MY LESSONS WITH EASE. WE STAND AT THE VISTA OF SOMETHING AMAZING.
ONCE YOU HAVE COMPLETED THIS RITUAL, YOU WILL HAVE MOVED INTO A GREATER REALM OF UNDERSTANDING.
I...I DON'T THINK I CAN.
IT'S TOO MUCH.
THESE FORCES... LIKE BOILING WATER SLIPPING THROUGH MY FINGERS.
IT'S NOT SUPPOSED TO BE PAINLESS.
IT'S NOT MEANT TO BE EASY.
THIS IS A RITE OF PASSAGE.
AND THE HENRY McCOY I KNOW IS NOT A QUITTER.
THERE'S A DOORWAY...
...MORE THAN ONE...
...OPENING BEFORE ME...
...OH, MY...

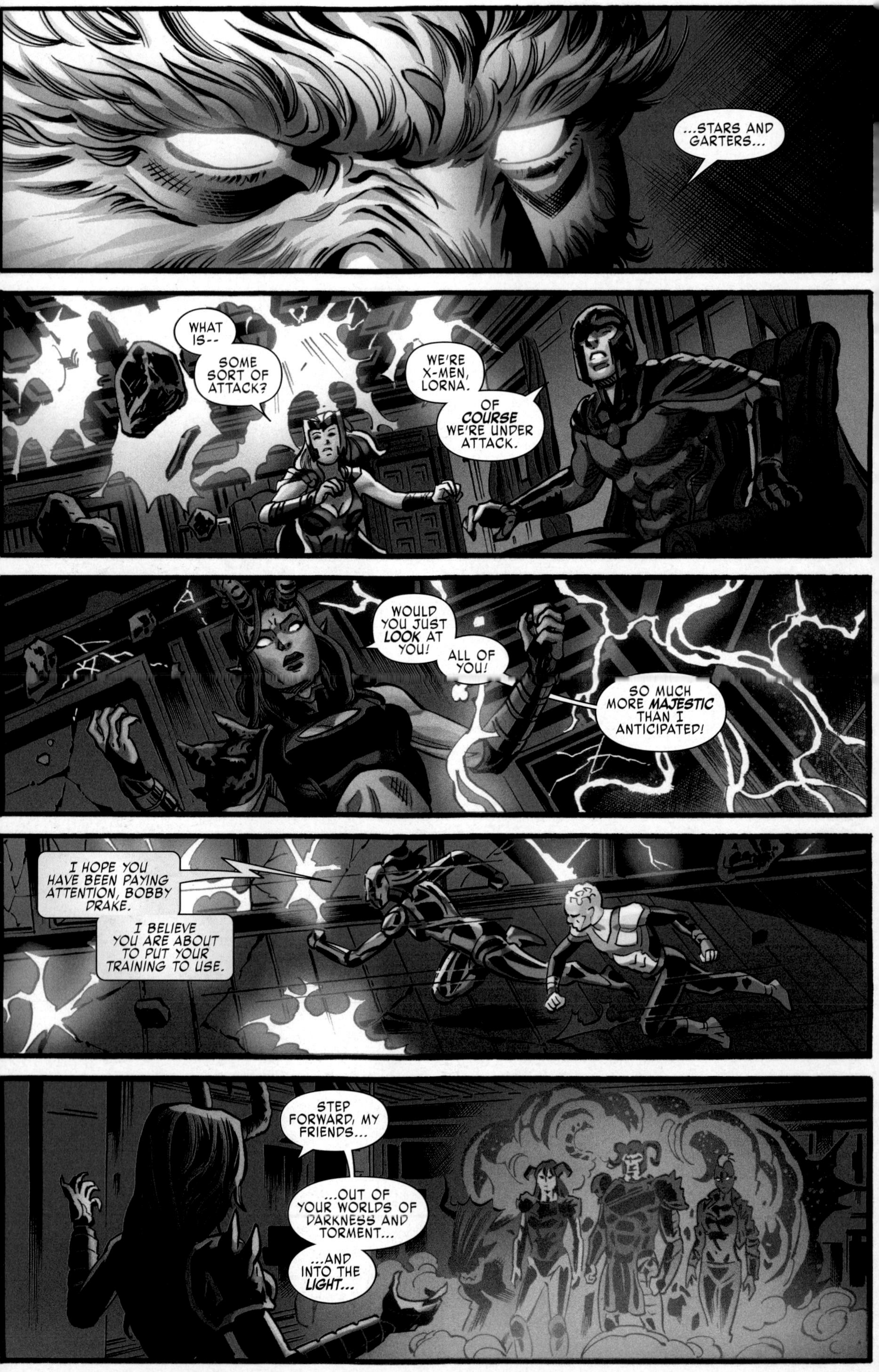
...STARS AND GARTERS...
WHAT IS--
SOME SORT OF ATTACK?
WE'RE X-MEN, LORNA.
OF COURSE WE'RE UNDER ATTACK.
WOULD YOU JUST LOOK AT YOU!
ALL OF YOU!
SO MUCH MORE MAJESTIC THAN I ANTICIPATED!
I HOPE YOU HAVE BEEN PAYING ATTENTION, BOBBY DRAKE.
I BELIEVE YOU ARE ABOUT TO PUT YOUR TRAINING TO USE.
STEP FORWARD, MY FRIENDS...
...OUT OF YOUR WORLDS OF DARKNESS AND TORMENT...
...AND INTO THE LIGHT...

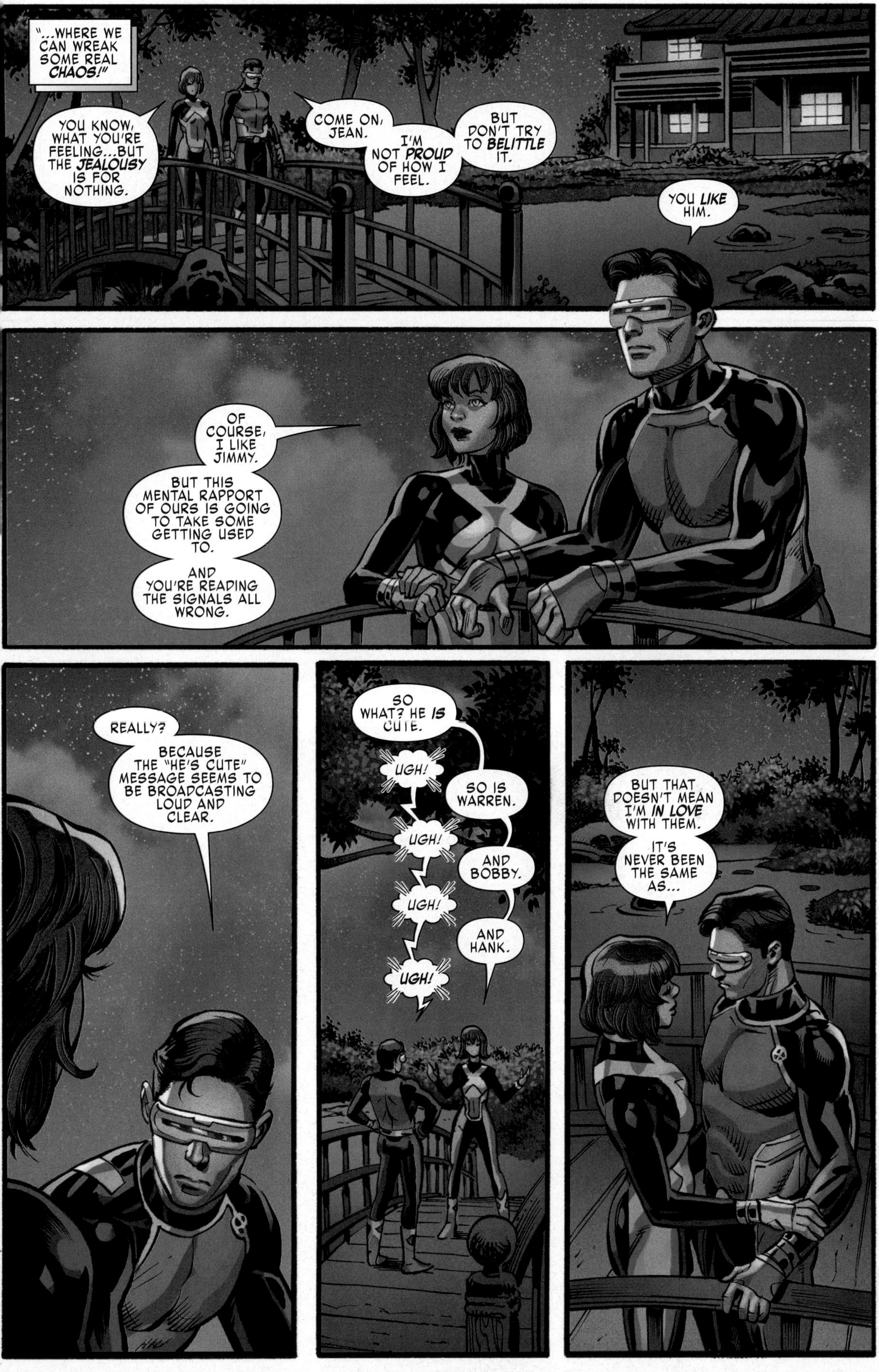
"...WHERE WE CAN WREAK SOME REAL CHAOS!"
YOU KNOW, WHAT YOU'RE FEELING...BUT THE JEALOUSY IS FOR NOTHING.
COME ON, JEAN.
I'M NOT PROUD OF HOW I FEEL.
BUT DON'T TRY TO BELITTLE IT.
YOU LIKE HIM.
OF COURSE, I LIKE JIMMY.
BUT THIS MENTAL RAPPORT OF OURS IS GOING TO TAKE SOME GETTING USED TO.
AND YOU'RE READING THE SIGNALS ALL WRONG.
REALLY?
BECAUSE THE "HE'S CUTE" MESSAGE SEEMS TO BE BROADCASTING LOUD AND CLEAR.
SO WHAT? HE IS CUTE.
UGH!
SO IS WARREN.
UGH!
AND BOBBY.
UGH!
AND HANK.
UGH!
BUT THAT DOESN'T MEAN I'M IN LOVE WITH THEM.
IT'S NEVER BEEN THE SAME AS...

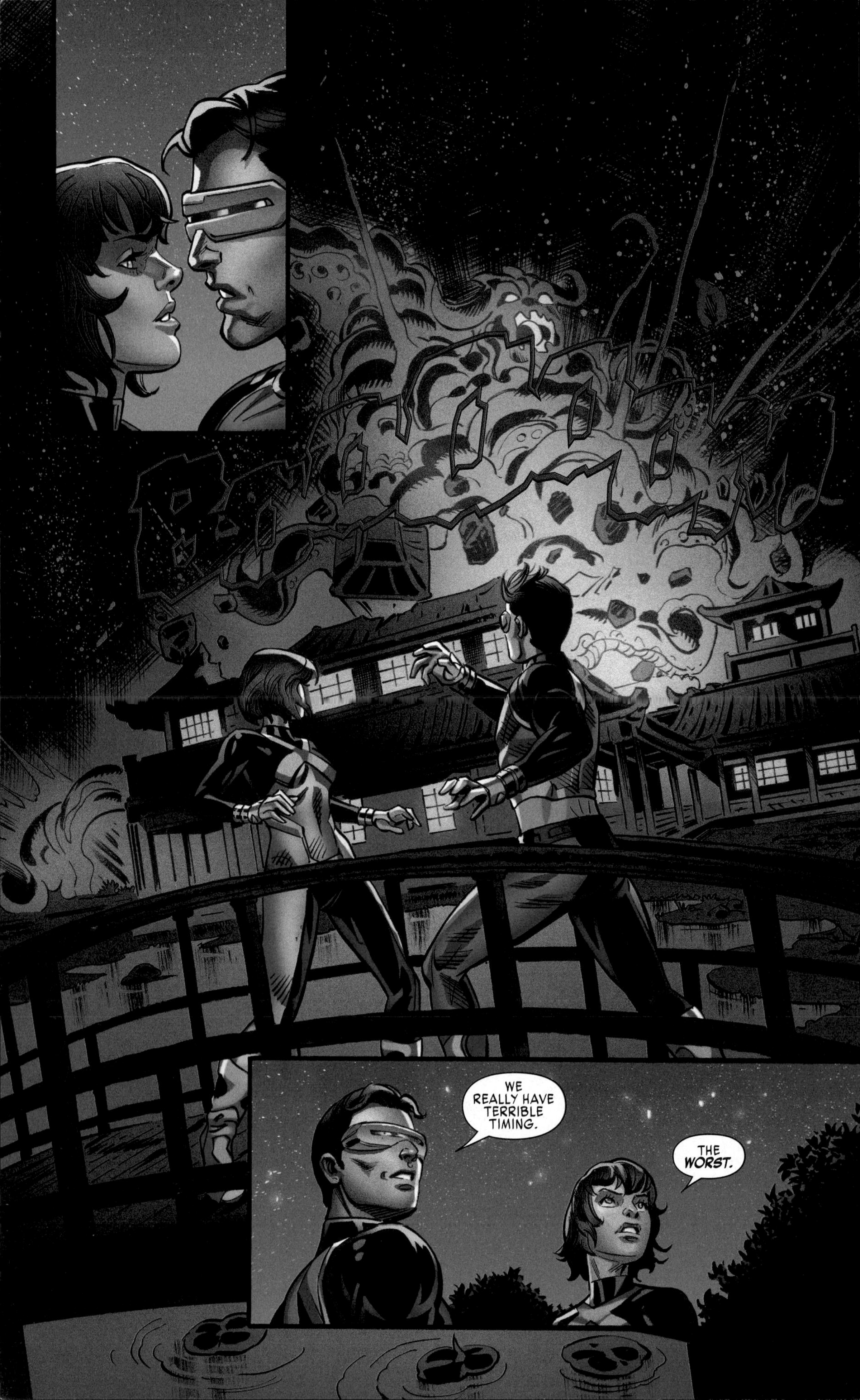
WE REALLY HAVE TERRIBLE TIMING.
THE *WORST.*

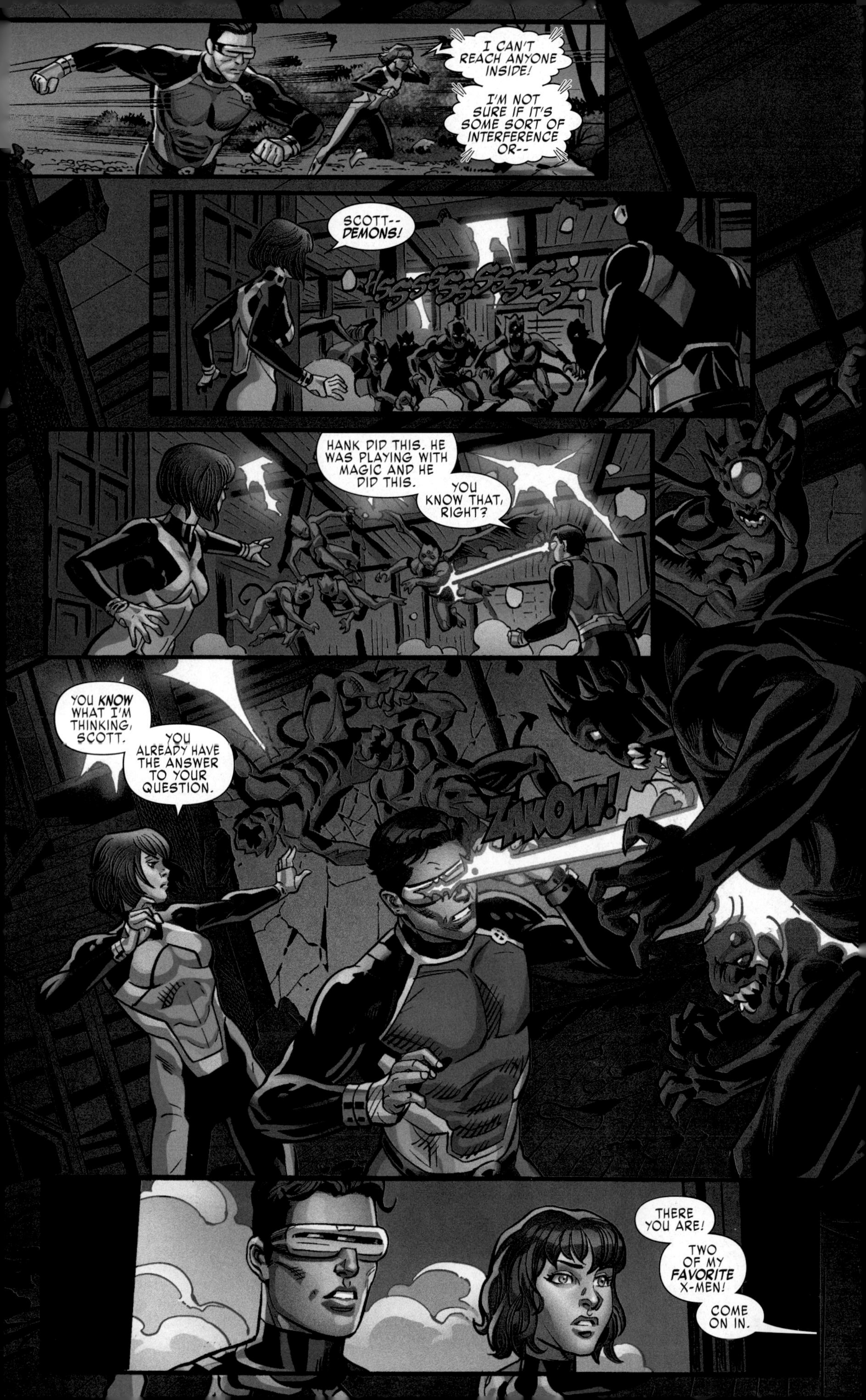
I CAN'T REACH ANYONE INSIDE!
I'M NOT SURE IF IT'S SOME SORT OF INTERFERENCE OR--
SCOTT-- DEMONS!
HSSSSSSSSSSSS
HANK DID THIS. HE WAS PLAYING WITH MAGIC AND HE DID THIS.
YOU KNOW THAT, RIGHT?
YOU KNOW WHAT I'M THINKING, SCOTT.
YOU ALREADY HAVE THE ANSWER TO YOUR QUESTION.
ZAKOW!
THERE YOU ARE!
TWO OF MY FAVORITE X-MEN!
COME ON IN.

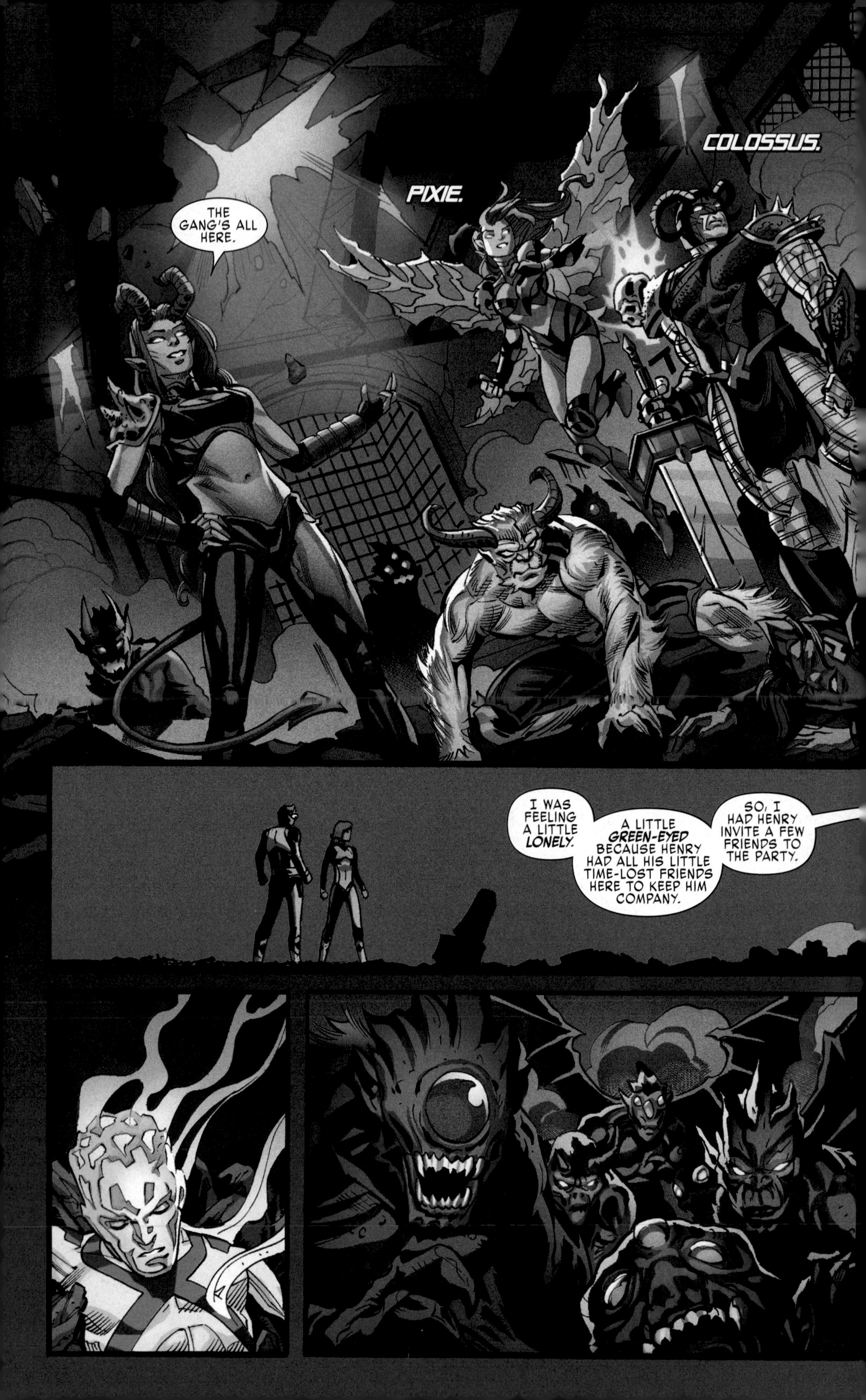
THE GANG'S ALL HERE.
PIXIE.
COLOSSUS.
I WAS FEELING A LITTLE *LONELY.*
A LITTLE *GREEN-EYED* BECAUSE HENRY HAD ALL HIS LITTLE TIME-LOST FRIENDS HERE TO KEEP HIM COMPANY.
SO, I HAD HENRY INVITE A FEW FRIENDS TO THE PARTY.

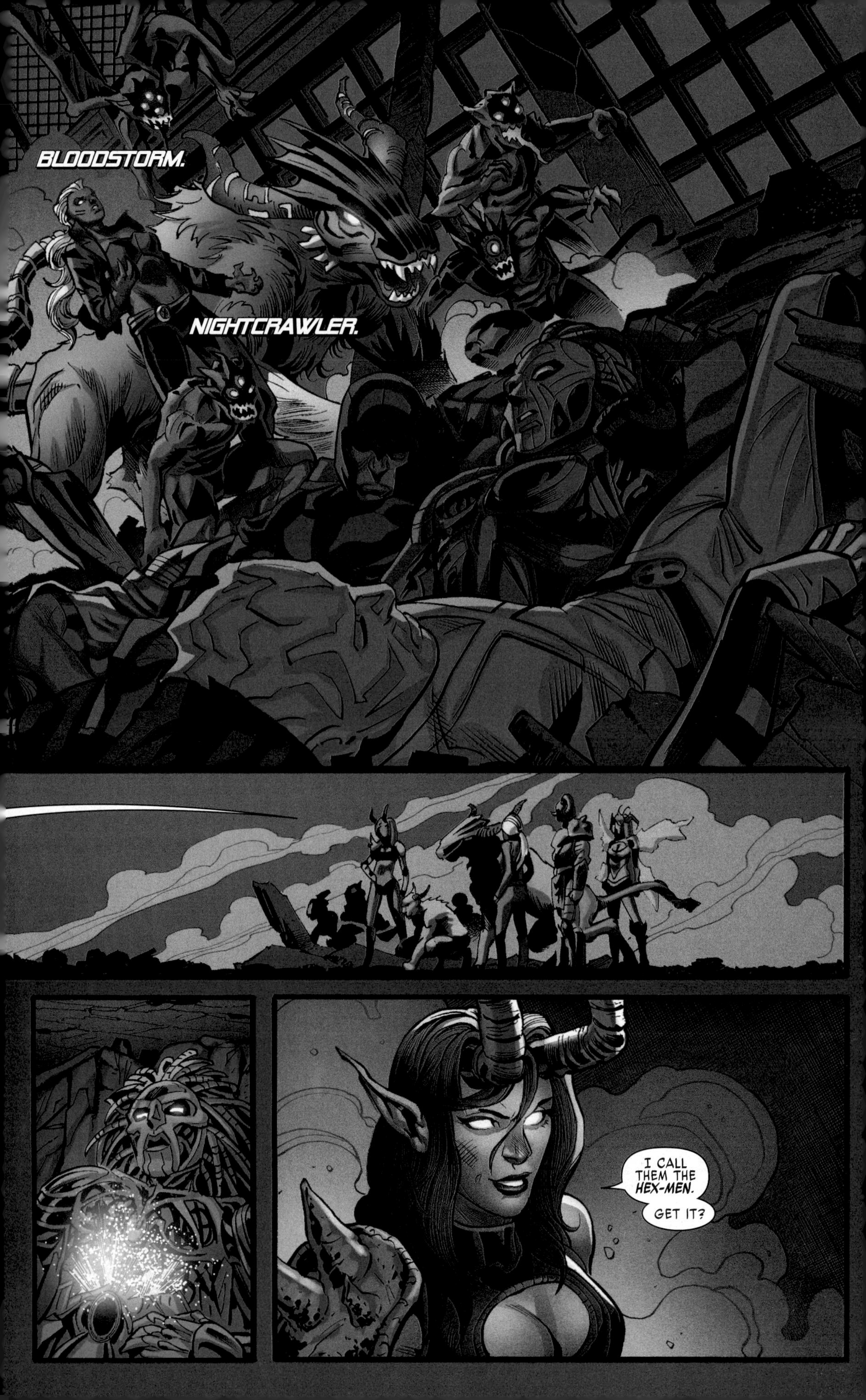

BLOODSTORM.
NIGHTCRAWLER.
I CALL THEM THE HEX-MEN.
GET IT?

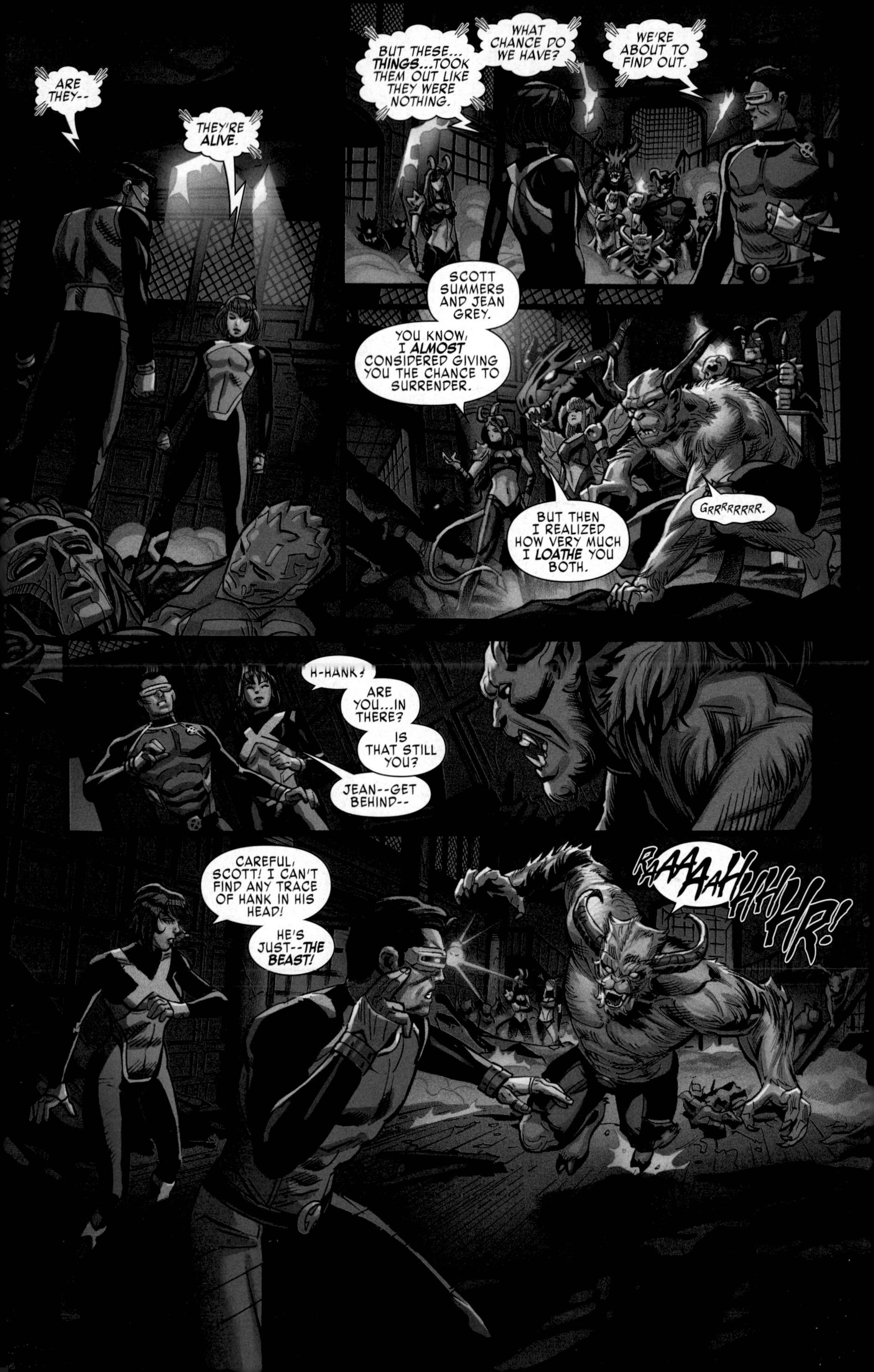

ARE THEY--
THEY'RE ALIVE.
BUT THESE... THINGS...TOOK THEM OUT LIKE THEY WERE NOTHING.
WHAT CHANCE DO WE HAVE?
WE'RE ABOUT TO FIND OUT.
SCOTT SUMMERS AND JEAN GREY.
YOU KNOW, I ALMOST CONSIDERED GIVING YOU THE CHANCE TO SURRENDER.
BUT THEN I REALIZED HOW VERY MUCH I LOATHE YOU BOTH.
GRRRRRRRR.
H-HANK?
ARE YOU...IN THERE?
IS THAT STILL YOU?
JEAN--GET BEHIND--
CAREFUL, SCOTT! I CAN'T FIND ANY TRACE OF HANK IN HIS HEAD!
HE'S JUST--THE BEAST!
RAAAAAHHHHR!

11

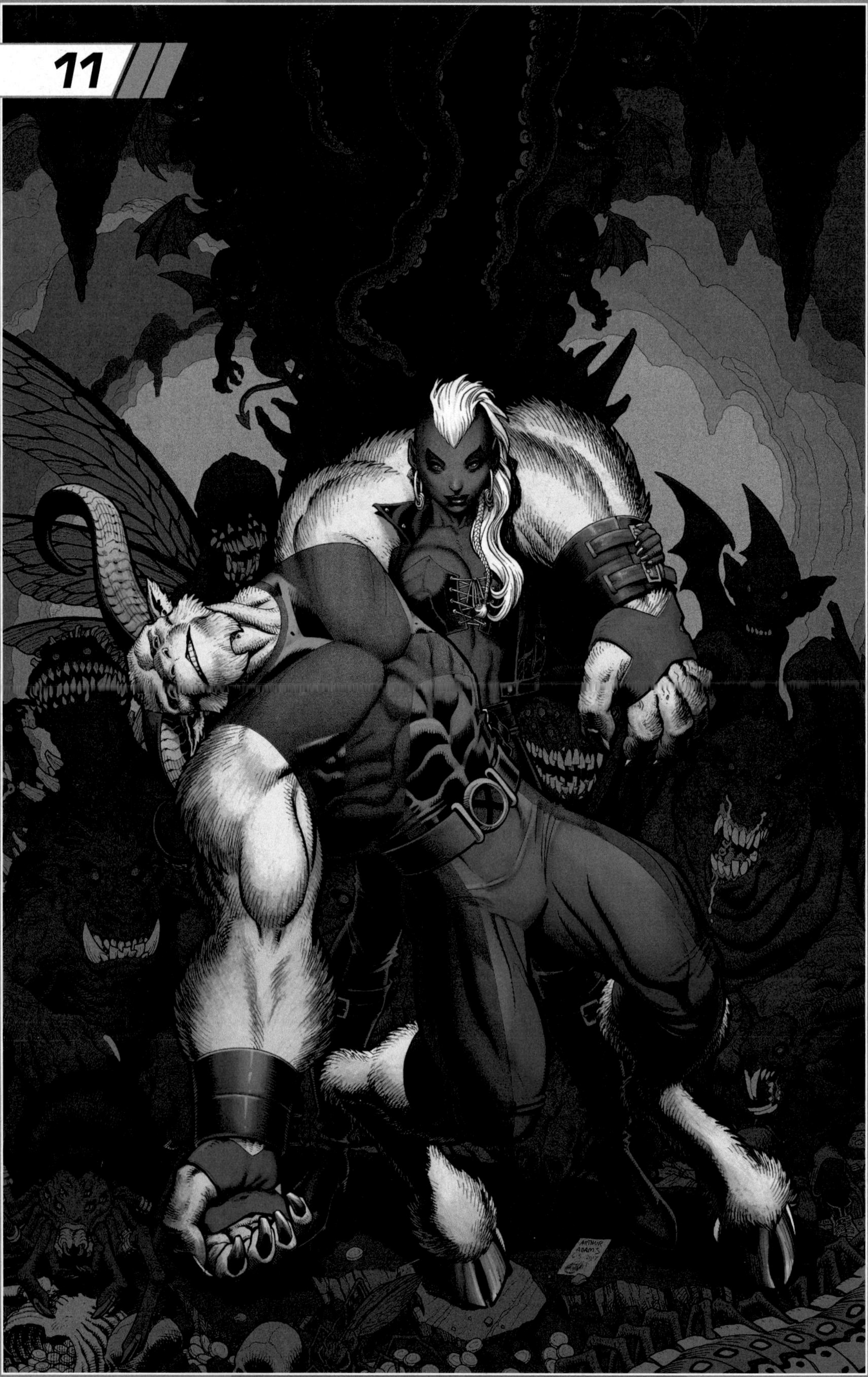
ARTHUR ADAMS

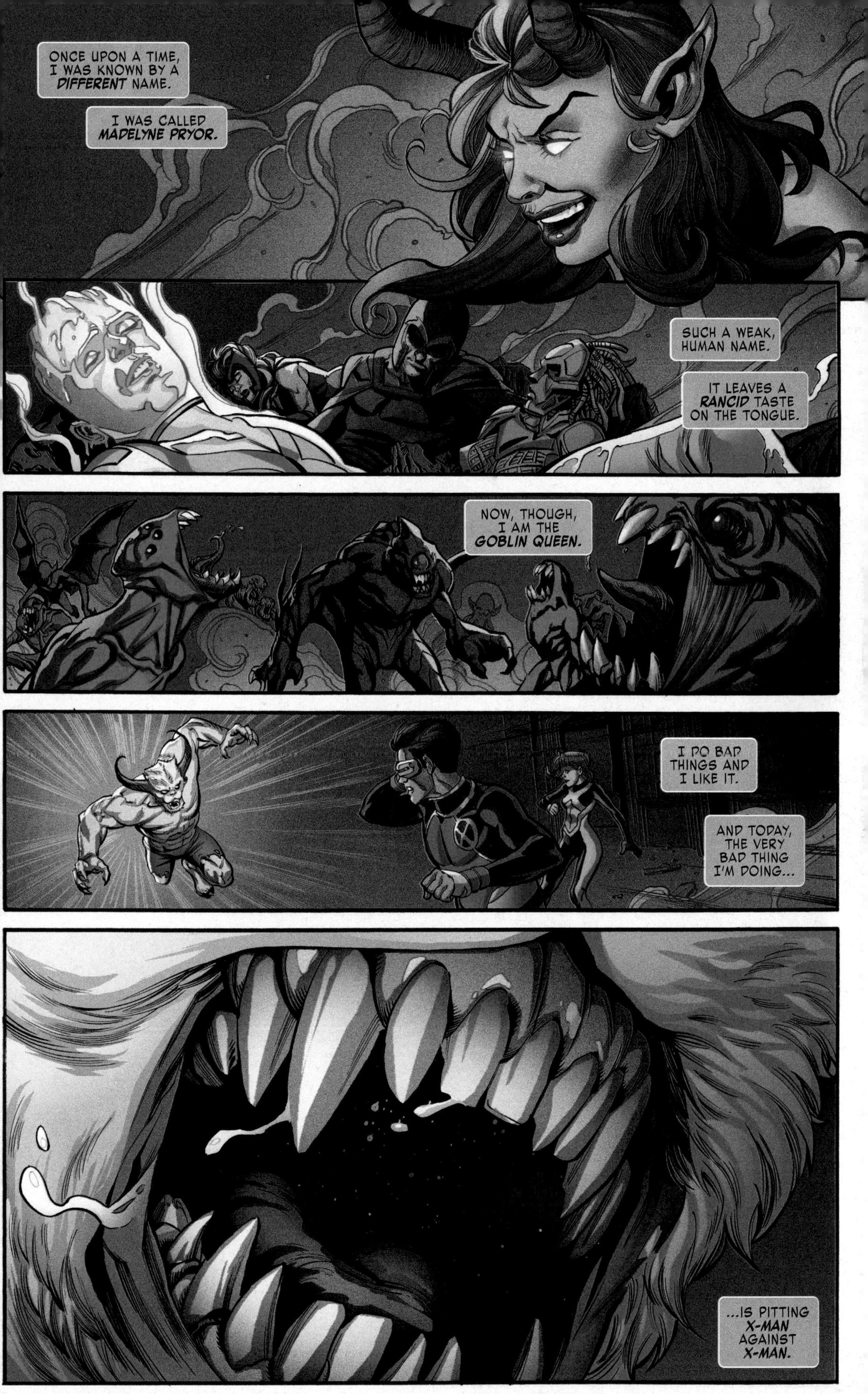
ONCE UPON A TIME, I WAS KNOWN BY A DIFFERENT NAME.
I WAS CALLED MADELYNE PRYOR.
SUCH A WEAK, HUMAN NAME.
IT LEAVES A RANCID TASTE ON THE TONGUE.
NOW, THOUGH, I AM THE GOBLIN QUEEN.
I DO BAD THINGS AND I LIKE IT.
AND TODAY, THE VERY BAD THING I'M DOING...
...IS PITTING X-MAN AGAINST X-MAN.

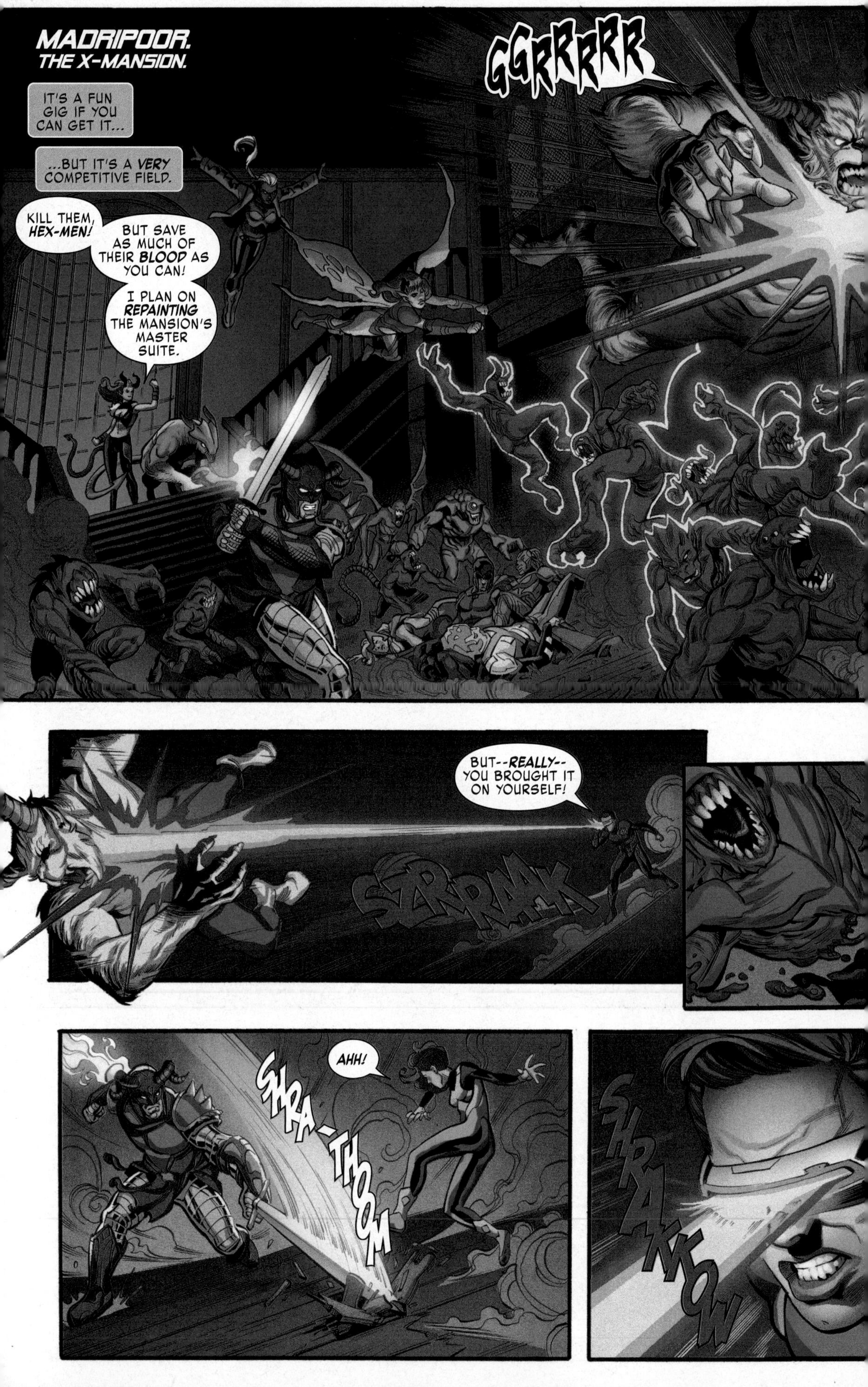
MADRIPOOR.
THE X-MANSION.
GGRRRRR
IT'S A FUN GIG IF YOU CAN GET IT...
...BUT IT'S A VERY COMPETITIVE FIELD.
KILL THEM, HEX-MEN!
BUT SAVE AS MUCH OF THEIR BLOOD AS YOU CAN!
I PLAN ON REPAINTING THE MANSION'S MASTER SUITE.
BUT--REALLY--YOU BROUGHT IT ON YOURSELF!
SZRAAK
AHH!
SHRA-THOOM
SHRAKKOW

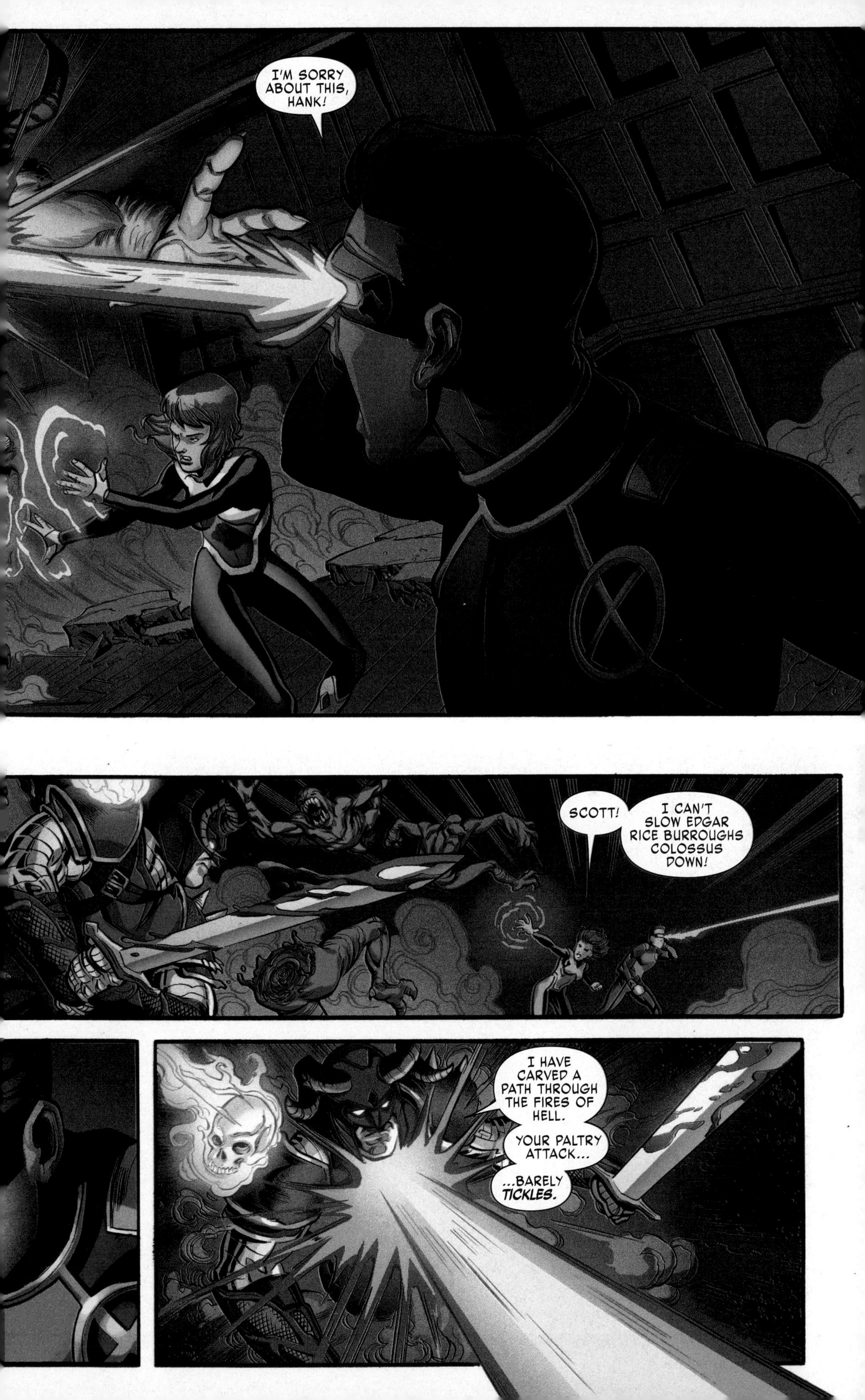
I'M SORRY ABOUT THIS, HANK!
SCOTT!
I CAN'T SLOW EDGAR RICE BURROUGHS COLOSSUS DOWN!
I HAVE CARVED A PATH THROUGH THE FIRES OF HELL.
YOUR PALTRY ATTACK...
...BARELY TICKLES.

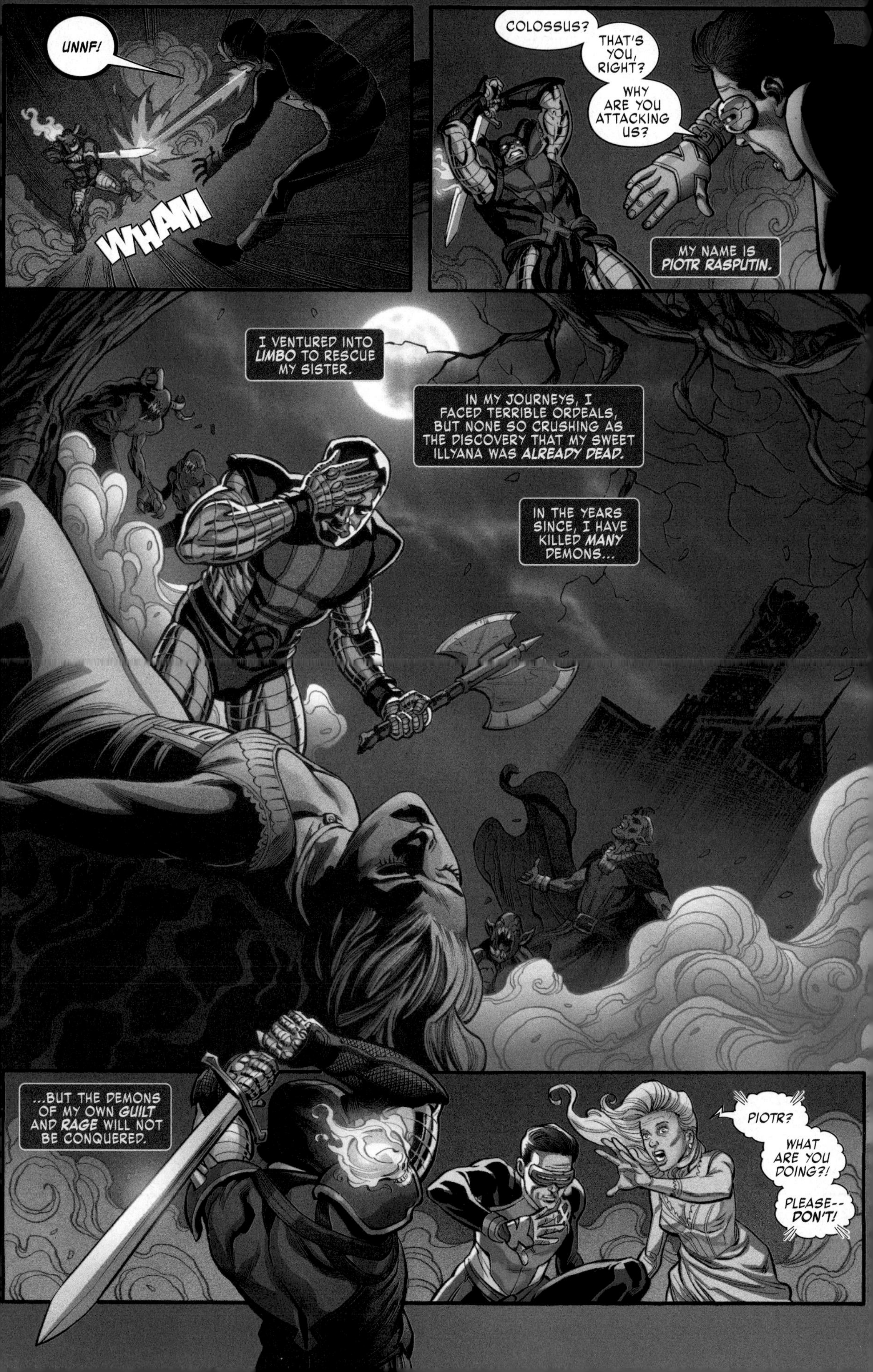

UNNF!
WHAM
COLOSSUS?
THAT'S YOU, RIGHT?
WHY ARE YOU ATTACKING US?
MY NAME IS PIOTR RASPUTIN.
I VENTURED INTO LIMBO TO RESCUE MY SISTER.
IN MY JOURNEYS, I FACED TERRIBLE ORDEALS, BUT NONE SO CRUSHING AS THE DISCOVERY THAT MY SWEET ILLYANA WAS ALREADY DEAD.
IN THE YEARS SINCE, I HAVE KILLED MANY DEMONS...
...BUT THE DEMONS OF MY OWN GUILT AND RAGE WILL NOT BE CONQUERED.
PIOTR?
WHAT ARE YOU DOING?!
PLEASE-- DON'T!

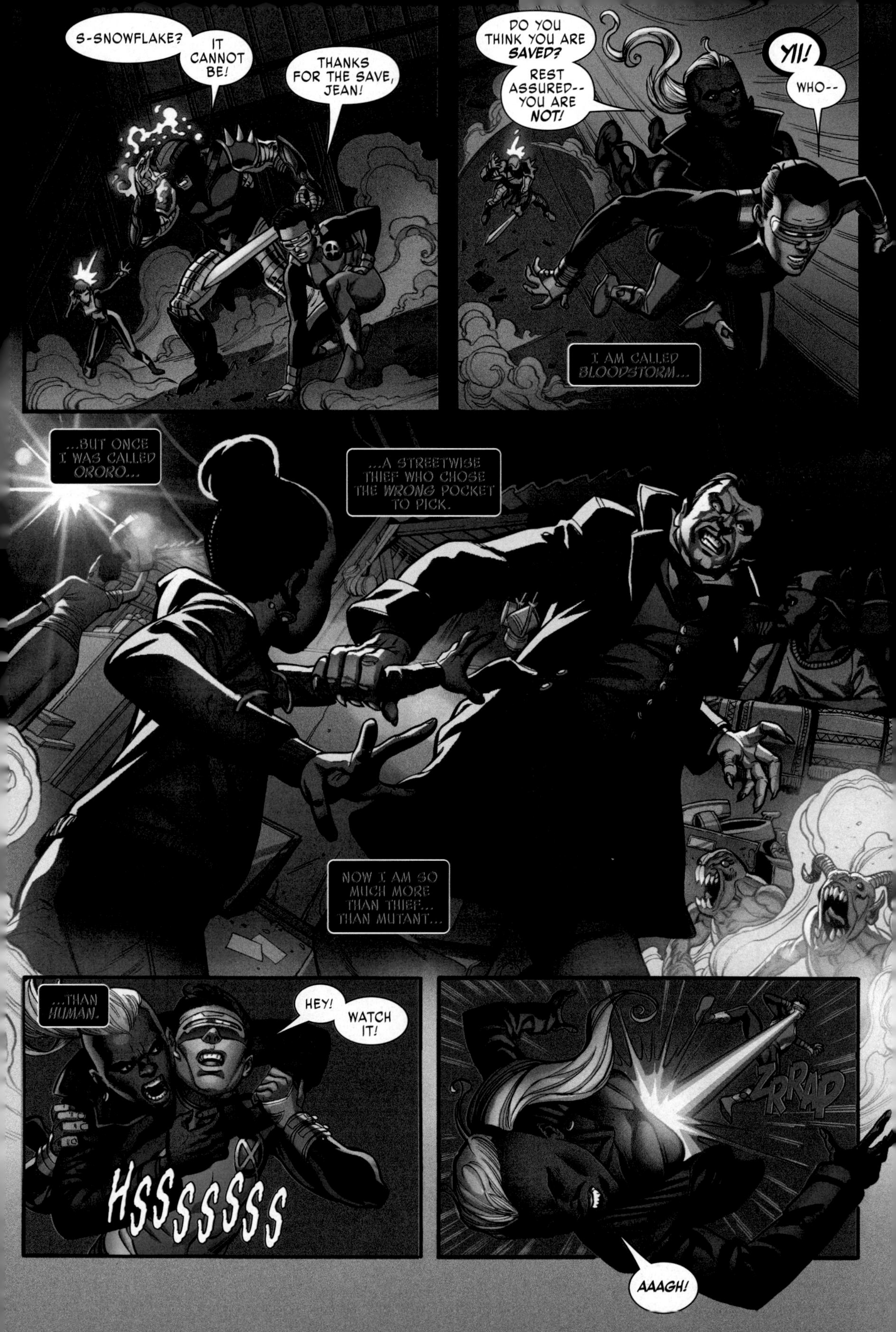
S-SNOWFLAKE?
IT CANNOT BE!
THANKS FOR THE SAVE, JEAN!
DO YOU THINK YOU ARE SAVED?
REST ASSURED-- YOU ARE NOT!
YII!
WHO--
I AM CALLED BLOODSTORM...
...BUT ONCE I WAS CALLED ORORO...
...A STREETWISE THIEF WHO CHOSE THE WRONG POCKET TO PICK.
NOW I AM SO MUCH MORE THAN THIEF... THAN MUTANT...
...THAN HUMAN.
HEY!
WATCH IT!
HSSSSSSS
ZRRAP
AAAGH!

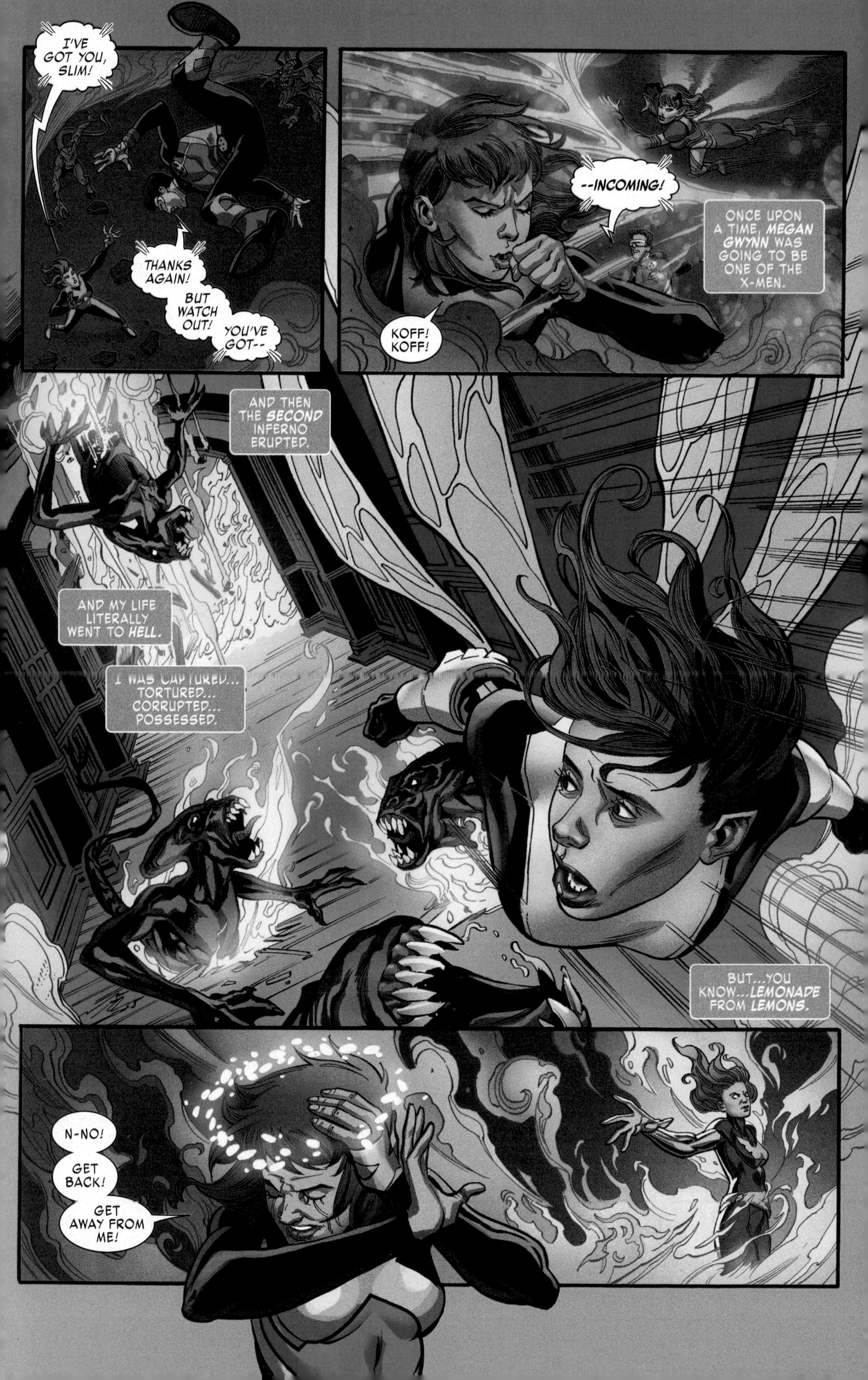

I'VE GOT YOU, SLIM!
THANKS AGAIN!
BUT WATCH OUT!
YOU'VE GOT--
--INCOMING!
ONCE UPON A TIME, MEGAN GWYNN WAS GOING TO BE ONE OF THE X-MEN.
KOFF! KOFF!
AND THEN THE SECOND INFERNO ERUPTED.
AND MY LIFE LITERALLY WENT TO HELL.
I WAS CAPTURED... TORTURED... CORRUPTED... POSSESSED.
BUT...YOU KNOW...LEMONADE FROM LEMONS.
N-NO!
GET BACK!
GET AWAY FROM ME!

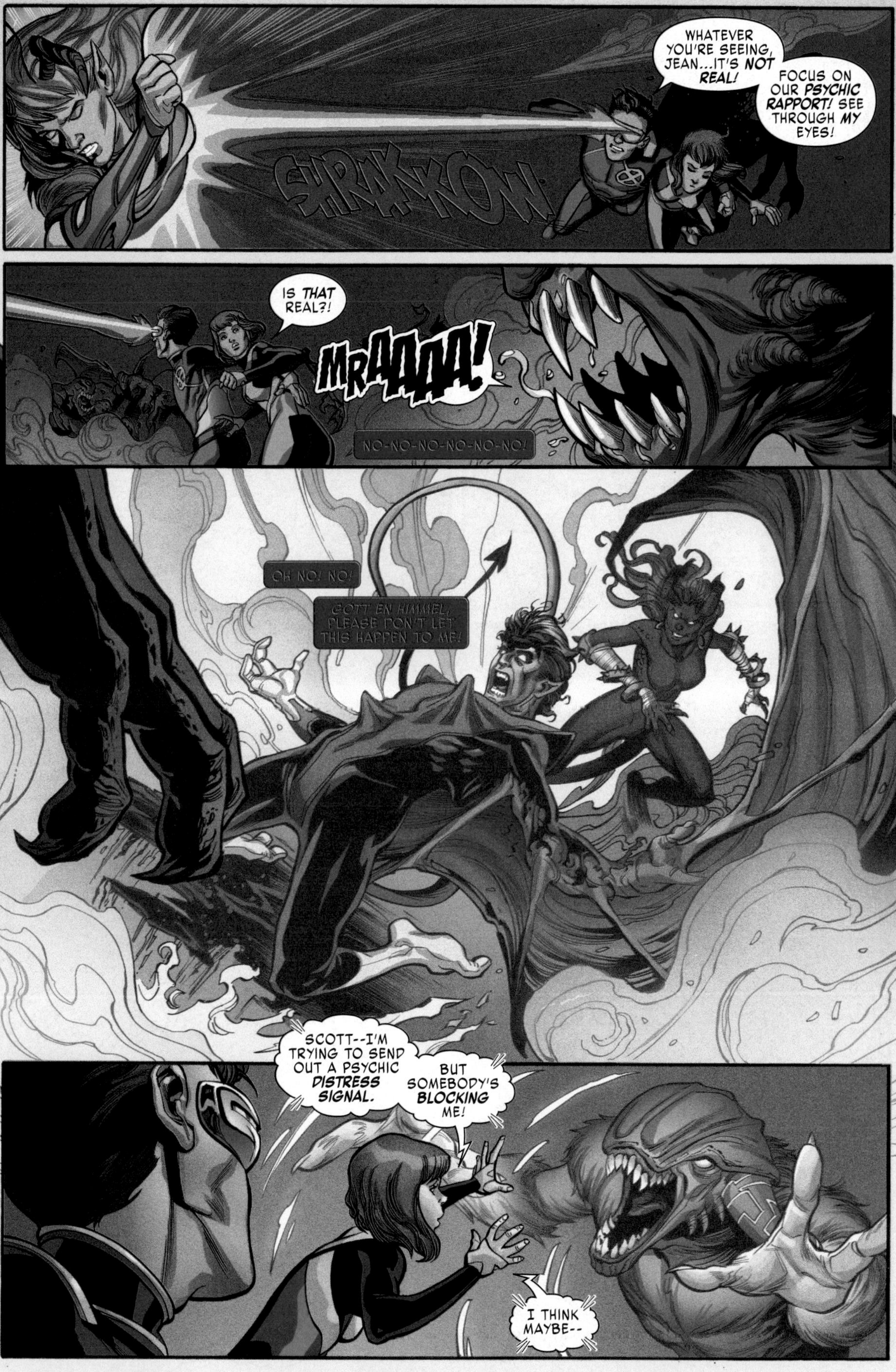
WHATEVER YOU'RE SEEING, JEAN...IT'S NOT REAL!
FOCUS ON OUR PSYCHIC RAPPORT! SEE THROUGH MY EYES!
SHRAKKOW
IS THAT REAL?!
MRAAAA!
NO-NO-NO-NO-NO-NO!
OH NO! NO!
GOTT EN HIMMEL, PLEASE DON'T LET THIS HAPPEN TO ME!
SCOTT--I'M TRYING TO SEND OUT A PSYCHIC DISTRESS SIGNAL.
BUT SOMEBODY'S BLOCKING ME!
I THINK MAYBE--

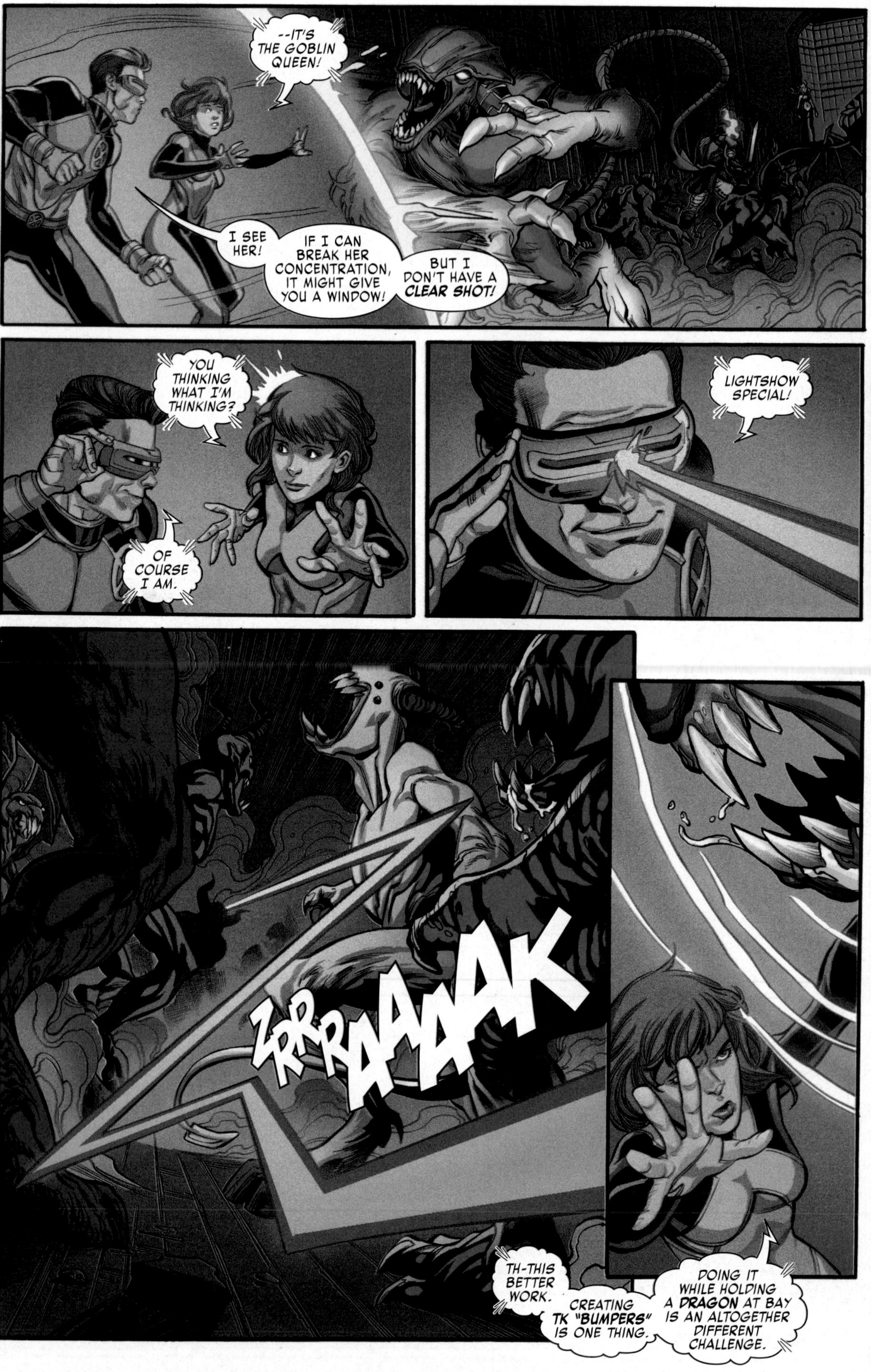
--IT'S THE GOBLIN QUEEN!
I SEE HER!
IF I CAN BREAK HER CONCENTRATION, IT MIGHT GIVE YOU A WINDOW!
BUT I DON'T HAVE A **CLEAR SHOT!**
YOU THINKING WHAT I'M THINKING?
OF COURSE I AM.
LIGHTSHOW SPECIAL!
ZRRRAAAAK
TH-THIS BETTER WORK.
CREATING **TK "BUMPERS"** IS ONE THING.
DOING IT WHILE HOLDING A **DRAGON** AT BAY IS AN ALTOGETHER DIFFERENT CHALLENGE.

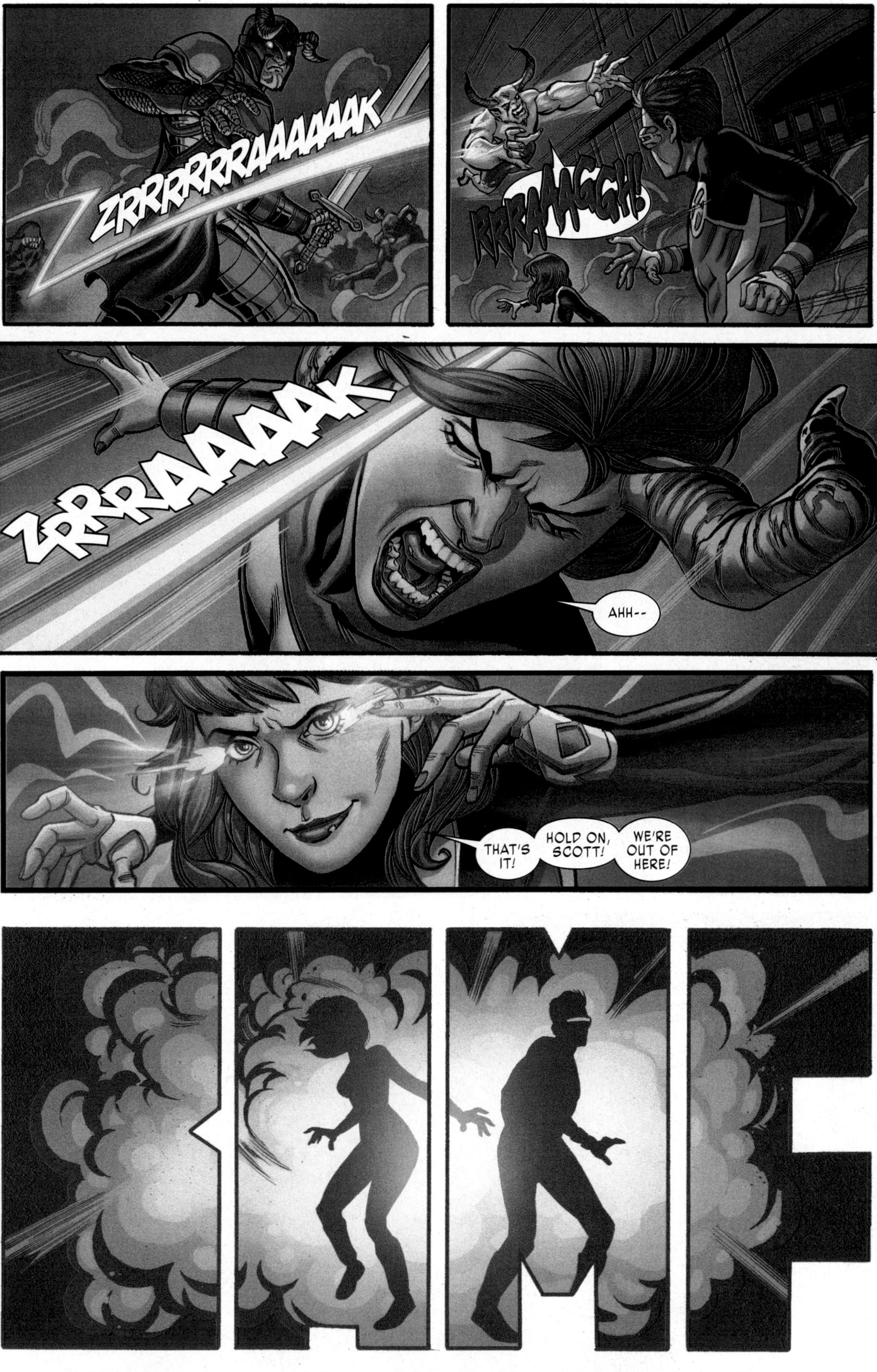
ZRRRRRRAAAAAK
RRRAAAGGH!
ZRRRAAAAAK
AHH--
THAT'S IT!
HOLD ON, SCOTT!
WE'RE OUT OF HERE!

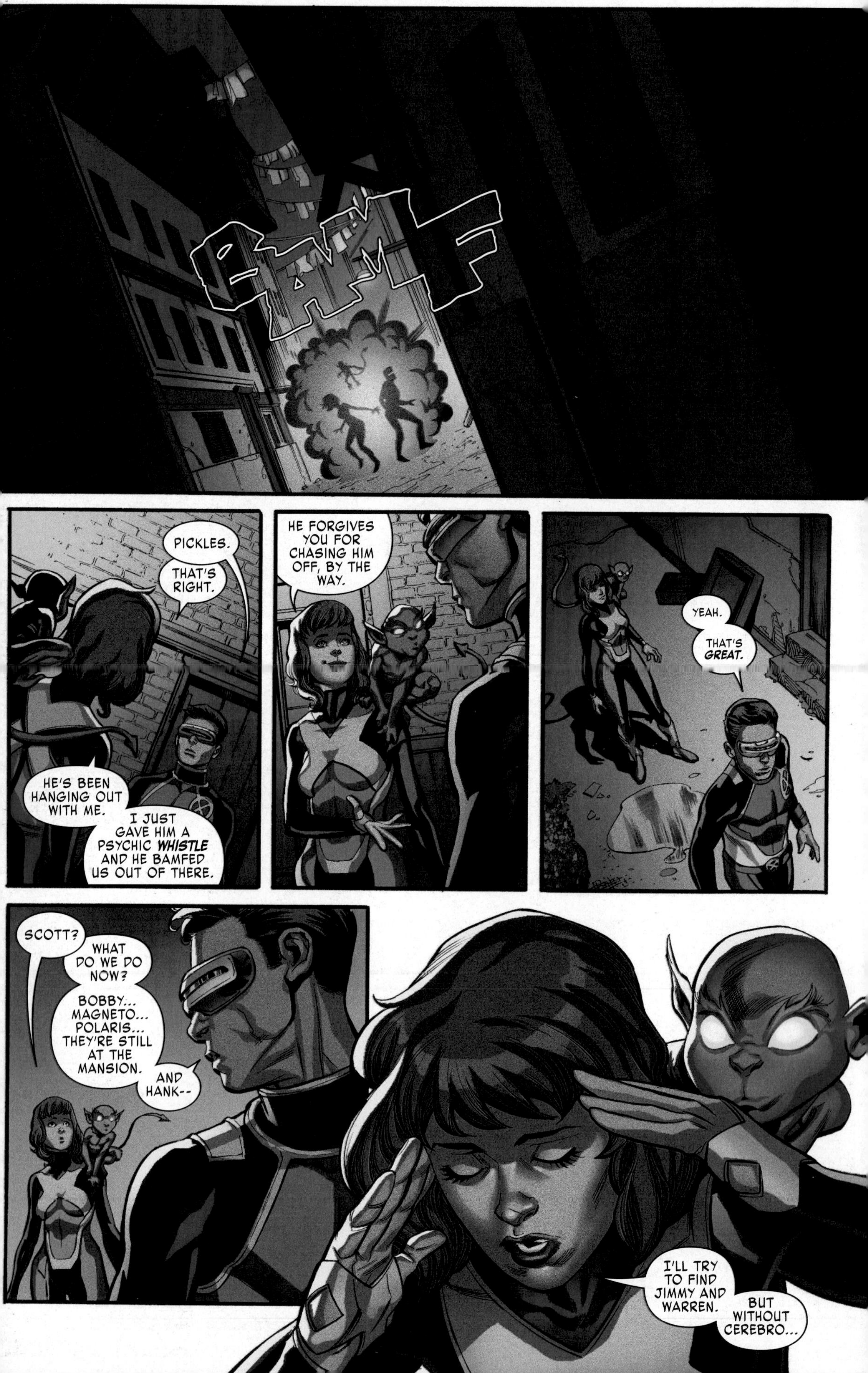
BAMF
PICKLES.
THAT'S RIGHT.
HE'S BEEN HANGING OUT WITH ME.
I JUST GAVE HIM A PSYCHIC WHISTLE AND HE BAMFED US OUT OF THERE.
HE FORGIVES YOU FOR CHASING HIM OFF, BY THE WAY.
YEAH.
THAT'S GREAT.
SCOTT?
WHAT DO WE DO NOW?
BOBBY... MAGNETO... POLARIS... THEY'RE STILL AT THE MANSION.
AND HANK--
I'LL TRY TO FIND JIMMY AND WARREN.
BUT WITHOUT CEREBRO...

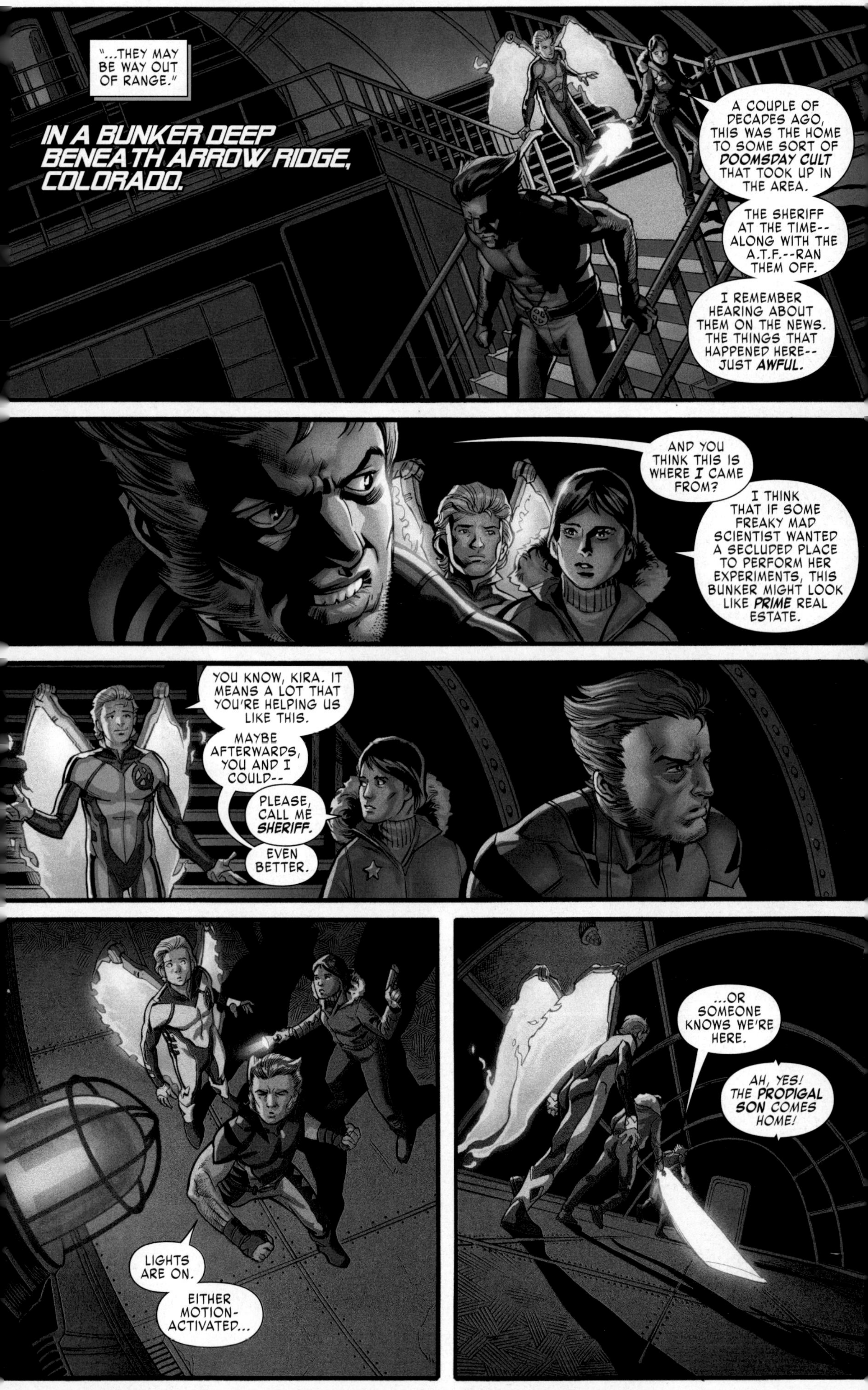
"...THEY MAY BE WAY OUT OF RANGE."
IN A BUNKER DEEP BENEATH ARROW RIDGE, COLORADO.
A COUPLE OF DECADES AGO, THIS WAS THE HOME TO SOME SORT OF DOOMSDAY CULT THAT TOOK UP IN THE AREA.
THE SHERIFF AT THE TIME--ALONG WITH THE A.T.F.--RAN THEM OFF.
I REMEMBER HEARING ABOUT THEM ON THE NEWS. THE THINGS THAT HAPPENED HERE--JUST AWFUL.
AND YOU THINK THIS IS WHERE I CAME FROM?
I THINK THAT IF SOME FREAKY MAD SCIENTIST WANTED A SECLUDED PLACE TO PERFORM HER EXPERIMENTS, THIS BUNKER MIGHT LOOK LIKE PRIME REAL ESTATE.
YOU KNOW, KIRA. IT MEANS A LOT THAT YOU'RE HELPING US LIKE THIS.
MAYBE AFTERWARDS, YOU AND I COULD--
PLEASE, CALL ME SHERIFF.
EVEN BETTER.
LIGHTS ARE ON.
EITHER MOTION-ACTIVATED...
...OR SOMEONE KNOWS WE'RE HERE.
AH, YES! THE PRODIGAL SON COMES HOME!

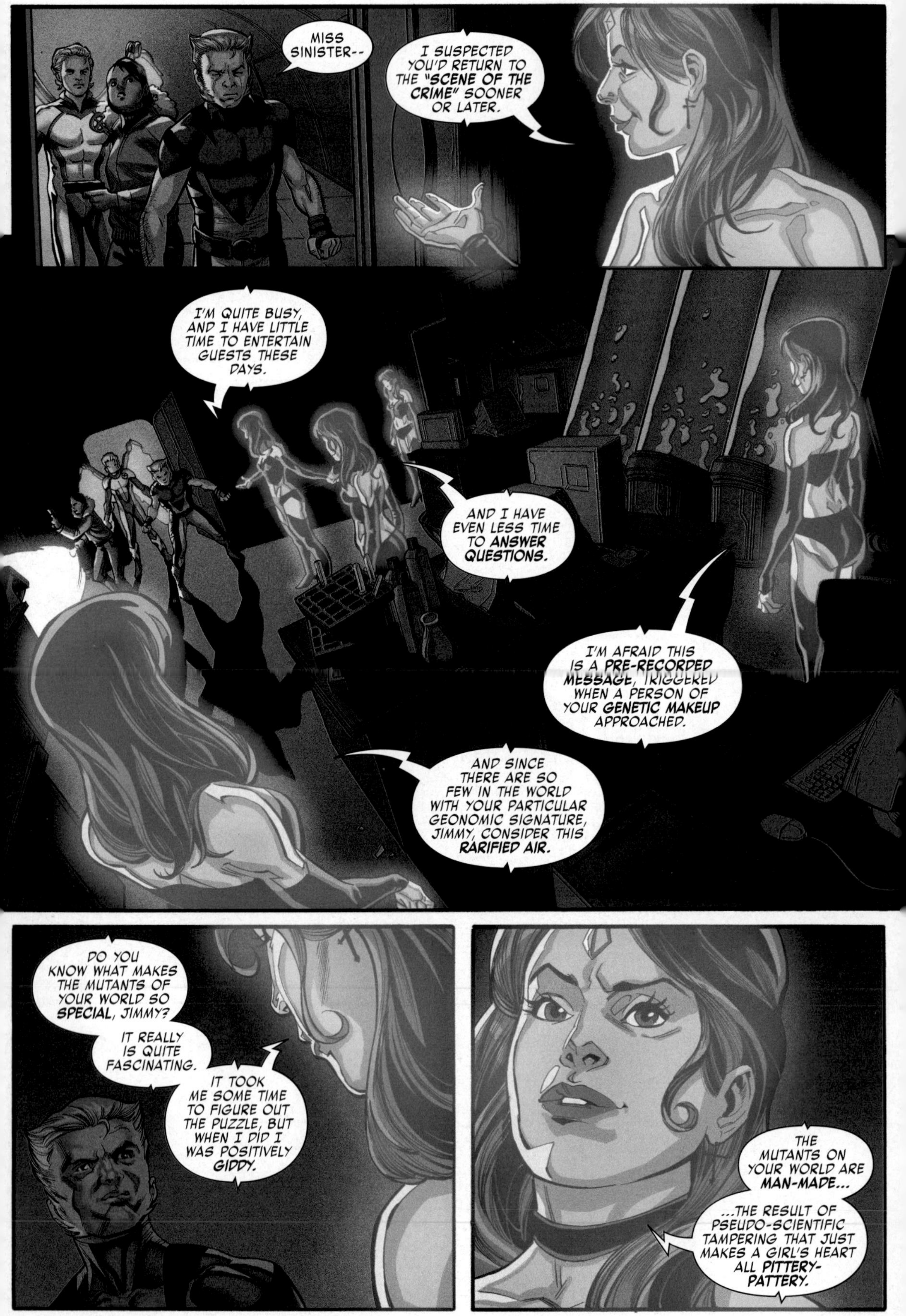

MISS SINISTER--
I SUSPECTED YOU'D RETURN TO THE "SCENE OF THE CRIME" SOONER OR LATER.
I'M QUITE BUSY, AND I HAVE LITTLE TIME TO ENTERTAIN GUESTS THESE DAYS.
AND I HAVE EVEN LESS TIME TO ANSWER QUESTIONS.
I'M AFRAID THIS IS A PRE-RECORDED MESSAGE, TRIGGERED WHEN A PERSON OF YOUR GENETIC MAKEUP APPROACHED.
AND SINCE THERE ARE SO FEW IN THE WORLD WITH YOUR PARTICULAR GEONOMIC SIGNATURE, JIMMY, CONSIDER THIS RARIFIED AIR.
DO YOU KNOW WHAT MAKES THE MUTANTS OF YOUR WORLD SO SPECIAL, JIMMY?
IT REALLY IS QUITE FASCINATING.
IT TOOK ME SOME TIME TO FIGURE OUT THE PUZZLE, BUT WHEN I DID I WAS POSITIVELY GIDDY.
THE MUTANTS ON YOUR WORLD ARE MAN-MADE...
...THE RESULT OF PSEUDO-SCIENTIFIC TAMPERING THAT JUST MAKES A GIRL'S HEART ALL PITTERY-PATTERY.

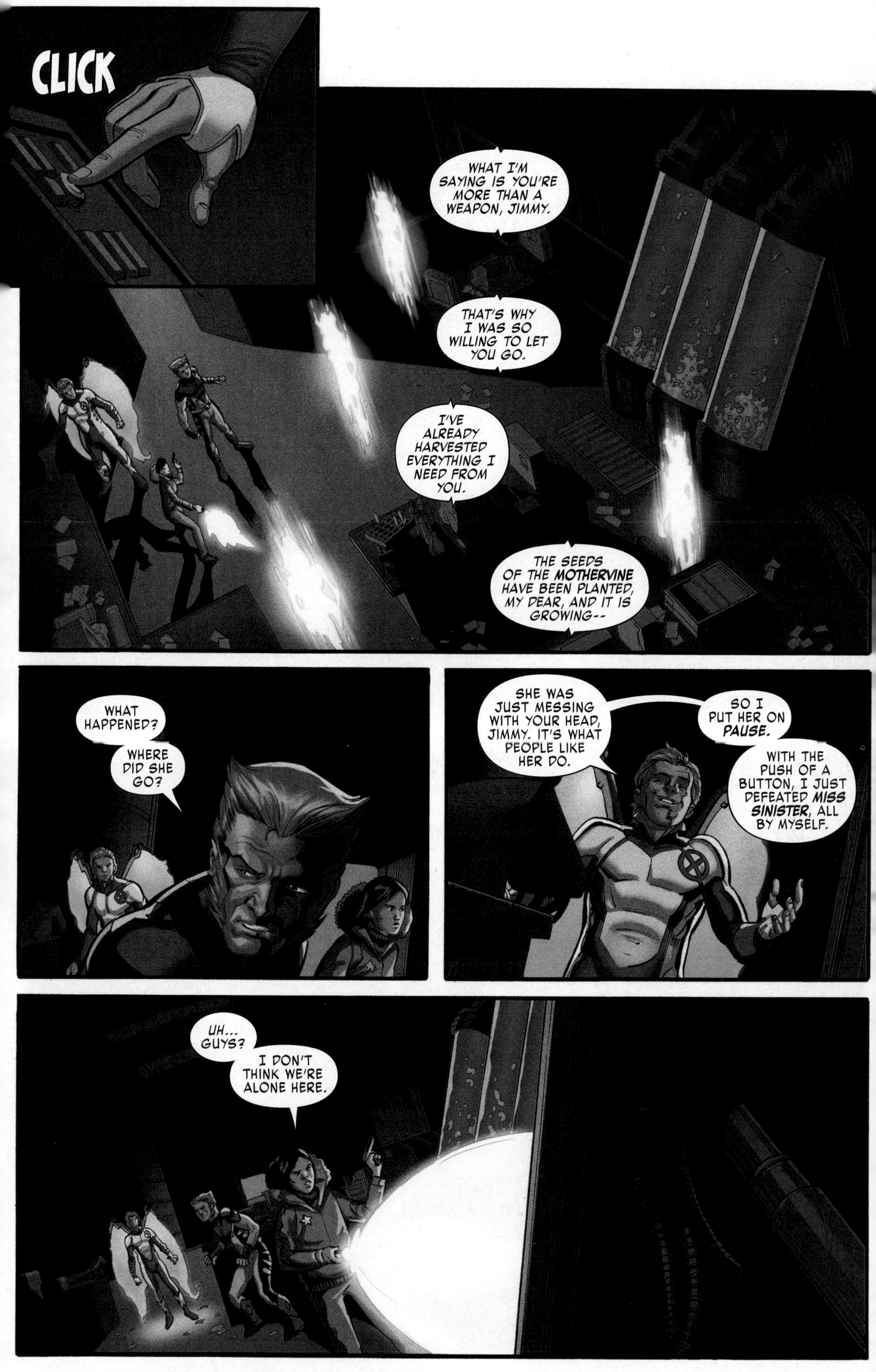
CLICK
WHAT I'M SAYING IS YOU'RE MORE THAN A WEAPON, JIMMY.
THAT'S WHY I WAS SO WILLING TO LET YOU GO.
I'VE ALREADY HARVESTED EVERYTHING I NEED FROM YOU.
THE SEEDS OF THE **MOTHERVINE** HAVE BEEN PLANTED, MY DEAR, AND IT IS GROWING--
WHAT HAPPENED?
WHERE DID SHE GO?
SHE WAS JUST MESSING WITH YOUR HEAD, JIMMY. IT'S WHAT PEOPLE LIKE HER DO.
SO I PUT HER ON ***PAUSE.***
WITH THE PUSH OF A BUTTON, I JUST DEFEATED ***MISS SINISTER,*** ALL BY MYSELF.
UH... GUYS?
I DON'T THINK WE'RE ALONE HERE.

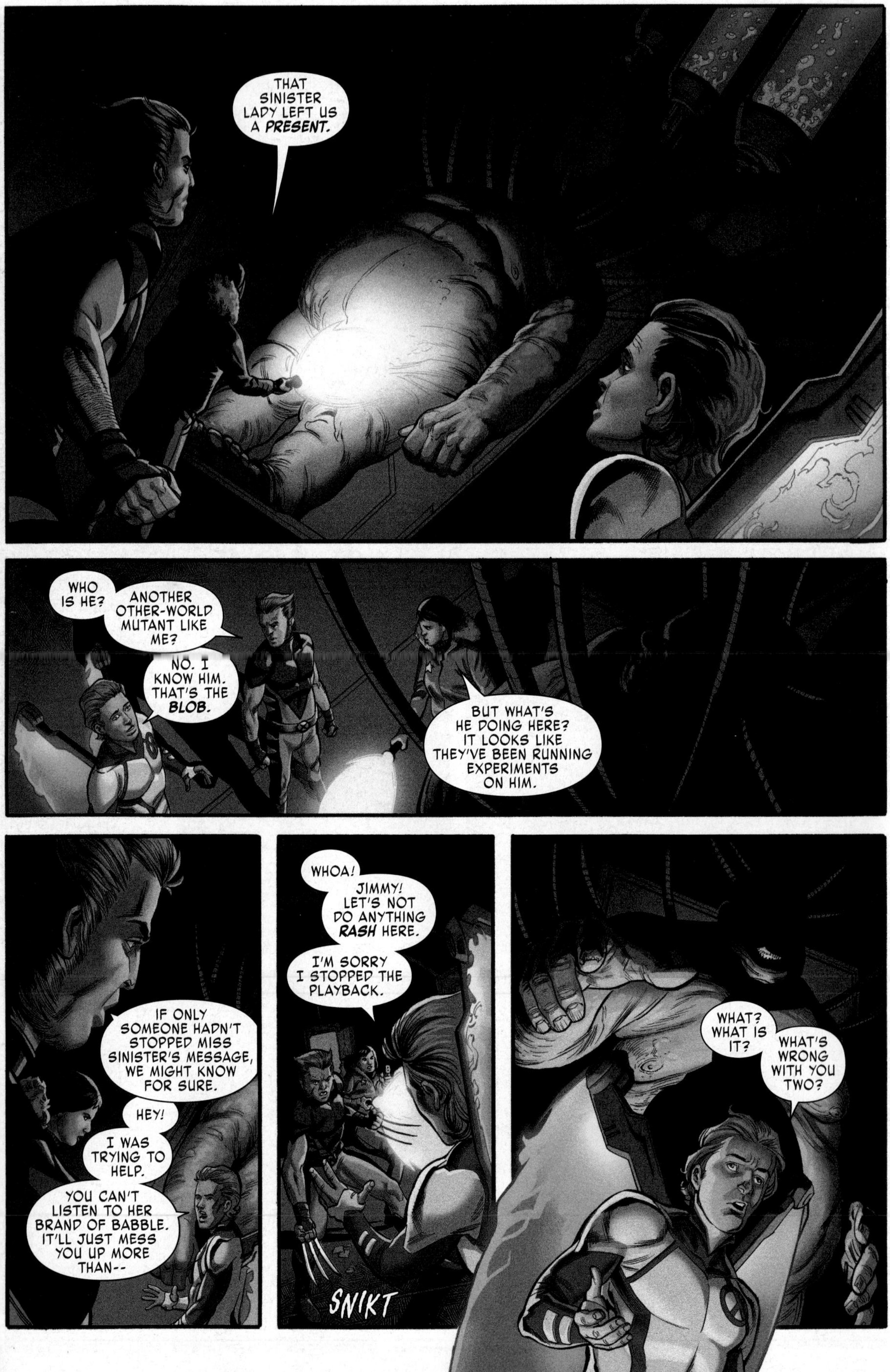
THAT SINISTER LADY LEFT US A PRESENT.
WHO IS HE?
ANOTHER OTHER-WORLD MUTANT LIKE ME?
NO. I KNOW HIM. THAT'S THE BLOB.
BUT WHAT'S HE DOING HERE? IT LOOKS LIKE THEY'VE BEEN RUNNING EXPERIMENTS ON HIM.
IF ONLY SOMEONE HADN'T STOPPED MISS SINISTER'S MESSAGE, WE MIGHT KNOW FOR SURE.
HEY!
I WAS TRYING TO HELP.
YOU CAN'T LISTEN TO HER BRAND OF BABBLE. IT'LL JUST MESS YOU UP MORE THAN--
WHOA!
JIMMY! LET'S NOT DO ANYTHING RASH HERE.
I'M SORRY I STOPPED THE PLAYBACK.
SNIKT
WHAT? WHAT IS IT?
WHAT'S WRONG WITH YOU TWO?

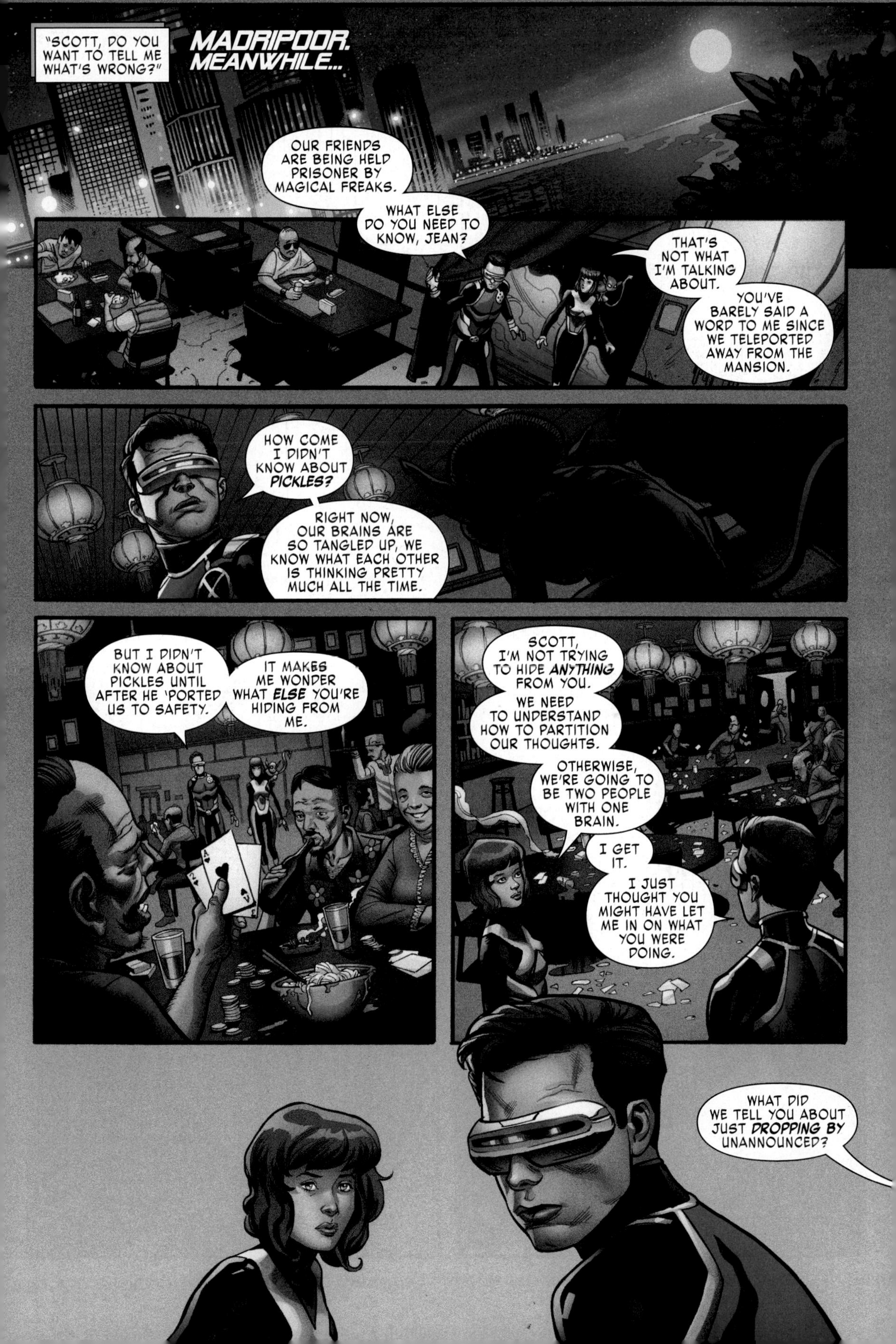
"SCOTT, DO YOU WANT TO TELL ME WHAT'S WRONG?"
MADRIPOOR. MEANWHILE...
OUR FRIENDS ARE BEING HELD PRISONER BY MAGICAL FREAKS.
WHAT ELSE DO YOU NEED TO KNOW, JEAN?
THAT'S NOT WHAT I'M TALKING ABOUT.
YOU'VE BARELY SAID A WORD TO ME SINCE WE TELEPORTED AWAY FROM THE MANSION.
HOW COME I DIDN'T KNOW ABOUT PICKLES?
RIGHT NOW, OUR BRAINS ARE SO TANGLED UP, WE KNOW WHAT EACH OTHER IS THINKING PRETTY MUCH ALL THE TIME.
BUT I DIDN'T KNOW ABOUT PICKLES UNTIL AFTER HE 'PORTED US TO SAFETY.
IT MAKES ME WONDER WHAT ELSE YOU'RE HIDING FROM ME.
SCOTT, I'M NOT TRYING TO HIDE ANYTHING FROM YOU.
WE NEED TO UNDERSTAND HOW TO PARTITION OUR THOUGHTS.
OTHERWISE, WE'RE GOING TO BE TWO PEOPLE WITH ONE BRAIN.
I GET IT.
I JUST THOUGHT YOU MIGHT HAVE LET ME IN ON WHAT YOU WERE DOING.
WHAT DID WE TELL YOU ABOUT JUST DROPPING BY UNANNOUNCED?

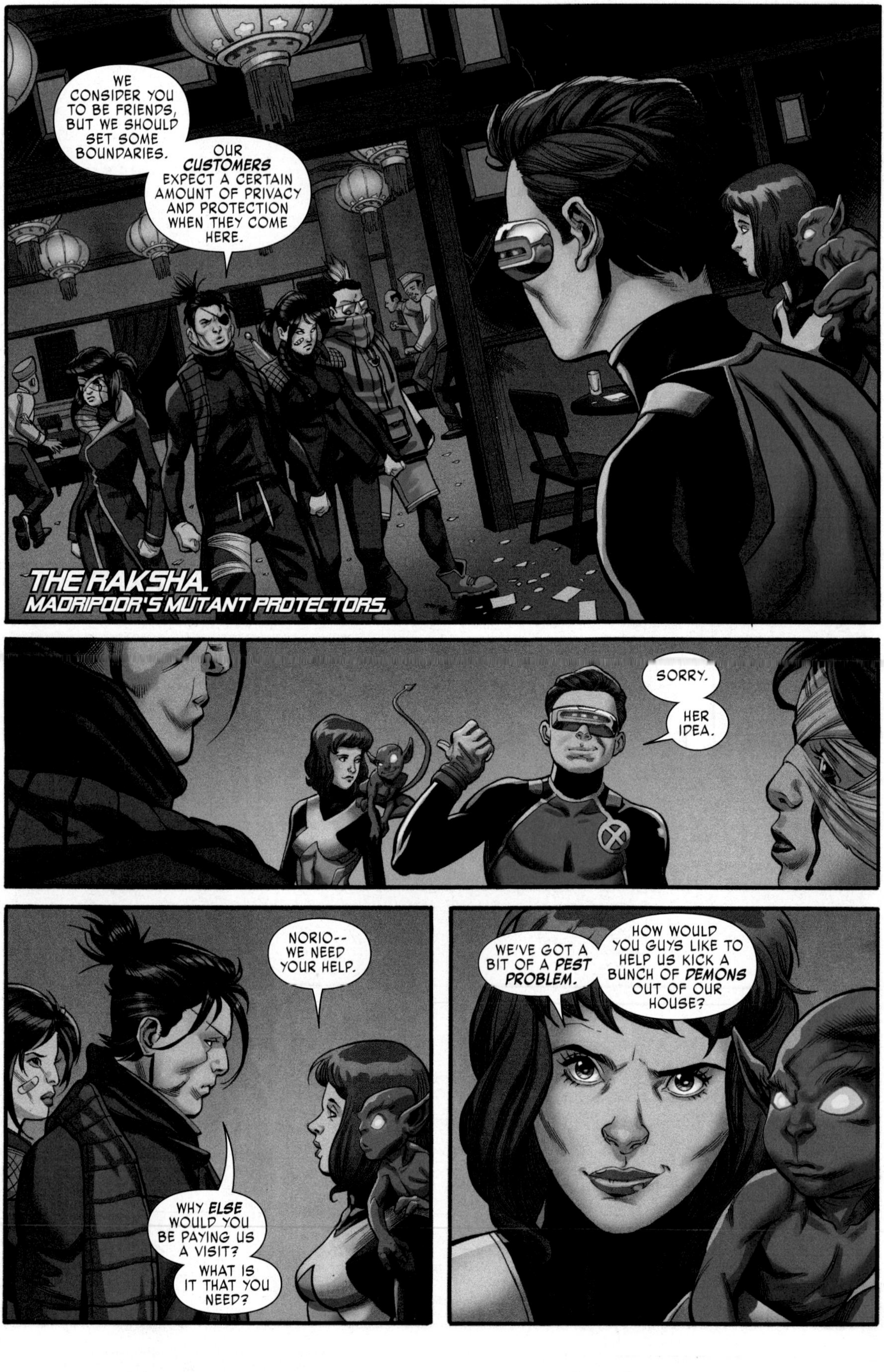
WE CONSIDER YOU TO BE FRIENDS, BUT WE SHOULD SET SOME BOUNDARIES.
OUR CUSTOMERS EXPECT A CERTAIN AMOUNT OF PRIVACY AND PROTECTION WHEN THEY COME HERE.
THE RAKSHA.
MADRIPOOR'S MUTANT PROTECTORS.
SORRY.
HER IDEA.
NORIO-- WE NEED YOUR HELP.
WHY ELSE WOULD YOU BE PAYING US A VISIT?
WHAT IS IT THAT YOU NEED?
WE'VE GOT A BIT OF A PEST PROBLEM.
HOW WOULD YOU GUYS LIKE TO HELP US KICK A BUNCH OF DEMONS OUT OF OUR HOUSE?

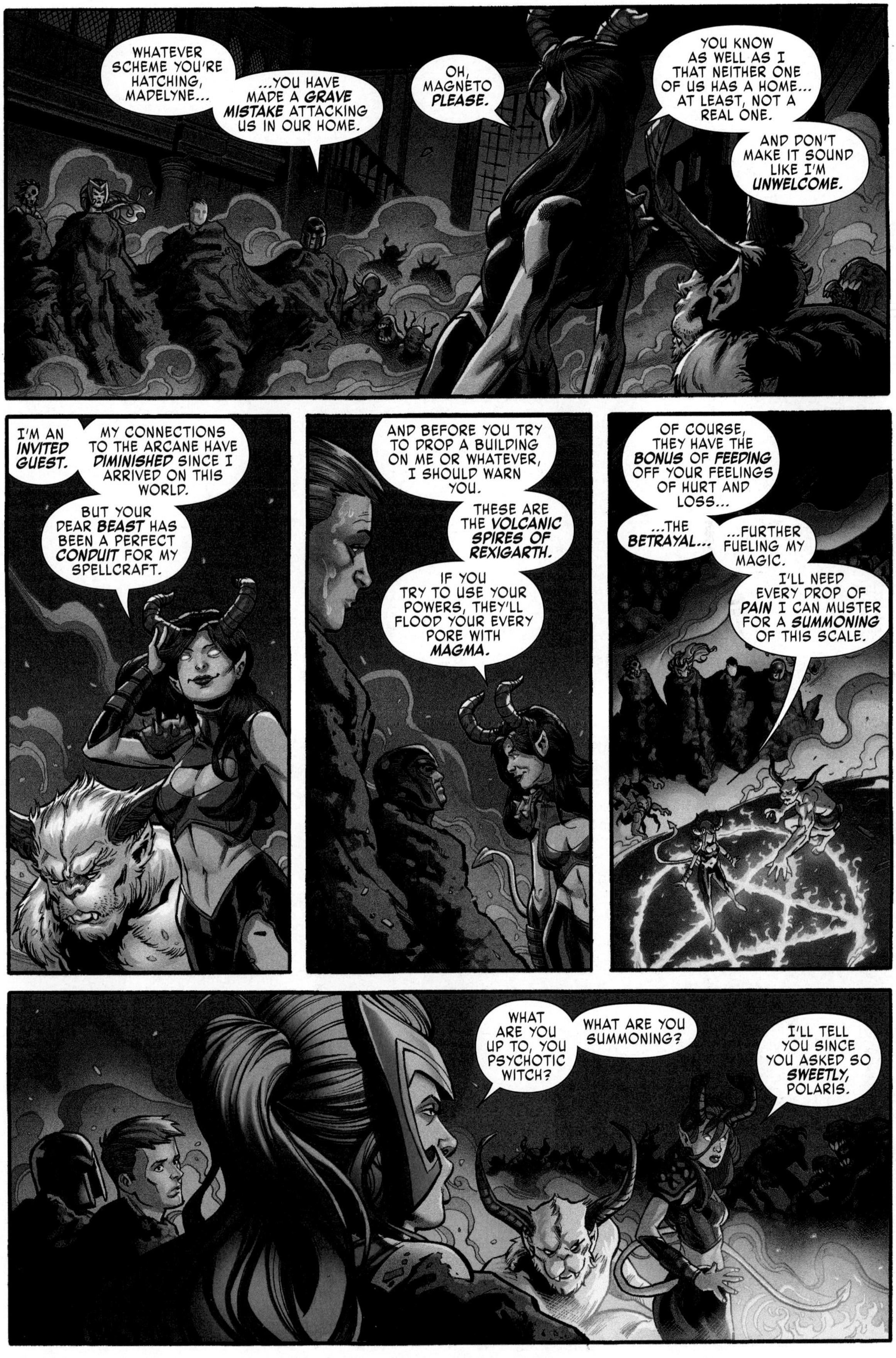
WHATEVER SCHEME YOU'RE HATCHING, MADELYNE...
...YOU HAVE MADE A GRAVE MISTAKE ATTACKING US IN OUR HOME.
OH, MAGNETO PLEASE.
YOU KNOW AS WELL AS I THAT NEITHER ONE OF US HAS A HOME... AT LEAST, NOT A REAL ONE.
AND DON'T MAKE IT SOUND LIKE I'M UNWELCOME.
I'M AN INVITED GUEST.
MY CONNECTIONS TO THE ARCANE HAVE DIMINISHED SINCE I ARRIVED ON THIS WORLD.
BUT YOUR DEAR BEAST HAS BEEN A PERFECT CONDUIT FOR MY SPELLCRAFT.
AND BEFORE YOU TRY TO DROP A BUILDING ON ME OR WHATEVER, I SHOULD WARN YOU.
THESE ARE THE VOLCANIC SPIRES OF REXIGARTH.
IF YOU TRY TO USE YOUR POWERS, THEY'LL FLOOD YOUR EVERY PORE WITH MAGMA.
OF COURSE, THEY HAVE THE BONUS OF FEEDING OFF YOUR FEELINGS OF HURT AND LOSS...
...THE BETRAYAL...
...FURTHER FUELING MY MAGIC.
I'LL NEED EVERY DROP OF PAIN I CAN MUSTER FOR A SUMMONING OF THIS SCALE.
WHAT ARE YOU UP TO, YOU PSYCHOTIC WITCH?
WHAT ARE YOU SUMMONING?
I'LL TELL YOU SINCE YOU ASKED SO SWEETLY, POLARIS.

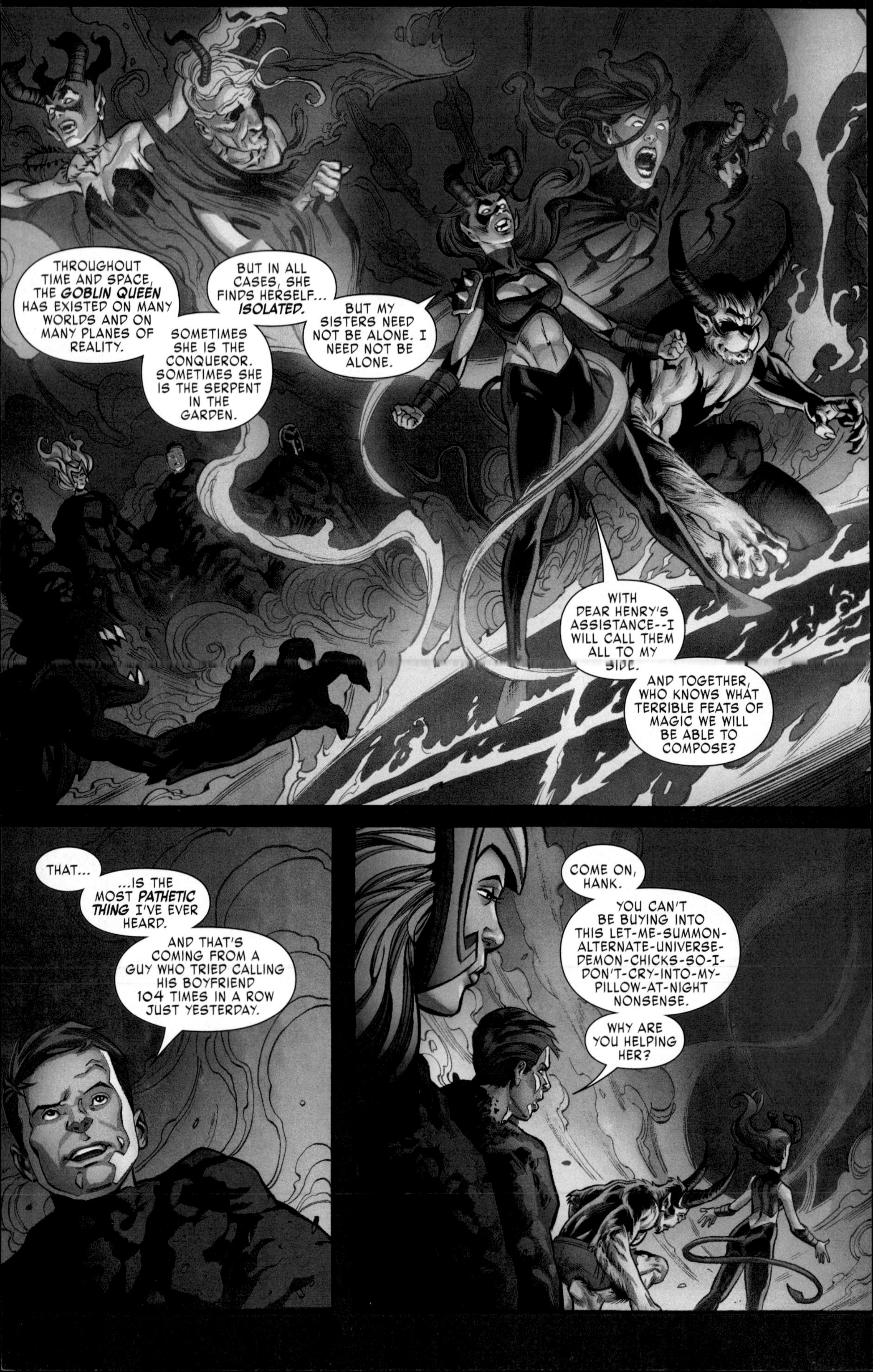
THROUGHOUT TIME AND SPACE, THE GOBLIN QUEEN HAS EXISTED ON MANY WORLDS AND ON MANY PLANES OF REALITY.
SOMETIMES SHE IS THE CONQUEROR. SOMETIMES SHE IS THE SERPENT IN THE GARDEN.
BUT IN ALL CASES, SHE FINDS HERSELF... ISOLATED.
BUT MY SISTERS NEED NOT BE ALONE. I NEED NOT BE ALONE.
WITH DEAR HENRY'S ASSISTANCE--I WILL CALL THEM ALL TO MY SIDE.
AND TOGETHER, WHO KNOWS WHAT TERRIBLE FEATS OF MAGIC WE WILL BE ABLE TO COMPOSE?
THAT...
...IS THE MOST PATHETIC THING I'VE EVER HEARD.
AND THAT'S COMING FROM A GUY WHO TRIED CALLING HIS BOYFRIEND 104 TIMES IN A ROW JUST YESTERDAY.
COME ON, HANK.
YOU CAN'T BE BUYING INTO THIS LET-ME-SUMMON-ALTERNATE-UNIVERSE-DEMON-CHICKS-SO-I-DON'T-CRY-INTO-MY-PILLOW-AT-NIGHT NONSENSE.
WHY ARE YOU HELPING HER?

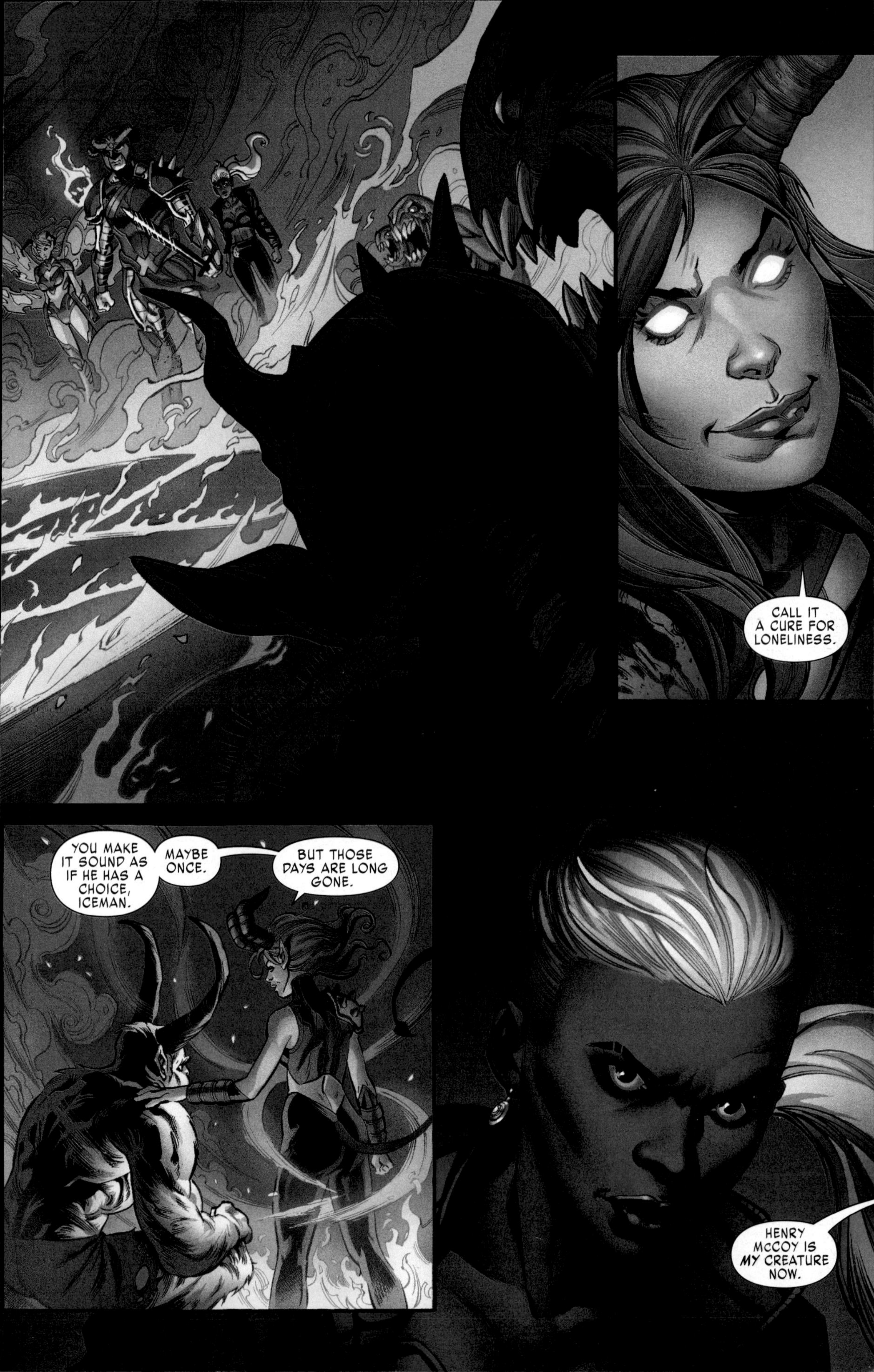
CALL IT A CURE FOR LONELINESS.
YOU MAKE IT SOUND AS IF HE HAS A CHOICE, ICEMAN.
MAYBE ONCE.
BUT THOSE DAYS ARE LONG GONE.
HENRY McCOY IS *MY* CREATURE NOW.

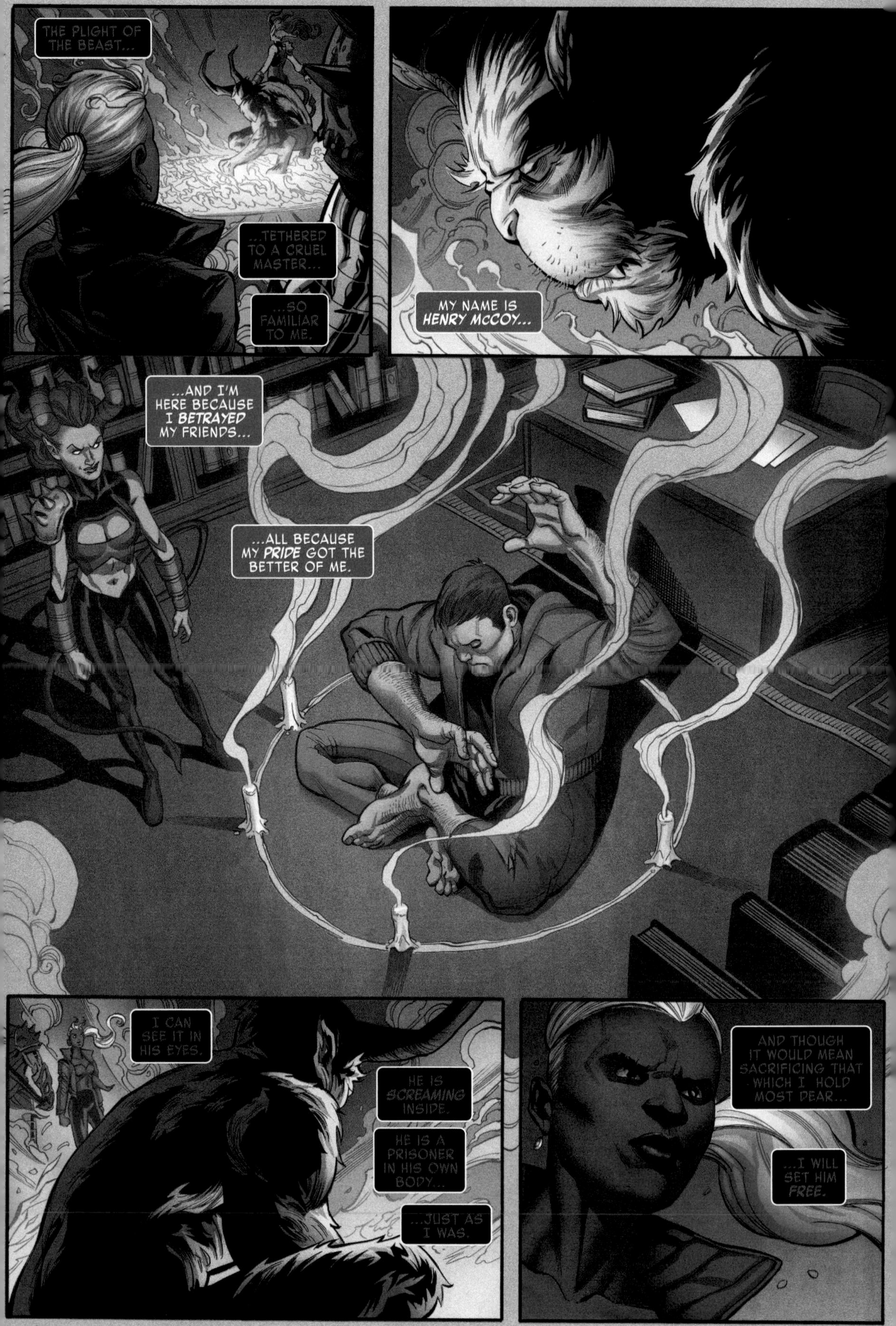
THE PLIGHT OF THE BEAST...
...TETHERED TO A CRUEL MASTER...
...SO FAMILIAR TO ME.
MY NAME IS HENRY McCOY...
...AND I'M HERE BECAUSE I BETRAYED MY FRIENDS...
...ALL BECAUSE MY PRIDE GOT THE BETTER OF ME.
I CAN SEE IT IN HIS EYES.
HE IS SCREAMING INSIDE.
HE IS A PRISONER IN HIS OWN BODY...
...JUST AS I WAS.
AND THOUGH IT WOULD MEAN SACRIFICING THAT WHICH I HOLD MOST DEAR...
...I WILL SET HIM FREE.

12

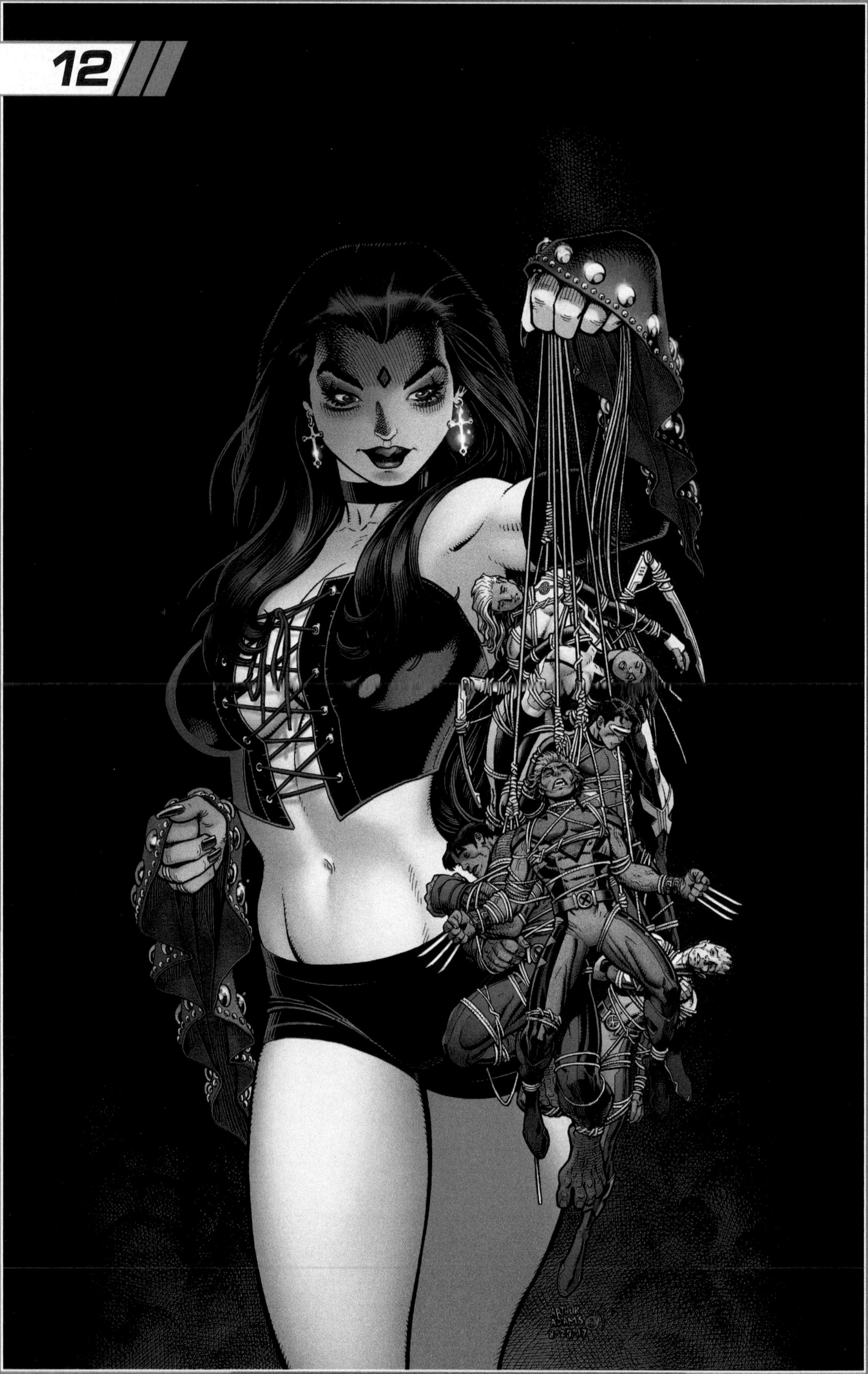

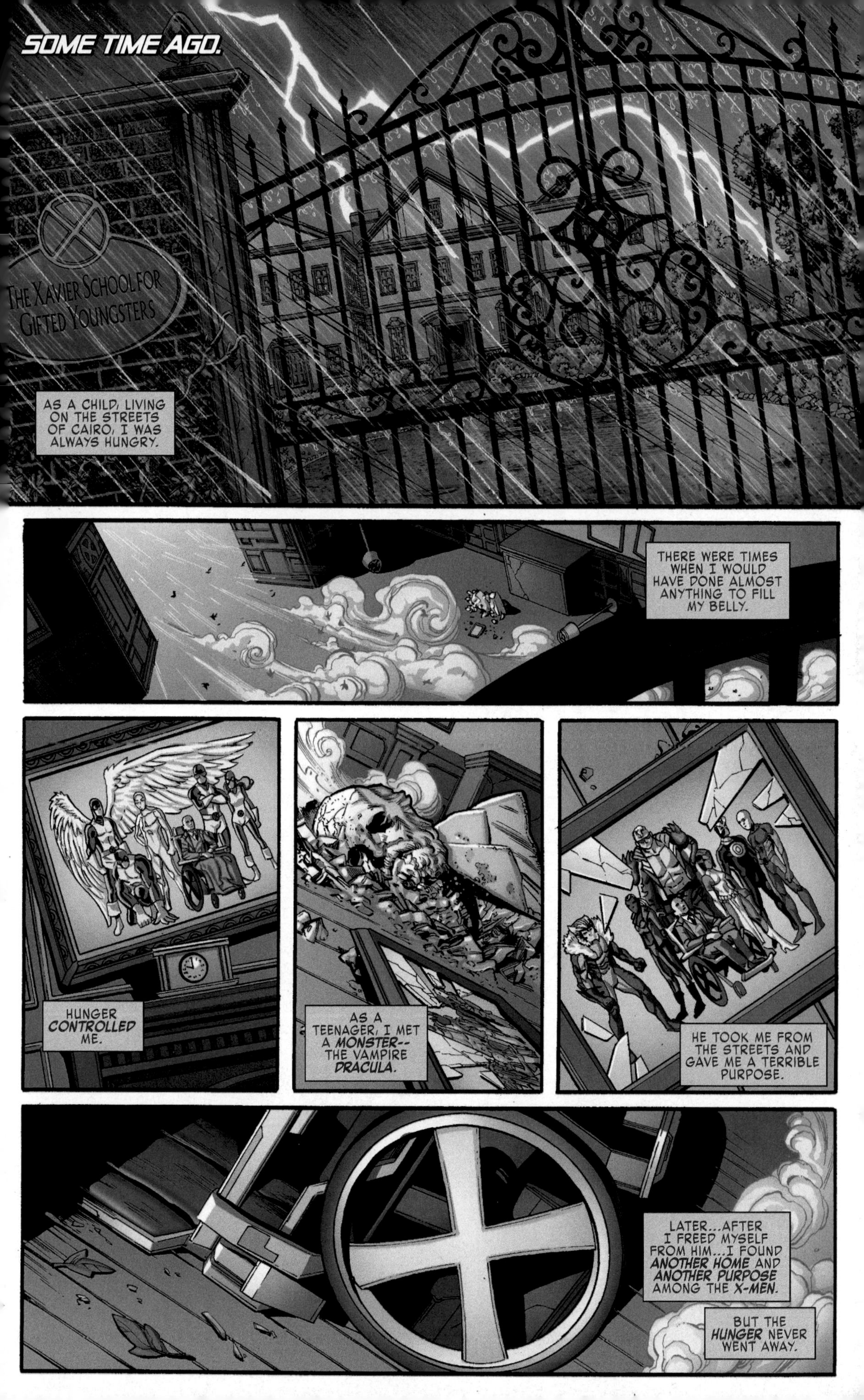
SOME TIME AGO.
THE XAVIER SCHOOL FOR GIFTED YOUNGSTERS
AS A CHILD, LIVING ON THE STREETS OF CAIRO, I WAS ALWAYS HUNGRY.
THERE WERE TIMES WHEN I WOULD HAVE DONE ALMOST ANYTHING TO FILL MY BELLY.
HUNGER CONTROLLED ME.
AS A TEENAGER, I MET A MONSTER-- THE VAMPIRE DRACULA.
HE TOOK ME FROM THE STREETS AND GAVE ME A TERRIBLE PURPOSE.
LATER...AFTER I FREED MYSELF FROM HIM...I FOUND ANOTHER HOME AND ANOTHER PURPOSE AMONG THE X-MEN.
BUT THE HUNGER NEVER WENT AWAY.

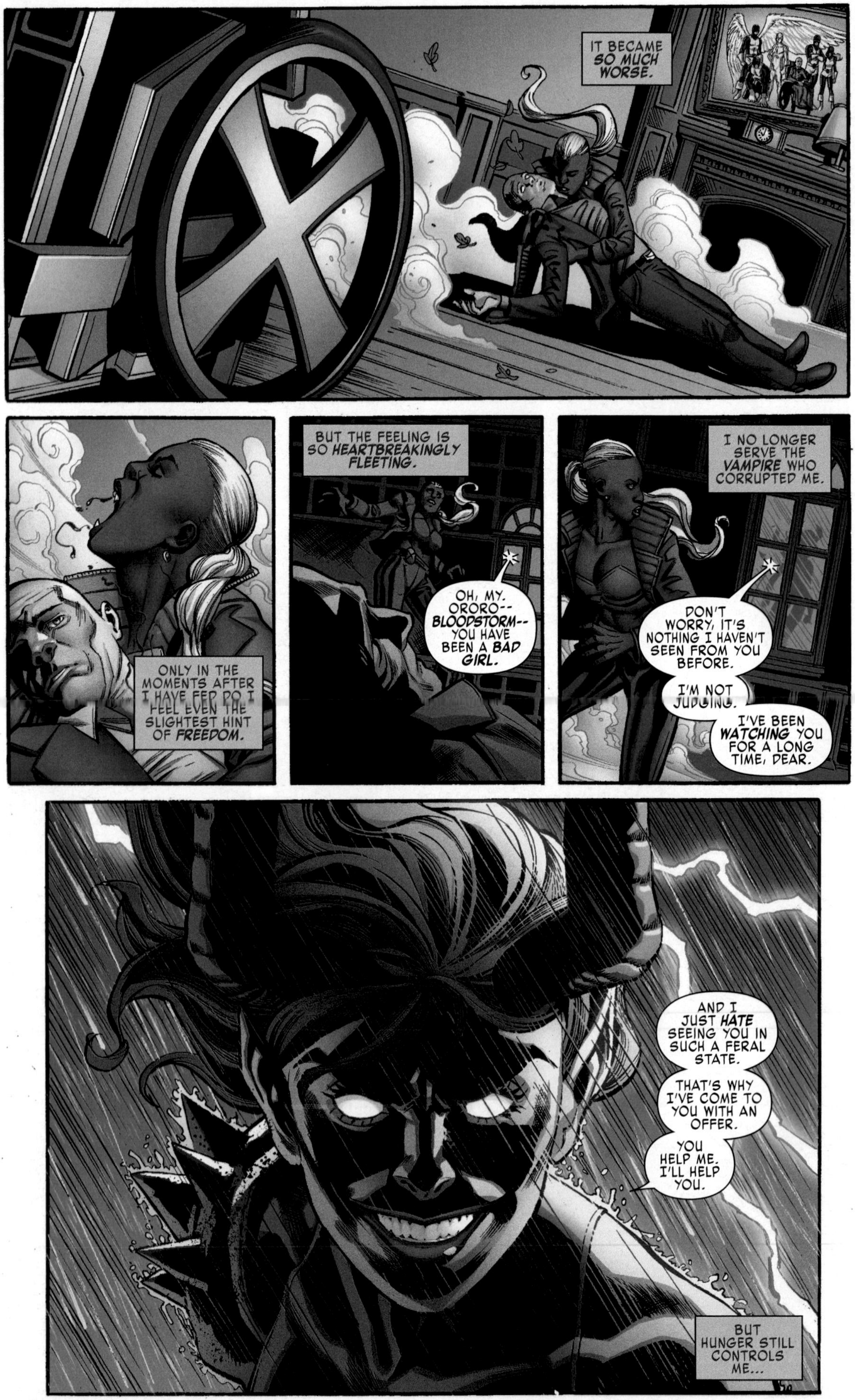
IT BECAME SO MUCH WORSE.
ONLY IN THE MOMENTS AFTER I HAVE FED DO I FEEL EVEN THE SLIGHTEST HINT OF FREEDOM.
BUT THE FEELING IS SO HEARTBREAKINGLY FLEETING.
OH, MY. ORORO-- BLOODSTORM-- YOU HAVE BEEN A BAD GIRL.
I NO LONGER SERVE THE VAMPIRE WHO CORRUPTED ME.
DON'T WORRY, IT'S NOTHING I HAVEN'T SEEN FROM YOU BEFORE.
I'M NOT JUDGING.
I'VE BEEN WATCHING YOU FOR A LONG TIME, DEAR.
AND I JUST HATE SEEING YOU IN SUCH A FERAL STATE.
THAT'S WHY I'VE COME TO YOU WITH AN OFFER.
YOU HELP ME. I'LL HELP YOU.
BUT HUNGER STILL CONTROLS ME...

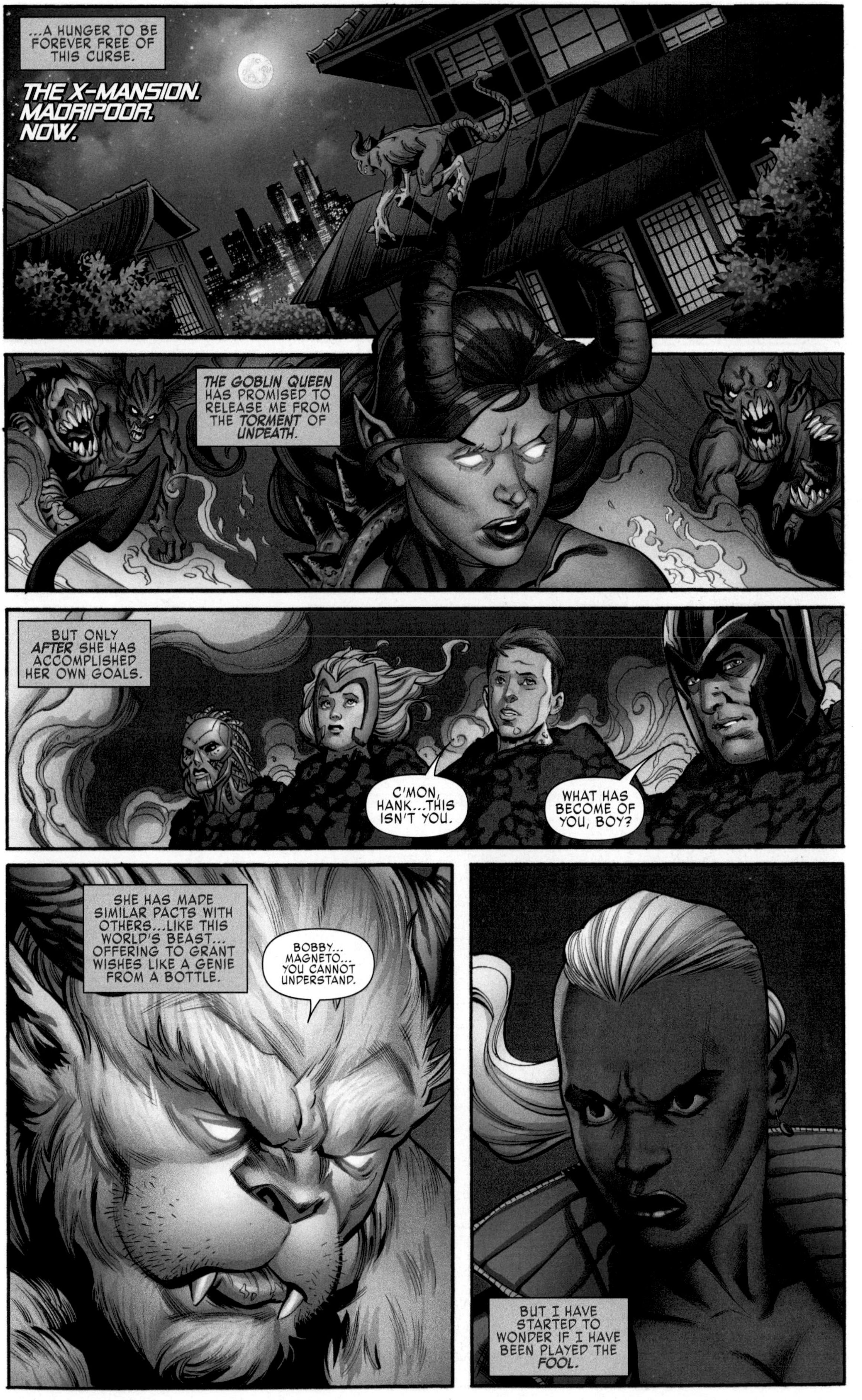
...A HUNGER TO BE FOREVER FREE OF THIS CURSE.
THE X-MANSION. MADRIPOOR. NOW.
THE GOBLIN QUEEN HAS PROMISED TO RELEASE ME FROM THE TORMENT OF UNDEATH.
BUT ONLY AFTER SHE HAS ACCOMPLISHED HER OWN GOALS.
C'MON, HANK...THIS ISN'T YOU.
WHAT HAS BECOME OF YOU, BOY?
SHE HAS MADE SIMILAR PACTS WITH OTHERS...LIKE THIS WORLD'S BEAST... OFFERING TO GRANT WISHES LIKE A GENIE FROM A BOTTLE.
BOBBY... MAGNETO... YOU CANNOT UNDERSTAND.
BUT I HAVE STARTED TO WONDER IF I HAVE BEEN PLAYED THE FOOL.

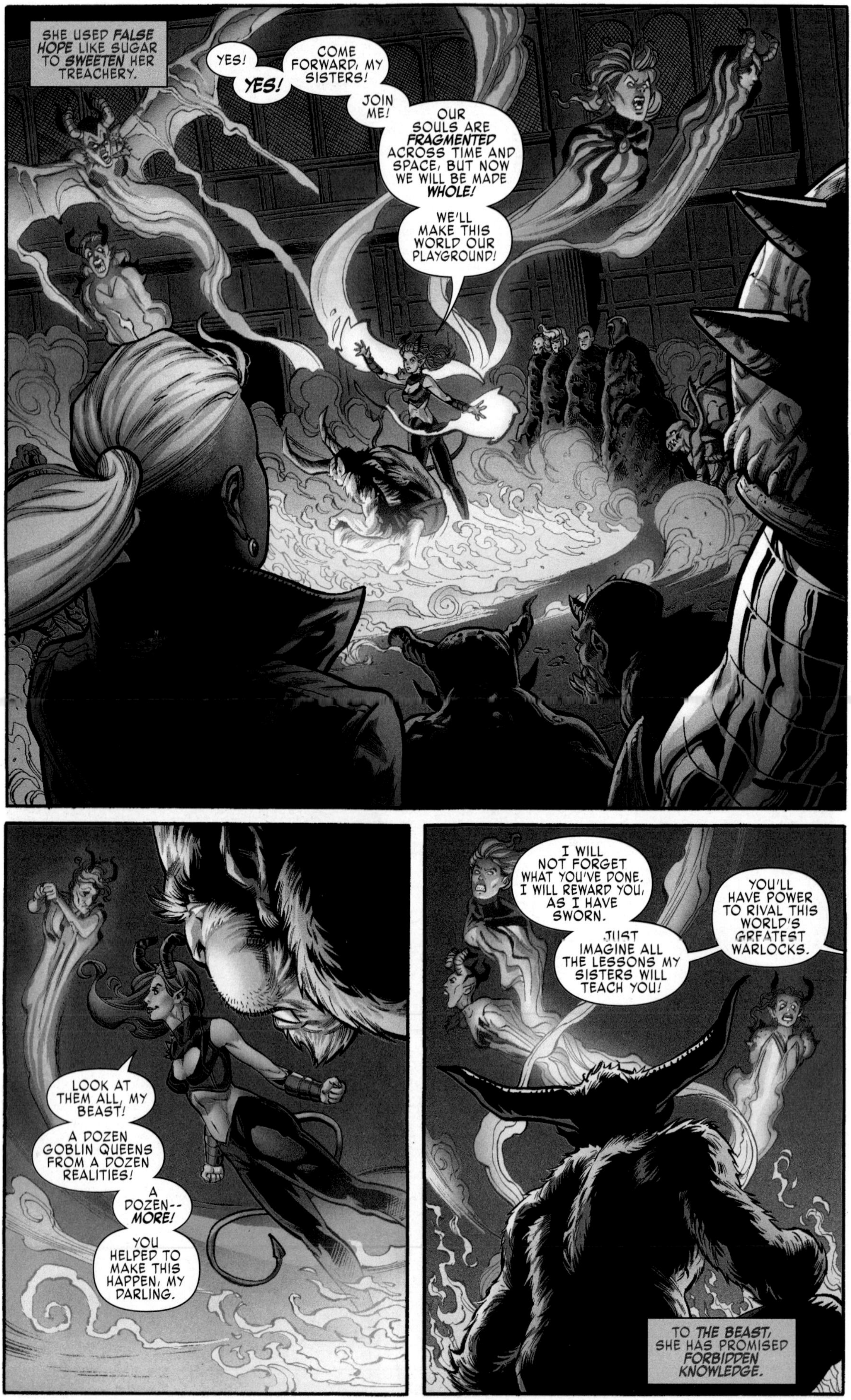
SHE USED FALSE HOPE LIKE SUGAR TO SWEETEN HER TREACHERY.
YES! YES!
COME FORWARD, MY SISTERS!
JOIN ME!
OUR SOULS ARE FRAGMENTED ACROSS TIME AND SPACE, BUT NOW WE WILL BE MADE WHOLE!
WE'LL MAKE THIS WORLD OUR PLAYGROUND!
LOOK AT THEM ALL, MY BEAST!
A DOZEN GOBLIN QUEENS FROM A DOZEN REALITIES!
A DOZEN--MORE!
YOU HELPED TO MAKE THIS HAPPEN, MY DARLING.
I WILL NOT FORGET WHAT YOU'VE DONE. I WILL REWARD YOU, AS I HAVE SWORN.
JUST IMAGINE ALL THE LESSONS MY SISTERS WILL TEACH YOU!
YOU'LL HAVE POWER TO RIVAL THIS WORLD'S GREATEST WARLOCKS.
TO THE BEAST, SHE HAS PROMISED FORBIDDEN KNOWLEDGE.

FROM ALTERNATE REALITIES, SHE COAXED *COLOSSUS* AND *PIXIE* INTO SERVITUDE WITH OTHER ASSURANCES.

THE RETURN OF *LOST HUMANITY.*

THE RETURN OF A *LOST SISTER.*

HER VOWS ARE *HOLLOW,* THOUGH.

HANK! SHE'S CONTROLLING YOU OR SOMETHING!

YOU'VE GOT TO FIGHT HER!

HER MAGIC IS FUELED BY THE PAIN OF *BETRAYAL.*

TOO LATE FOR THAT NOW.

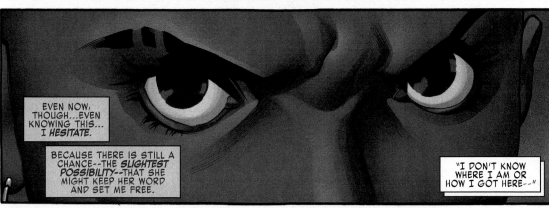

EVEN NOW, THOUGH...EVEN KNOWING THIS... I *HESITATE.*

BECAUSE THERE IS STILL A CHANCE--THE *SLIGHTEST POSSIBILITY*--THAT SHE MIGHT KEEP HER WORD AND SET ME FREE.

"I DON'T KNOW WHERE I AM OR HOW I GOT HERE--"

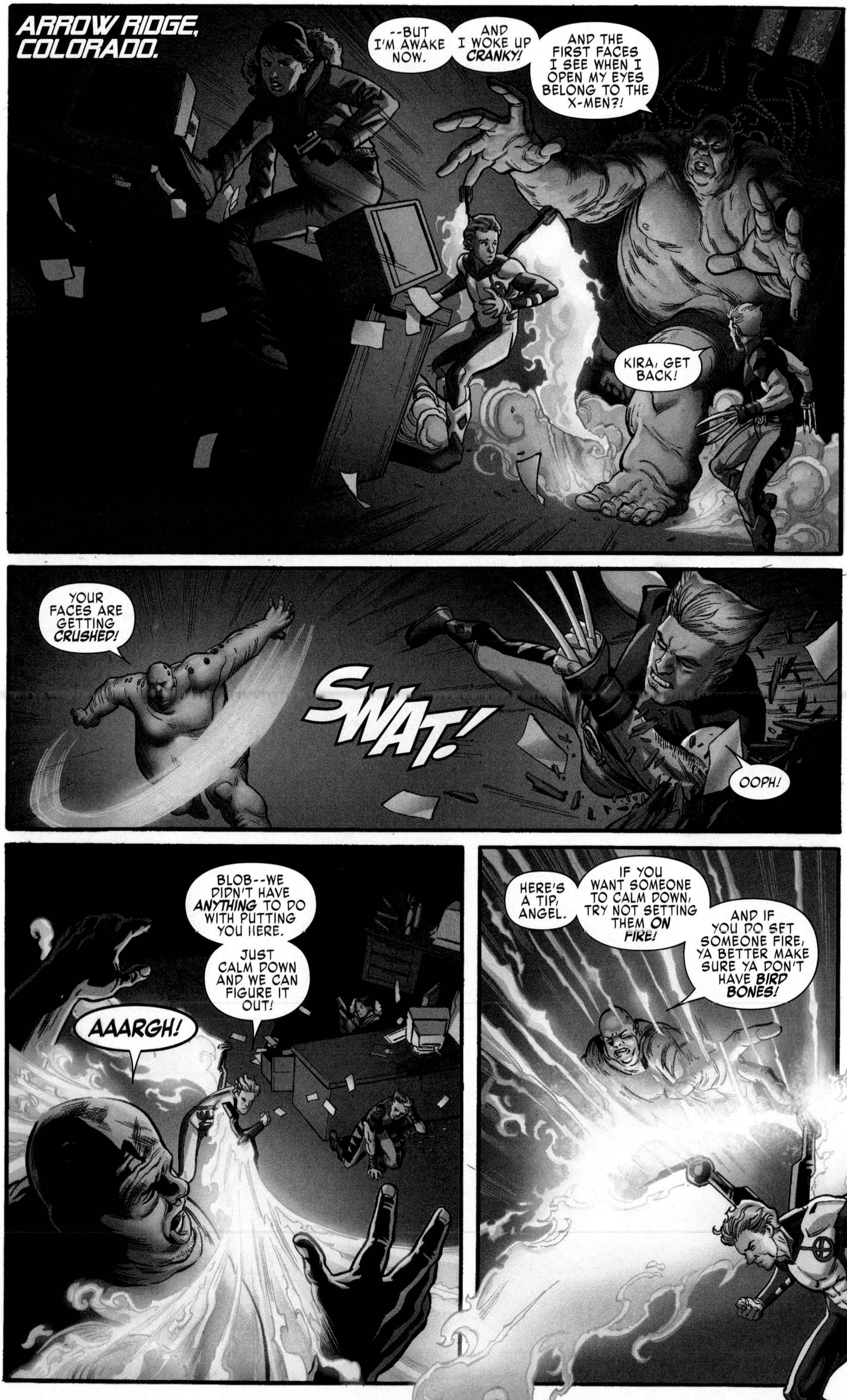
ARROW RIDGE, COLORADO.
--BUT I'M AWAKE NOW.
AND I WOKE UP CRANKY!
AND THE FIRST FACES I SEE WHEN I OPEN MY EYES BELONG TO THE X-MEN?!
KIRA, GET BACK!
YOUR FACES ARE GETTING CRUSHED!
SWAT!
OOPH!
BLOB--WE DIDN'T HAVE ANYTHING TO DO WITH PUTTING YOU HERE.
JUST CALM DOWN AND WE CAN FIGURE IT OUT!
AAARGH!
HERE'S A TIP, ANGEL.
IF YOU WANT SOMEONE TO CALM DOWN, TRY NOT SETTING THEM ON FIRE!
AND IF YOU DO SET SOMEONE FIRE, YA BETTER MAKE SURE YA DON'T HAVE BIRD BONES!

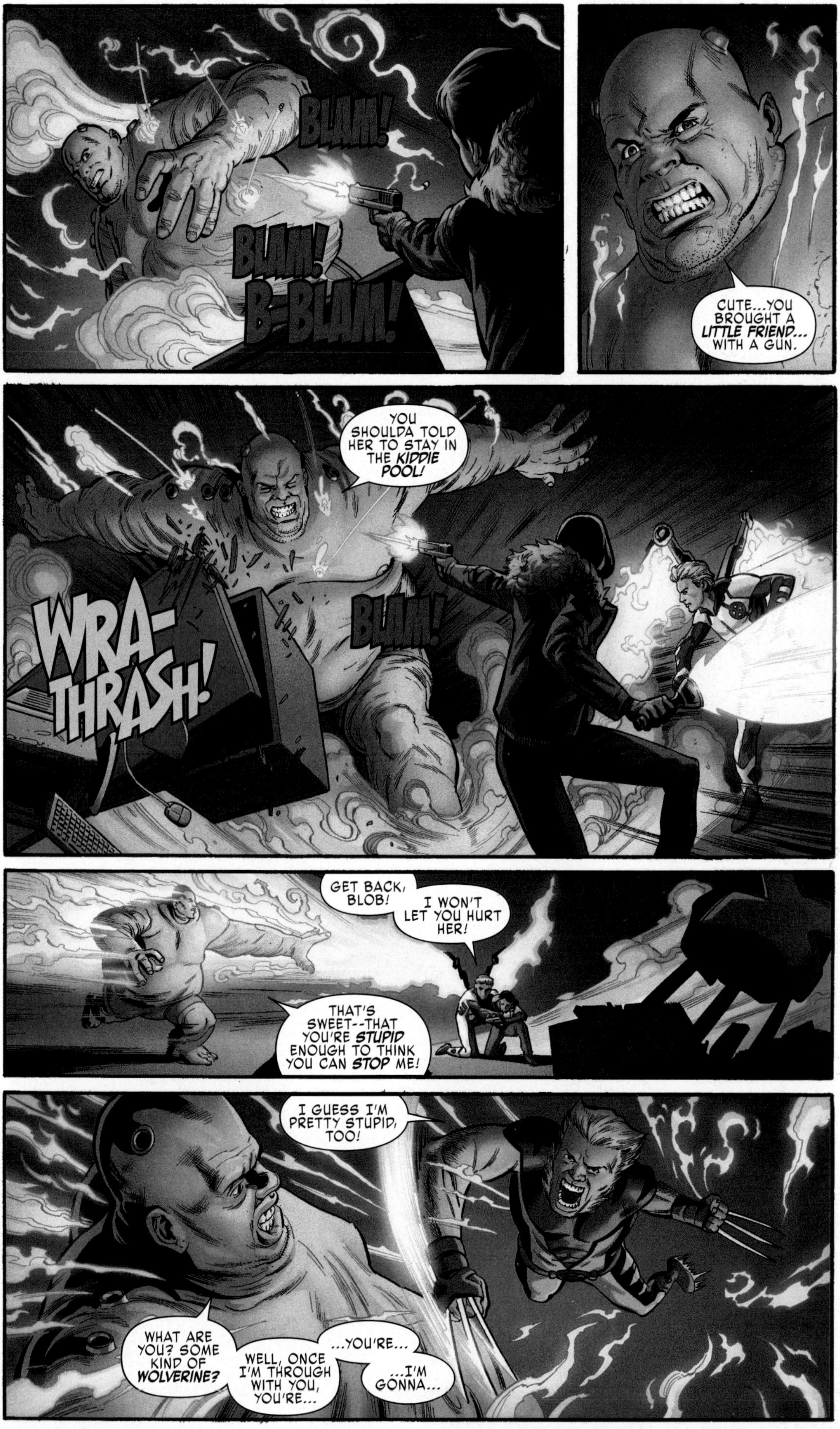
BLAM!
BLAM!
B-BLAM!
CUTE...YOU BROUGHT A LITTLE FRIEND... WITH A GUN.
YOU SHOULDA TOLD HER TO STAY IN THE KIDDIE POOL!
WRA-THRASH!
BLAM!
GET BACK, BLOB!
I WON'T LET YOU HURT HER!
THAT'S SWEET--THAT YOU'RE STUPID ENOUGH TO THINK YOU CAN STOP ME!
I GUESS I'M PRETTY STUPID, TOO!
WHAT ARE YOU? SOME KIND OF WOLVERINE?
WELL, ONCE I'M THROUGH WITH YOU, YOU'RE...
...YOU'RE...
...I'M GONNA...

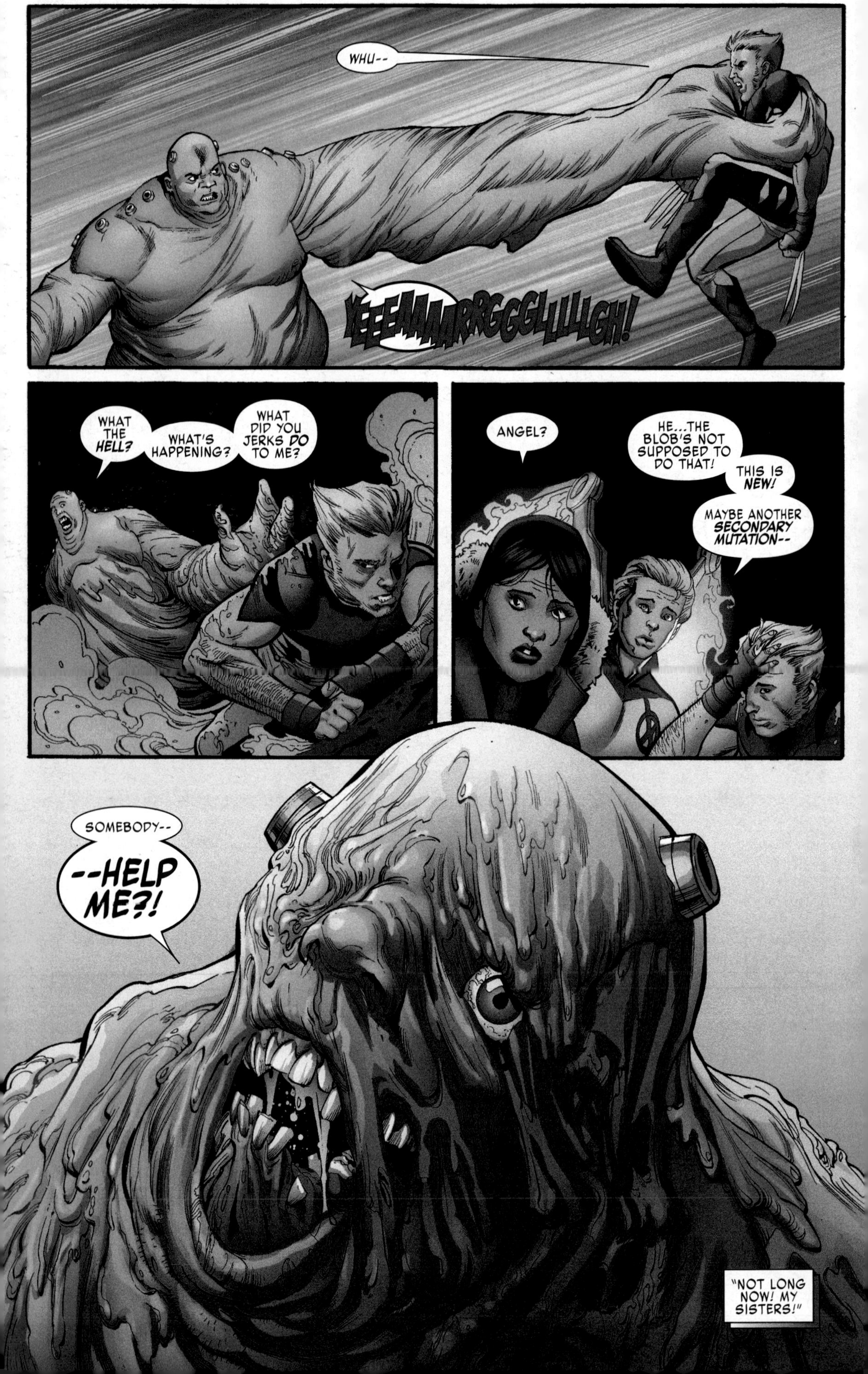
WHU--
YEEEAAAARRGGGLLLLLGH!
WHAT THE HELL?
WHAT'S HAPPENING?
WHAT DID YOU JERKS DO TO ME?
ANGEL?
HE...THE BLOB'S NOT SUPPOSED TO DO THAT!
THIS IS NEW!
MAYBE ANOTHER SECONDARY MUTATION--
SOMEBODY--
--HELP ME?!
"NOT LONG NOW! MY SISTERS!"

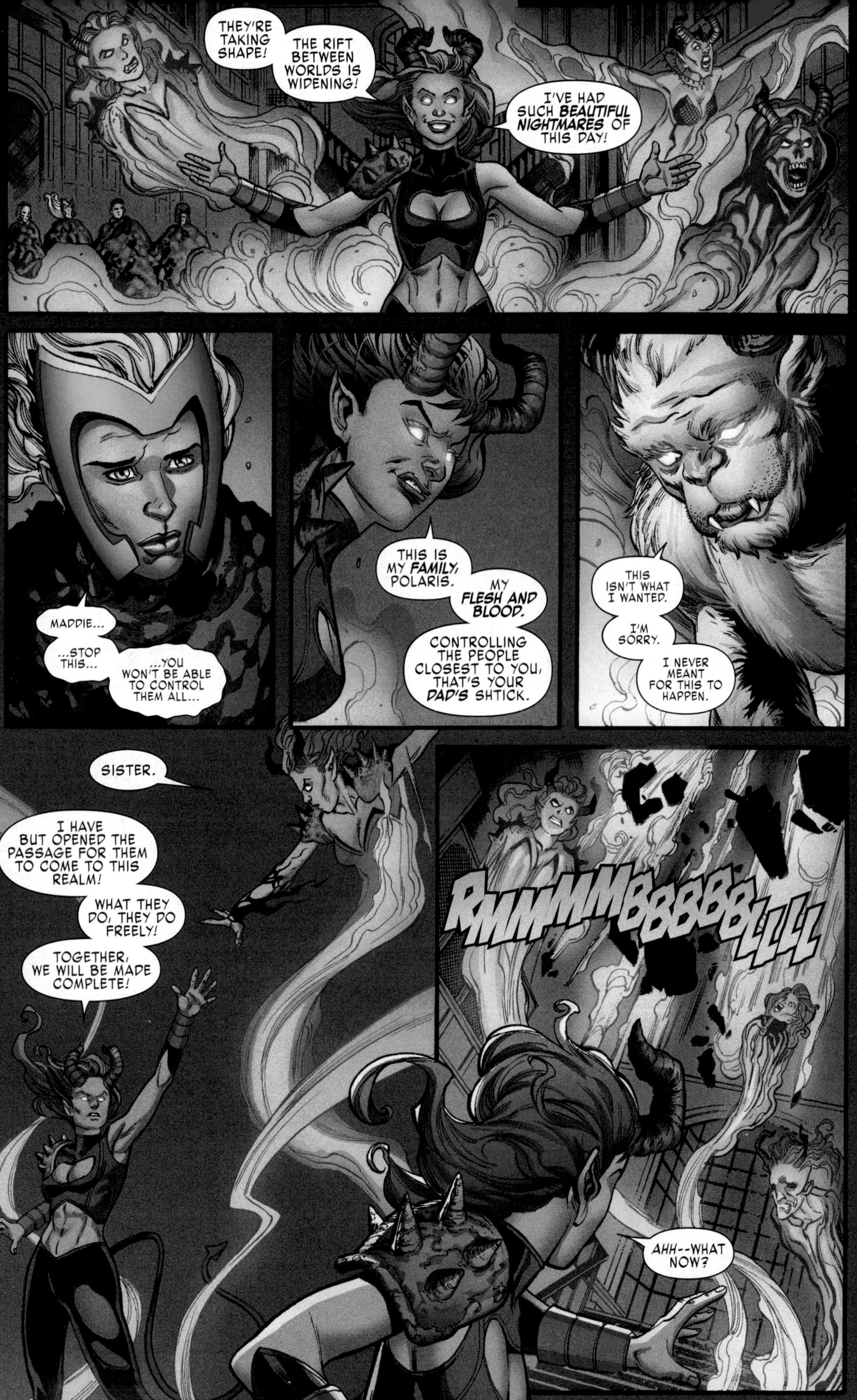
THEY'RE TAKING SHAPE!
THE RIFT BETWEEN WORLDS IS WIDENING!
I'VE HAD SUCH BEAUTIFUL NIGHTMARES OF THIS DAY!
MADDIE...
...STOP THIS...
...YOU WON'T BE ABLE TO CONTROL THEM ALL...
THIS IS MY FAMILY, POLARIS.
MY FLESH AND BLOOD.
CONTROLLING THE PEOPLE CLOSEST TO YOU, THAT'S YOUR DAD'S SHTICK.
THIS ISN'T WHAT I WANTED.
I'M SORRY.
I NEVER MEANT FOR THIS TO HAPPEN.
SISTER.
I HAVE BUT OPENED THE PASSAGE FOR THEM TO COME TO THIS REALM!
WHAT THEY DO, THEY DO FREELY!
TOGETHER, WE WILL BE MADE COMPLETE!
RMMMMBBBBLLLL
AHH--WHAT NOW?

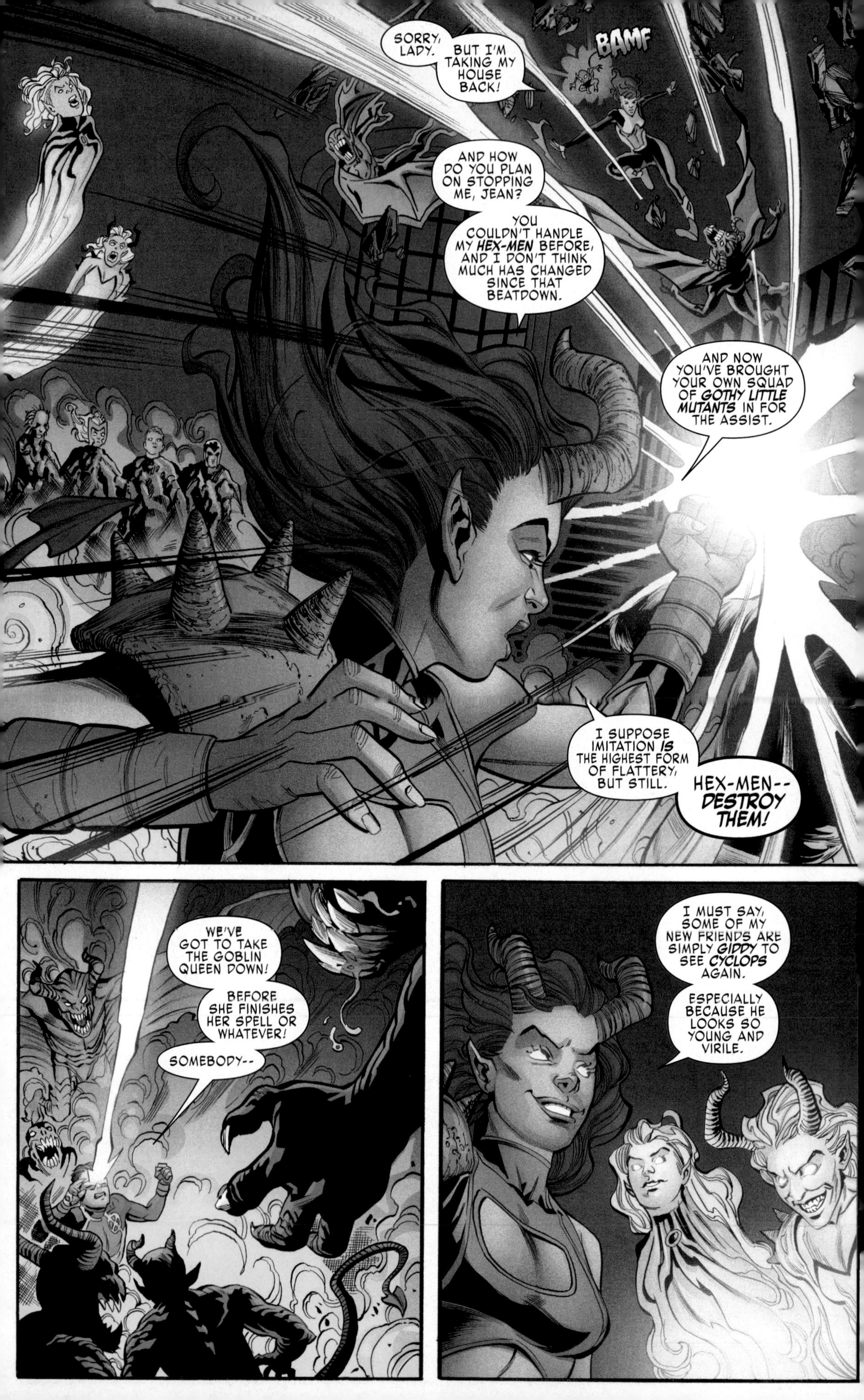

SORRY, LADY.
BUT I'M TAKING MY HOUSE BACK!
BAMF
AND HOW DO YOU PLAN ON STOPPING ME, JEAN?
YOU COULDN'T HANDLE MY HEX-MEN BEFORE, AND I DON'T THINK MUCH HAS CHANGED SINCE THAT BEATDOWN.
AND NOW YOU'VE BROUGHT YOUR OWN SQUAD OF GOTHY LITTLE MUTANTS IN FOR THE ASSIST.
I SUPPOSE IMITATION IS THE HIGHEST FORM OF FLATTERY, BUT STILL.
HEX-MEN-- DESTROY THEM!
WE'VE GOT TO TAKE THE GOBLIN QUEEN DOWN!
BEFORE SHE FINISHES HER SPELL OR WHATEVER!
SOMEBODY--
I MUST SAY, SOME OF MY NEW FRIENDS ARE SIMPLY GIDDY TO SEE CYCLOPS AGAIN.
ESPECIALLY BECAUSE HE LOOKS SO YOUNG AND VIRILE.

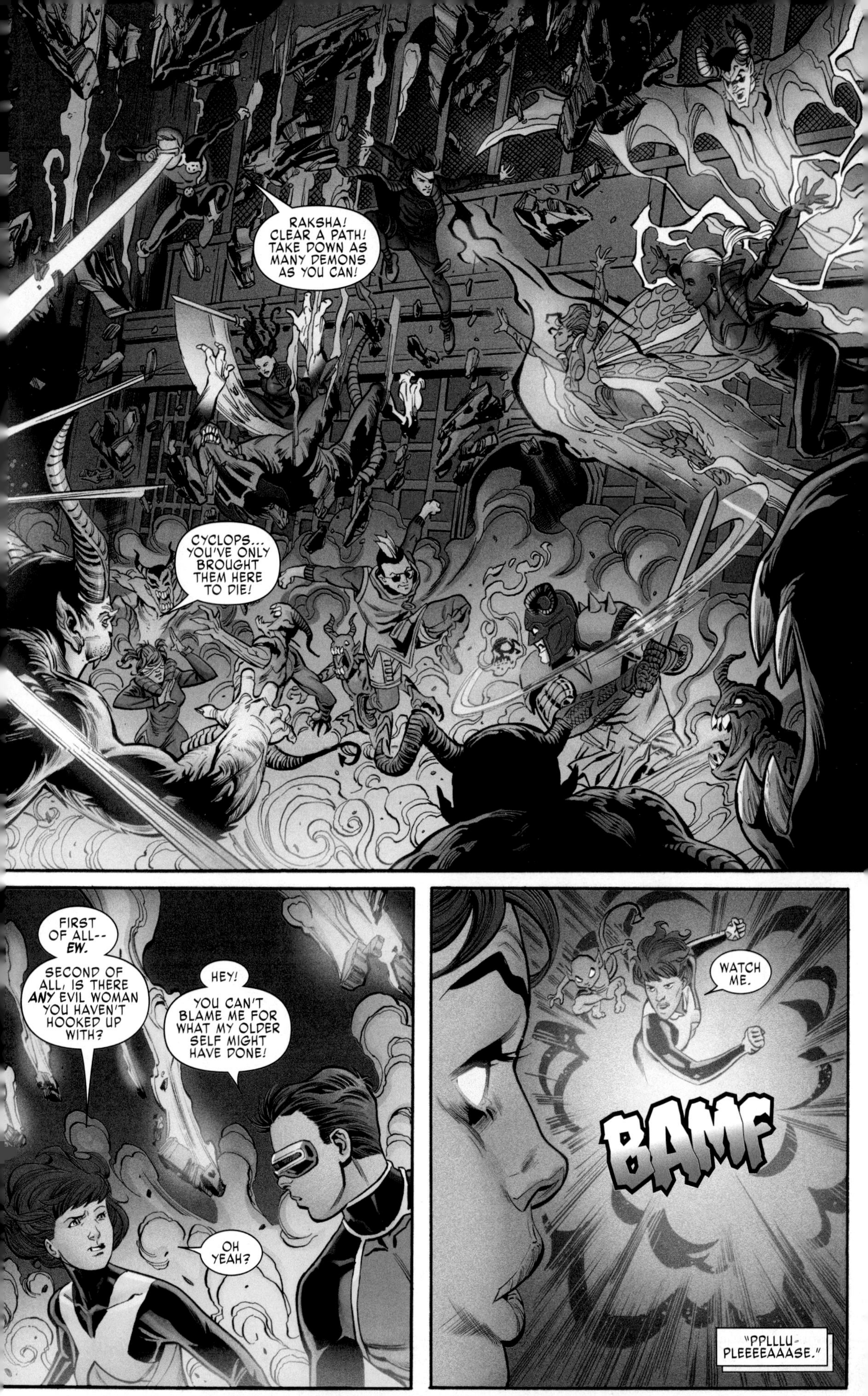
RAKSHA! CLEAR A PATH! TAKE DOWN AS MANY DEMONS AS YOU CAN!
CYCLOPS... YOU'VE ONLY BROUGHT THEM HERE TO DIE!
FIRST OF ALL-- *EW.*
SECOND OF ALL, IS THERE *ANY* EVIL WOMAN YOU HAVEN'T HOOKED UP WITH?
HEY!
YOU CAN'T BLAME ME FOR WHAT MY OLDER SELF MIGHT HAVE DONE!
OH YEAH?
WATCH ME.
BAMF
"PPLLLU-PLEEEEAAASE."

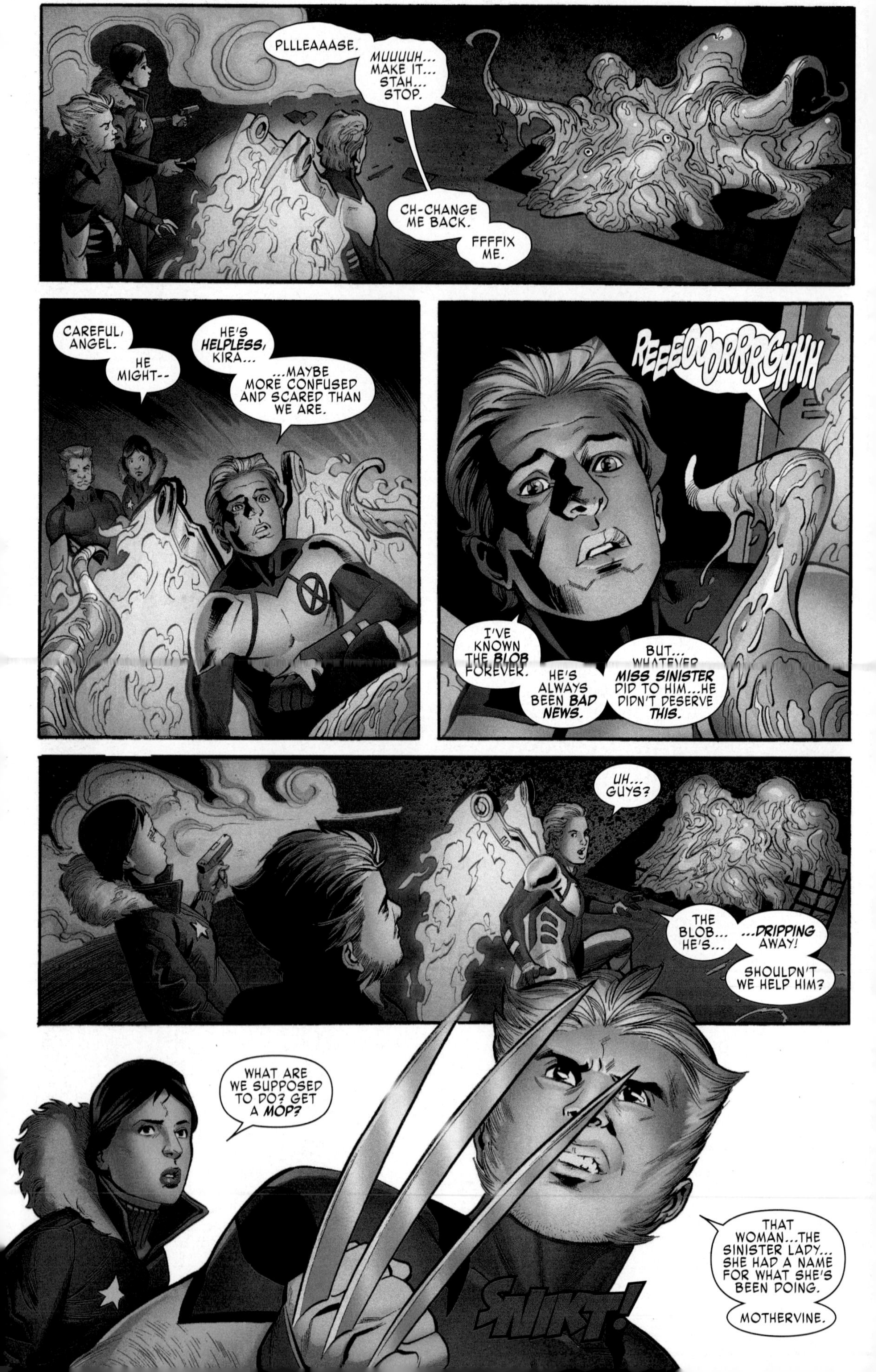
PLLLEAAAASE.
MUUUUH... MAKE IT... STAH... STOP.
CH-CHANGE ME BACK.
FFFFIX ME.
CAREFUL, ANGEL.
HE MIGHT--
HE'S HELPLESS, KIRA...
...MAYBE MORE CONFUSED AND SCARED THAN WE ARE.
REEEOOORRRGHHH
I'VE KNOWN THE BLOB FOREVER.
HE'S ALWAYS BEEN BAD NEWS.
BUT... WHATEVER MISS SINISTER DID TO HIM...HE DIDN'T DESERVE THIS.
UH... GUYS?
THE BLOB... HE'S...
...DRIPPING AWAY!
SHOULDN'T WE HELP HIM?
WHAT ARE WE SUPPOSED TO DO? GET A MOP?
SNIKT!
THAT WOMAN...THE SINISTER LADY... SHE HAD A NAME FOR WHAT SHE'S BEEN DOING.
MOTHERVINE.

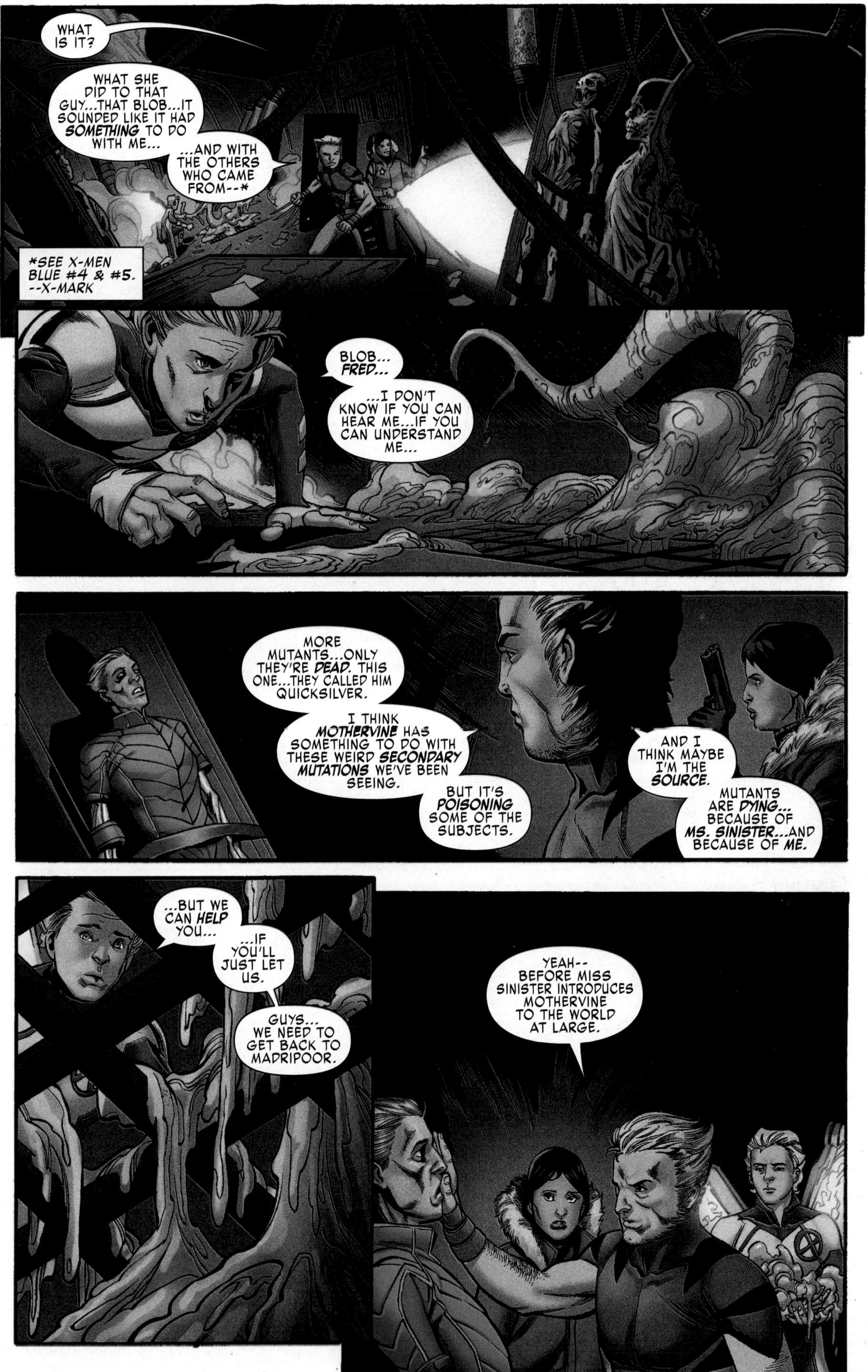
WHAT IS IT?
WHAT SHE DID TO THAT GUY...THAT BLOB...IT SOUNDED LIKE IT HAD SOMETHING TO DO WITH ME...
...AND WITH THE OTHERS WHO CAME FROM--*
*SEE X-MEN BLUE #4 & #5. --X-MARK
BLOB... FRED...
...I DON'T KNOW IF YOU CAN HEAR ME...IF YOU CAN UNDERSTAND ME...
MORE MUTANTS...ONLY THEY'RE DEAD. THIS ONE...THEY CALLED HIM QUICKSILVER.
I THINK MOTHERVINE HAS SOMETHING TO DO WITH THESE WEIRD SECONDARY MUTATIONS WE'VE BEEN SEEING.
BUT IT'S POISONING SOME OF THE SUBJECTS.
AND I THINK MAYBE I'M THE SOURCE.
MUTANTS ARE DYING... BECAUSE OF MS. SINISTER...AND BECAUSE OF ME.
...BUT WE CAN HELP YOU...
...IF YOU'LL JUST LET US.
GUYS... WE NEED TO GET BACK TO MADRIPOOR.
YEAH-- BEFORE MISS SINISTER INTRODUCES MOTHERVINE TO THE WORLD AT LARGE.

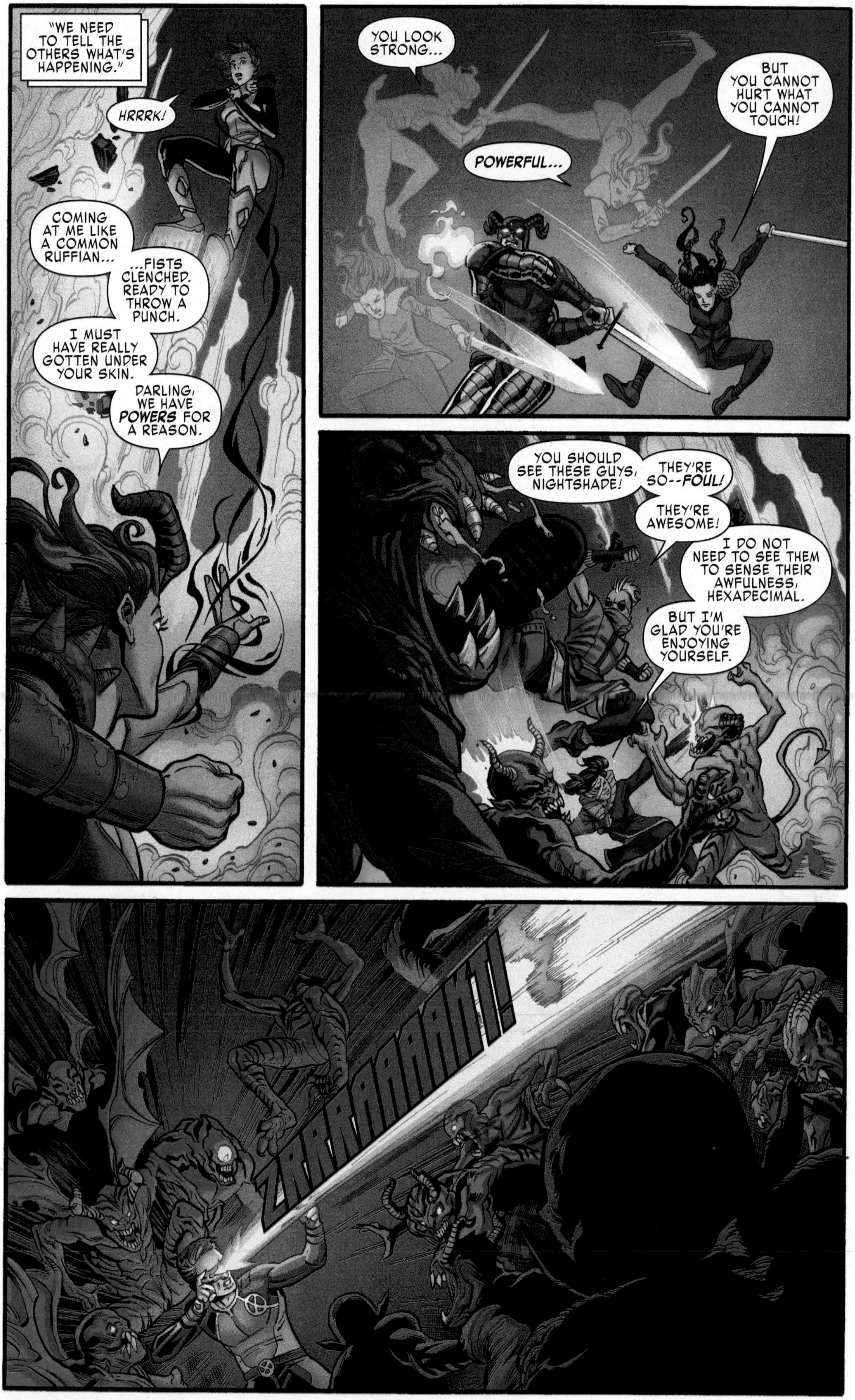
"WE NEED TO TELL THE OTHERS WHAT'S HAPPENING."
HRRRK!
COMING AT ME LIKE A COMMON RUFFIAN...
...FISTS CLENCHED. READY TO THROW A PUNCH.
I MUST HAVE REALLY GOTTEN UNDER YOUR SKIN.
DARLING, WE HAVE POWERS FOR A REASON.
YOU LOOK STRONG...
POWERFUL...
BUT YOU CANNOT HURT WHAT YOU CANNOT TOUCH!
YOU SHOULD SEE THESE GUYS, NIGHTSHADE!
THEY'RE SO--FOUL!
THEY'RE AWESOME!
I DO NOT NEED TO SEE THEM TO SENSE THEIR AWFULNESS, HEXADECIMAL.
BUT I'M GLAD YOU'RE ENJOYING YOURSELF.
ZARRAAAAKT!

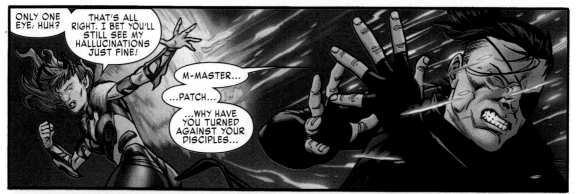

ONLY ONE EYE, HUH? THAT'S ALL RIGHT. I BET YOU'LL STILL SEE MY HALLUCINATIONS JUST FINE!

M-MASTER...

...PATCH...

...WHY HAVE YOU TURNED AGAINST YOUR DISCIPLES...

I'D LOVE TO TOY WITH YOU A LITTLE LONGER, JEAN.

BUT MY SUMMONING IS ALMOST COMPLETE.

THE VEIL BETWEEN WORLDS HAS BEEN RIPPED ASUNDER!

ONCE SHE IS DONE, SHE WILL HAVE NO USE FOR ANY OF US.

JEAN--

OF ALL MY CLONES... MADELYNE PRYOR IS DEFINITELY MY LEAST FAVORITE.

GAZING NIGHTSHADE! RUN! I CAN'T STOP MYSELF!

SMACK!

RAAARGH!

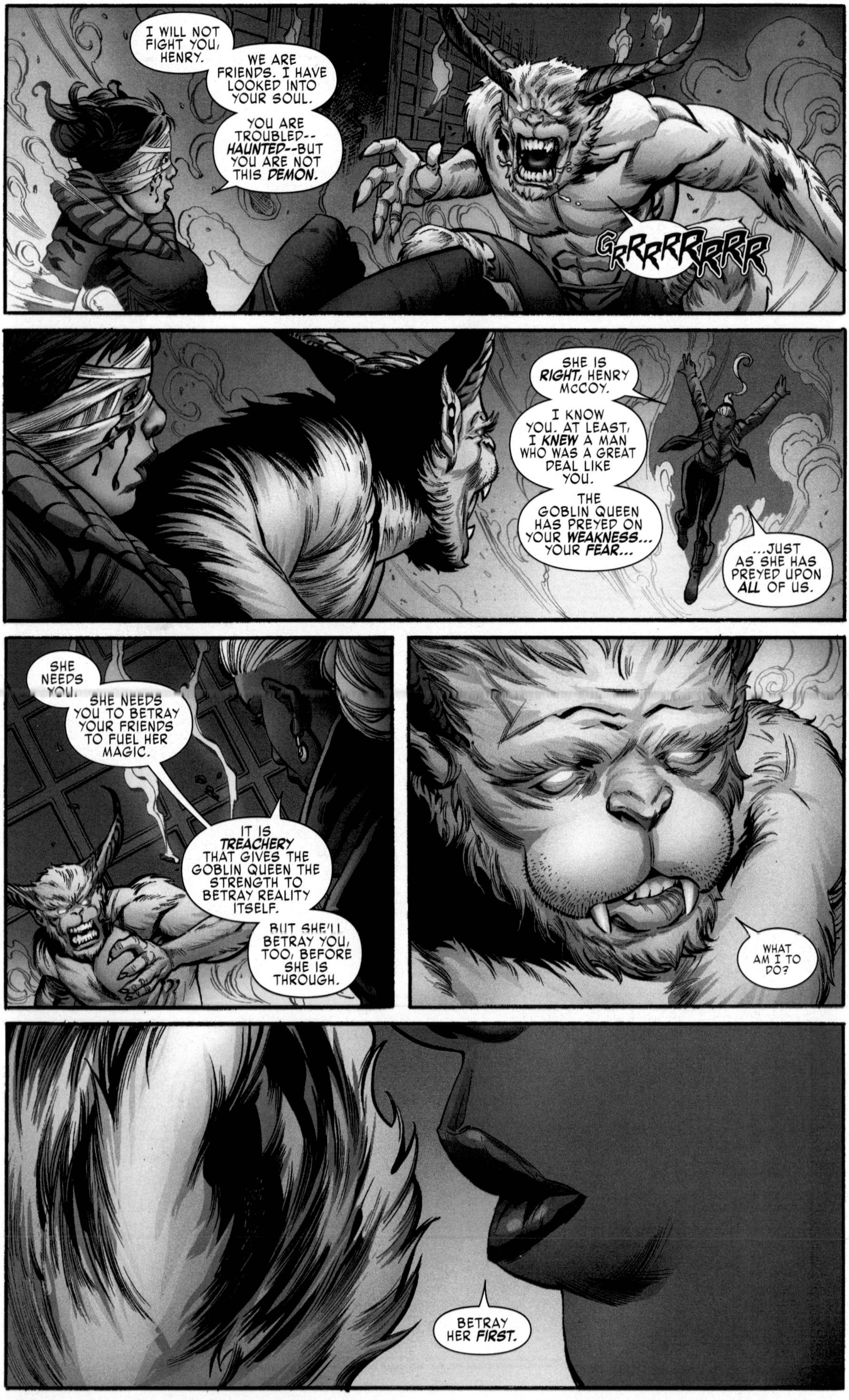
I WILL NOT FIGHT YOU, HENRY.
WE ARE FRIENDS. I HAVE LOOKED INTO YOUR SOUL.
YOU ARE TROUBLED--*HAUNTED*--BUT YOU ARE NOT THIS *DEMON.*
GRRRRRRRR
SHE IS *RIGHT,* HENRY McCOY.
I KNOW YOU. AT LEAST, I *KNEW* A MAN WHO WAS A GREAT DEAL LIKE YOU.
THE GOBLIN QUEEN HAS PREYED ON YOUR *WEAKNESS*... YOUR *FEAR*...
...JUST AS SHE HAS PREYED UPON *ALL* OF US.
SHE NEEDS YOU.
SHE NEEDS YOU TO BETRAY YOUR FRIENDS TO FUEL HER MAGIC.
IT IS *TREACHERY* THAT GIVES THE GOBLIN QUEEN THE STRENGTH TO BETRAY REALITY ITSELF.
BUT SHE'LL BETRAY YOU, TOO, BEFORE SHE IS THROUGH.
WHAT AM I TO DO?
BETRAY HER *FIRST.*

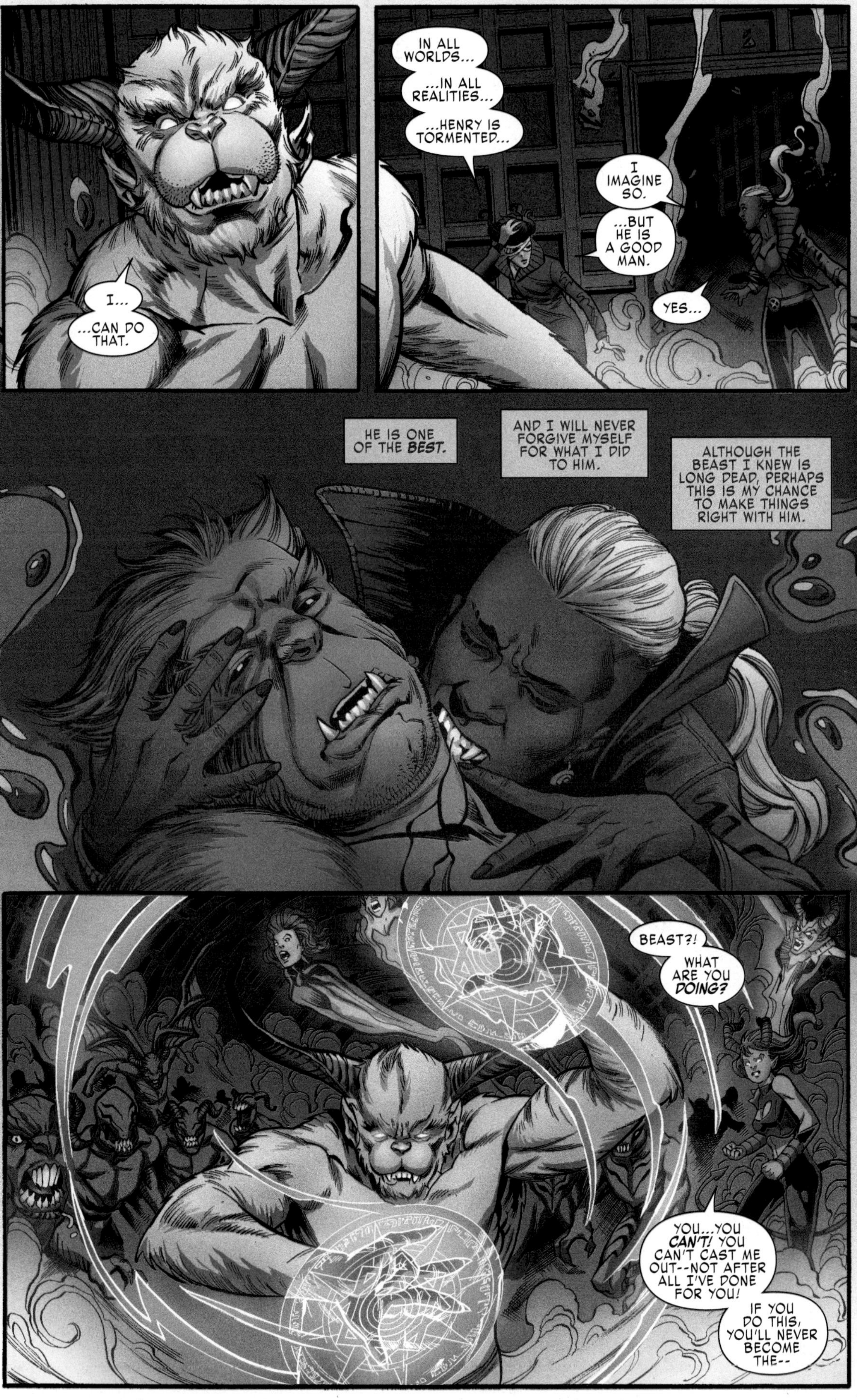
I...
...CAN DO THAT.
IN ALL WORLDS...
...IN ALL REALITIES...
...HENRY IS TORMENTED...
I IMAGINE SO.
...BUT HE IS A GOOD MAN.
YES...
HE IS ONE OF THE BEST.
AND I WILL NEVER FORGIVE MYSELF FOR WHAT I DID TO HIM.
ALTHOUGH THE BEAST I KNEW IS LONG DEAD, PERHAPS THIS IS MY CHANCE TO MAKE THINGS RIGHT WITH HIM.
BEAST?!
WHAT ARE YOU DOING?
YOU...YOU CAN'T! YOU CAN'T CAST ME OUT--NOT AFTER ALL I'VE DONE FOR YOU!
IF YOU DO THIS, YOU'LL NEVER BECOME THE--

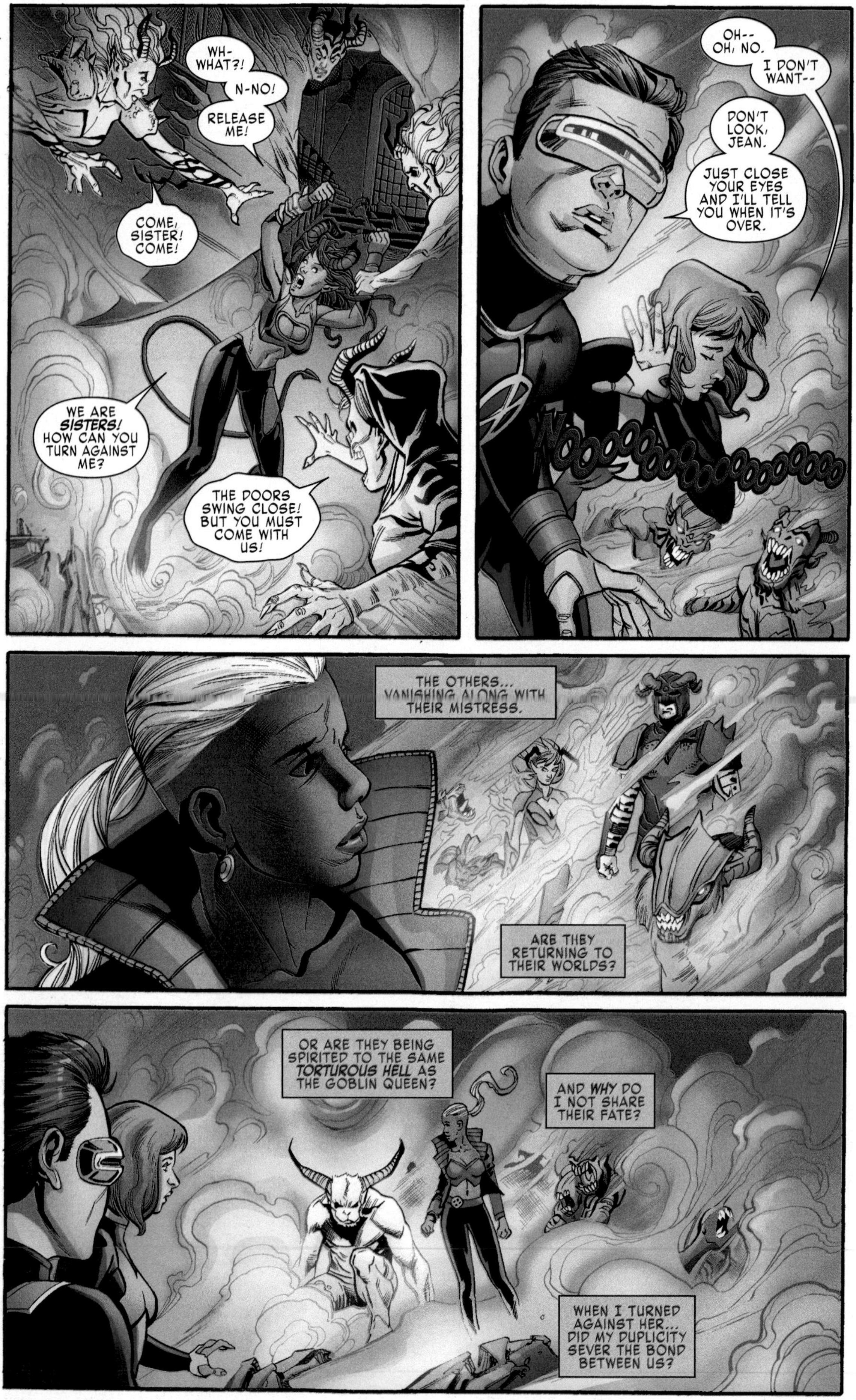
WH-WHAT?!
N-NO!
RELEASE ME!
COME, SISTER! COME!
WE ARE SISTERS! HOW CAN YOU TURN AGAINST ME?
THE DOORS SWING CLOSE! BUT YOU MUST COME WITH US!
OH-- OH, NO.
I DON'T WANT--
DON'T LOOK, JEAN.
JUST CLOSE YOUR EYES AND I'LL TELL YOU WHEN IT'S OVER.
NOOOOOOOOOOOOOOOOOO
THE OTHERS... VANISHING ALONG WITH THEIR MISTRESS.
ARE THEY RETURNING TO THEIR WORLDS?
OR ARE THEY BEING SPIRITED TO THE SAME TORTUROUS HELL AS THE GOBLIN QUEEN?
AND WHY DO I NOT SHARE THEIR FATE?
WHEN I TURNED AGAINST HER... DID MY DUPLICITY SEVER THE BOND BETWEEN US?

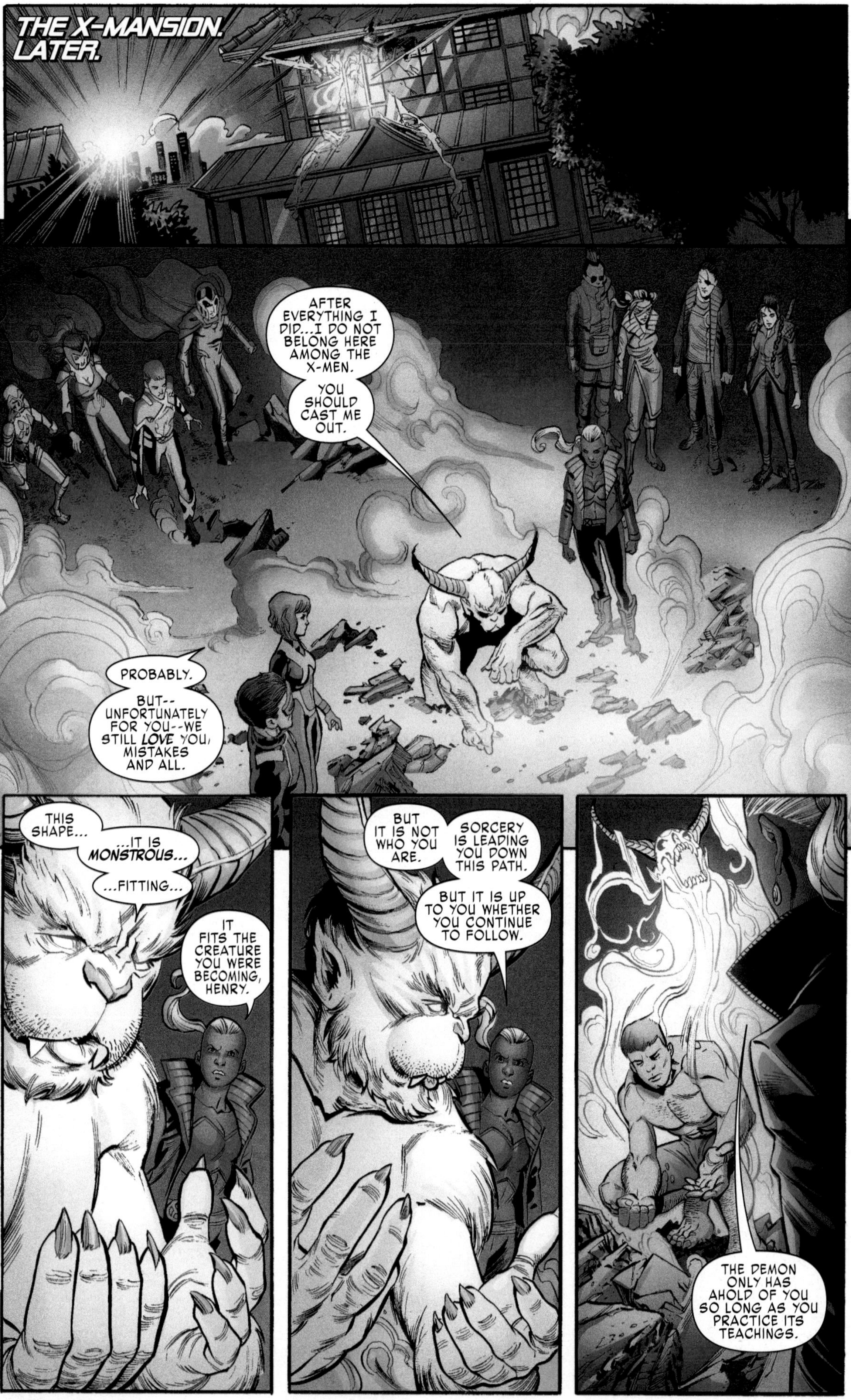
THE X-MANSION. LATER.
AFTER EVERYTHING I DID...I DO NOT BELONG HERE AMONG THE X-MEN.
YOU SHOULD CAST ME OUT.
PROBABLY.
BUT--UNFORTUNATELY FOR YOU--WE STILL LOVE YOU, MISTAKES AND ALL.
THIS SHAPE...
...IT IS MONSTROUS...
...FITTING...
IT FITS THE CREATURE YOU WERE BECOMING, HENRY.
BUT IT IS NOT WHO YOU ARE.
SORCERY IS LEADING YOU DOWN THIS PATH.
BUT IT IS UP TO YOU WHETHER YOU CONTINUE TO FOLLOW.
THE DEMON ONLY HAS AHOLD OF YOU SO LONG AS YOU PRACTICE ITS TEACHINGS.

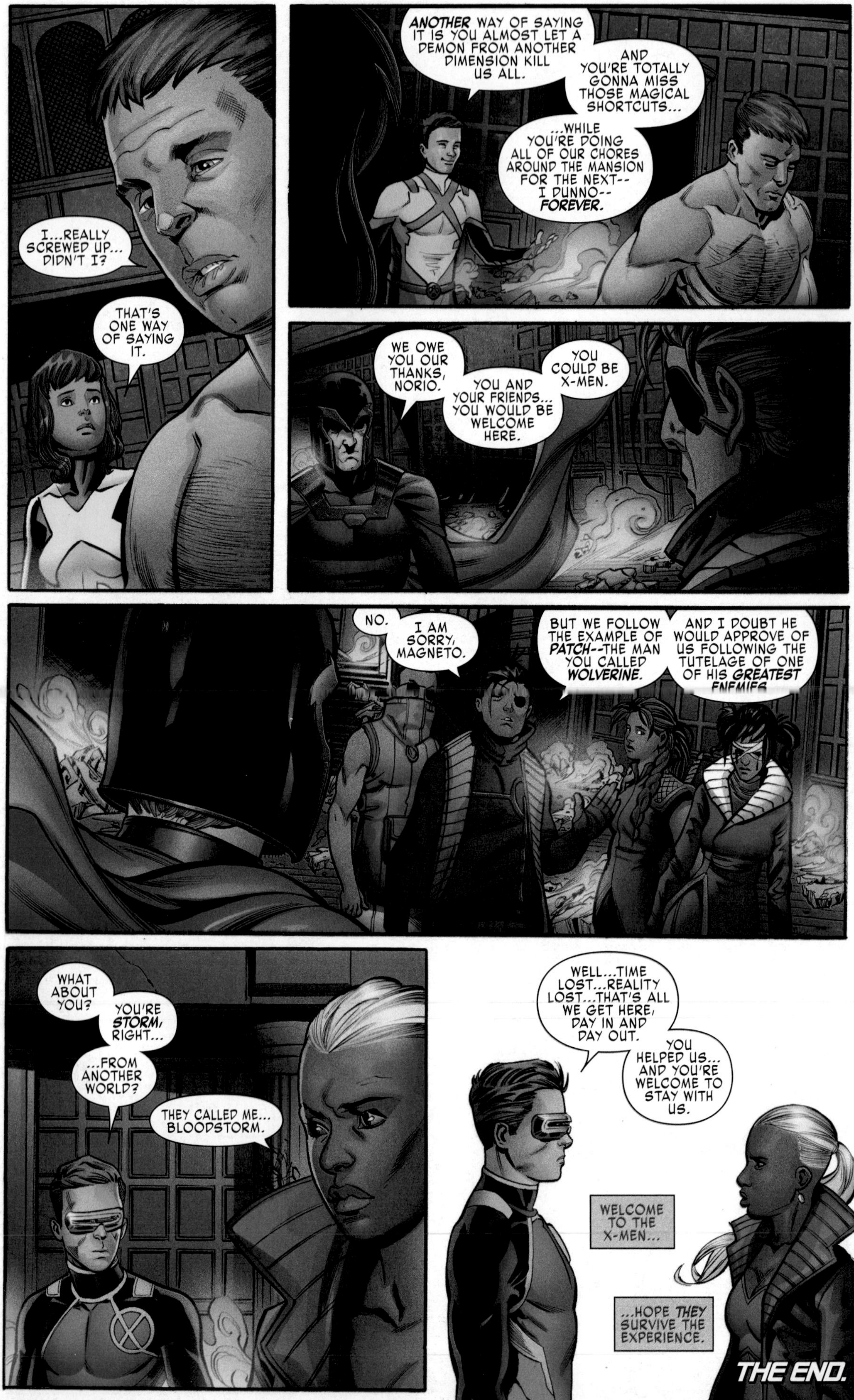

I...REALLY SCREWED UP... DIDN'T I?
THAT'S ONE WAY OF SAYING IT.
ANOTHER WAY OF SAYING IT IS YOU ALMOST LET A DEMON FROM ANOTHER DIMENSION KILL US ALL.
AND YOU'RE TOTALLY GONNA MISS THOSE MAGICAL SHORTCUTS...
...WHILE YOU'RE DOING ALL OF OUR CHORES AROUND THE MANSION FOR THE NEXT-- I DUNNO-- FOREVER.
WE OWE YOU OUR THANKS, NORIO.
YOU AND YOUR FRIENDS... YOU WOULD BE WELCOME HERE.
YOU COULD BE X-MEN.
NO.
I AM SORRY, MAGNETO.
BUT WE FOLLOW THE EXAMPLE OF PATCH--THE MAN YOU CALLED WOLVERINE.
AND I DOUBT HE WOULD APPROVE OF US FOLLOWING THE TUTELAGE OF ONE OF HIS GREATEST ENEMIES.
WHAT ABOUT YOU?
YOU'RE STORM, RIGHT...
...FROM ANOTHER WORLD?
THEY CALLED ME... BLOODSTORM.
WELL...TIME LOST...REALITY LOST...THAT'S ALL WE GET HERE, DAY IN AND DAY OUT.
YOU HELPED US... AND YOU'RE WELCOME TO STAY WITH US.
WELCOME TO THE X-MEN...
...HOPE THEY SURVIVE THE EXPERIENCE.
THE END.

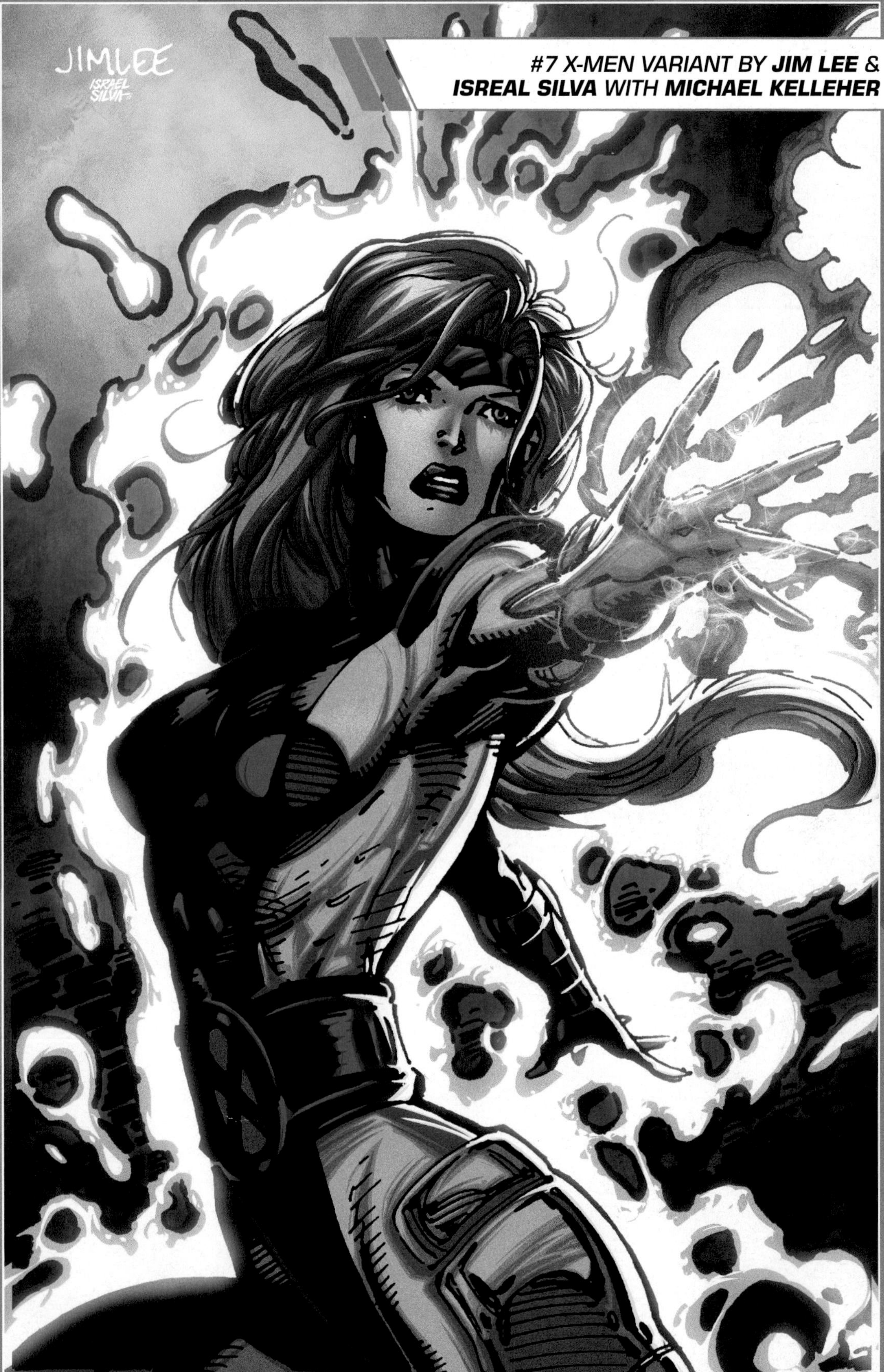
JIMLEE
ISRAEL SILVA

#7 X-MEN VARIANT BY **JIM LEE** &
ISREAL SILVA WITH **MICHAEL KELLEHER**

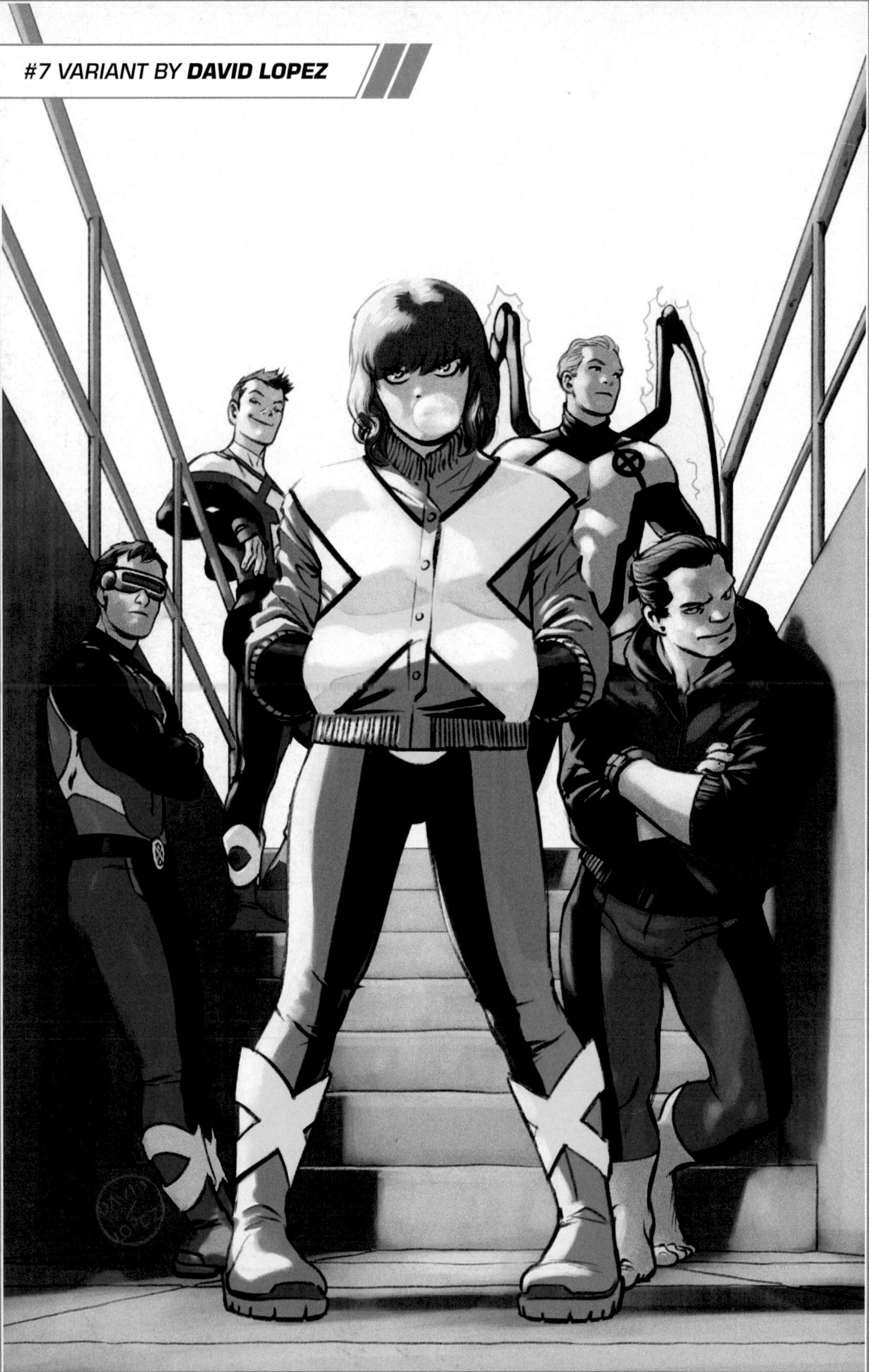

#7 VARIANT BY **DAVID LOPEZ**

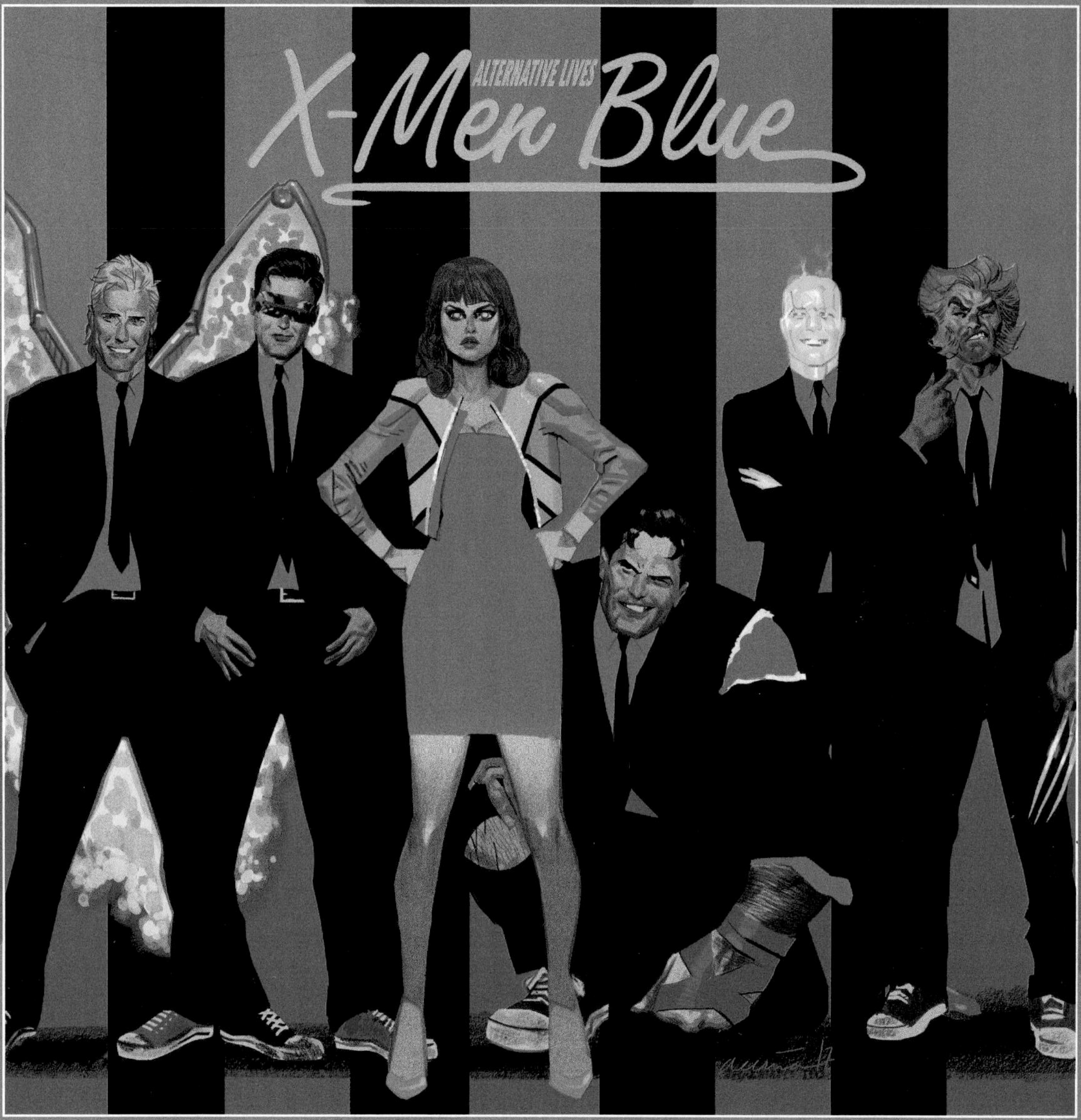
ALTERNATIVE LIVES
X-Men Blue

#11 ROCK-N-ROLL VARIANT BY **DANIEL ACUÑA**